André & Oscar

André & Oscar

THE LITERARY FRIENDSHIP OF ANDRÉ GIDE AND OSCAR WILDE

JONATHAN FRYER

ST. MARTIN'S PRESS ⚙ NEW YORK

ANDRÉ & OSCAR: THE LITERARY FRIENDSHIP OF ANDRÉ GIDE
AND OSCAR WILDE. Copyright © 1997 by Jonathan Fryer. All
rights reserved. Printed in the United States of America. No
part of this book may be used or reproduced in any manner
whatsoever without written permission except in the case of
brief quotations embodied in critical articles or reviews. For
information, address St. Martin's Press, 175 Fifth Avenue,
New York, N.Y. 10010.

Library of Congress Cataloging-in-Publication Data

Fryer, Jonathan.
    André & Oscar : the literary friendship of André Gide
and Oscar Wilde / Jonathan Fryer.
        p.   cm.
    Includes bibliographical references and index.
    ISBN 0-312-18039-x
    1. Gide, André, 1869–1951—Friends and associates. 2.
Wilde, Oscar, 1854–1900—Friends and associates. 3.
Authors, French—20th century—Biography. 4. Authors,
Irish—19th century—Biography.
    I. Title.
PQ2613.I2Z62774   1998
848'.91209—dc21   98-2918
                                                      CIP

First published in Great Britain by Constable
and Company Limited

First U.S. Edition: May 1998

10 9 8 7 6 5 4 3 2 1

for

FRANCIS KING

truest and most generous of friends

Contents

List of Illustrations

between pages 128 and 129

9

Acknowledgements

The author would like particularly to thank André Gide's daughter, Catherine Gide, and Oscar Wilde's grandson, Merlin Holland, for permission to quote from letters and other material still in copyright.

He also wishes to record his sincere appreciation to Alice Tassel and Gallimard for assistance with the André Gide estate, Sheila Colman for her permission to quote the brief extract from Lord Alfred Douglas's *Autobiography*, and Francis King and the publishers John Murray for permission to quote from *A Literary Companion: Florence*.

Carol O'Brien, editor at Constable, was a tower of strength and patience, while in their separate and individual ways, Michael Bloch, Jennifer Kavanagh, Peter Lewis-Crown and Ardon Seales all provided invaluable encouragement and moral support, for which the author is immensely grateful.

Don Mead and other members of the Oscar Wilde Society were enthusiastic and helpful. The London Library Staff were, as ever, efficient and indispensable.

André & Oscar

CHAPTER ONE

Paris 1891

THE BOULEVARDS of Paris were made for Oscar Wilde: new yet fashionable; elegant, yet accessible to any casual labourer or street urchin who fancied chancing his luck. Emile Zola decried the way that Baron Haussmann, to flatter the vanity of the Emperor Napoleon III, had in the 1850s and 1860s cut great swathes through the medieval city, opening up fresh vistas and creating new gardens, squares and promenades where the bourgeoisie could strut. But Oscar was enchanted.

Seated in one of the many cafés along the boulevards, Oscar could watch and be seen. Away from the domestic pressures of wife and children, friends and foes, he could ruminate over a glass of absinthe, savouring the spectacle before his eyes. He took delight in the most mundane things that distinguished Paris from his adopted home, London. Even the newspaper kiosks of the boulevards were a source of wonder, as he told the editor of the *Speaker*, employing a characteristic tone of extravagant irony:

[December 1891]
Sir, I have just, at a price that for any other English sixpenny paper I would have considered exorbitant, purchased a copy of the

Speaker at one of the charming kiosks that decorate Paris; institutions, by the way, that I think we should at once introduce into London. The kiosk is a delightful object, and, when illuminated at night from within, as lovely as a fantastic Chinese lantern, especially when the transparent advertisements are from the clever pencil of M. Cheret.[1] In London we have merely the ill-clad newsvendors, whose voice, in spite of the admirable efforts of the Royal College of Music to make England a really musical nation, is always out of tune, and whose rags, badly designed and badly worn, merely emphasize a painful note of uncomely misery, without conveying that impression of picturesqueness which is the only thing that makes the spectacle of the poverty of others at all bearable.

Oscar's first encounter with Paris had been in the summer of 1874, at the impressionable age of nineteen, in the company of his formidable mother, Lady Wilde – a fiery Irish nationalist poet who had abandoned her indulgence in inflammatory rhetoric for the marginally less precarious role of society hostess. Like her, Oscar developed considerable fluency in the French language, though when he was writing it his spelling and grammar left a lot to be desired. This was rather odd, as he had excelled in classical languages in his university studies in both Dublin and Oxford, and he read a great deal of French literature and was much affected by it, notably Balzac, Baudelaire, Flaubert (for Oscar, the 'sinless master') and Gautier.

In 1882 Oscar had made his legendary lecture tour of the United States and Canada, during which he developed the pose of the languid, lily-bearing aesthete to its limits. After this he felt he needed to recover somewhere more stimulating than London. His classic bent, and the desire to complete his second play (a rather dreadful

1. Jules Cheret, a successful French poster-artist, who had lived in England for
   several years as a young man.

historical melodrama entitled *The Duchess of Padua*) made him think initially of Athens, Rome or Venice. Instead, he opted for Paris in January 1883, settling into the same hotel as that in which he had stayed with his mother nearly a decade before: the Hôtel Voltaire on the Quai Voltaire, on the Left Bank. He had a small suite, with a splendid view; but when William Wordsworth's great-grandson Robert Sherard commented on this, Oscar responded dismissively: 'Oh, that is altogether immaterial, except to the innkeeper, who of course charges it in the bill. A gentleman never looks out of the window.'

Blond, twenty-one, masculine and obtuse, Sherard was one of a long series of bewitched young admirers whose attentions Oscar so savoured, though until his seduction by the young Robert Ross in 1886, Oscar seems not to have given physical expression to his desire for youthful male bodies. Indeed, Robert Sherard later maintained that he had been completely unaware that there was anything odd about Wilde's interest in him, despite the fact that Oscar once kissed him full on the lips. Comradely affection and the use of endearments between men were much more common between Englishmen before Wilde's disgrace than they are today. Besides, Sherard was dazzled, as so many other young men had been and would be. Oscar, for his part, delighted in having such a sturdy acolyte, whose looks he likened to those of a later Roman Emperor who had reigned but one day. During the four months that Wilde spent in Paris in 1883 Sherard saw him virtually daily and would, with time, become one of his most persistent, though not most perceptive, biographers. Oscar enjoyed shocking him and used him as a confidant – perhaps realising that his confessions would be recorded for posterity. Oscar dutifully reported to the young man a session he had had with a well-known woman prostitute, though not his interests in other directions.

Sherard had met Oscar at the Paris home of the Greek beauty Maria Cassavetti-Zambaco, and had been appalled at the Irishman's outfit, which reportedly turned heads on the boulevards. The knee-breeches that had helped make him a regular target of satirical magazines on both sides of the Atlantic before 1883 had given way to garments considered more in keeping with Continental decadence: tight trousers, fancy shirt cuffs turned back over jacket sleeves, vivid silk handkerchiefs and a flamboyant hairstyle (initially long, but then shortened and curled by a cooperative Parisian barber, after the fashion of the Emperor Nero).

Oscar had come to Paris with a stock of copies of his *Poems*, published at his own expense two years earlier, to a largely hostile critical reception. Combined with letters of introduction to various French men of letters and hostesses, the little volume nonetheless made more impression than a mere visiting card. Perhaps the poetry's weaknesses (and debt to other poets) were not so obvious to French speakers. During this visit to Paris the doors of many literary salons and artists' studios were opened to him. As in London, he acquired a reputation that far exceeded the merit of his as yet feeble literary output. But not everyone was favourably impressed. Edmond de Goncourt, novelist and acerbic diarist, who first received Oscar in April 1883, was not for a moment taken in, mocking Wilde as being an 'individual of doubtful gender, with a ham actor's turn of phrase and tall stories', while acknowledging the Irishman's skills as a gossip. The painter Edgar Degas (to whose studio Oscar climbed up a ladder, in the company of his friend, artistic mentor and future sparring partner James McNeill Whistler) declared that Oscar seemed to be playing the role of Lord Byron in a suburban theatre.

Oscar did not just count on his appearance for making an effect. He kept a notebook in French of *bons mots* that he had used, or would use, in conversation, or wished he had thought of himself. He amused some of his Parisian acquaintances and outraged others with such remarks as 'In order to write, I must have yellow satin', or 'I need lions in gilded cages. It's frightful: after human flesh, lions like bones, and people never give them any.' But Oscar was not just show, a heavy, exotic clown performing centre-stage. He was also observing, analysing and absorbing what was around him, from the pictures of Corot and the Impressionists like Monet and Pissarro to the developing schools of French poetry. Inspired by the latter's example, he started thinking more seriously about a long poem that had been slowly germinating in his mind, *The Sphinx*.

Oscar had to leave Paris in May 1883 because his money was running out. But the city had so ingrained itself in his mind that he took his new wife Constance there (as well as to Dieppe) for their honeymoon in June of the following year. In Paris they occupied a suite of rooms at the Hôtel Wagram, in the rue de Rivoli, overlooking the Tuileries. A journalist who visited Oscar there was surprised to find him stretched out reading Stendhal's *Le rouge et le noir* (*Scarlet and Black*). He would have been even more surprised had he discovered Oscar reading another book which really caught his imagination during his honeymoon: Joris-Karl Huysmans' *A rebours* (*Against Nature*), which had been published only weeks before.

In that novel, Huysmans portrays the decadent interests of the wealthy young Duc des Esseintes, not just in art and literature, but also in the realm of love. Des Esseintes (like Proust's Baron Charlus in *A la recherche du temps perdu – Remembrance of Things Past*) was largely based on Whistler's friend, the Comte Robert de Montesquiou, poet, aesthete and socialite, whose extravagant tastes and bizarre mannerisms made him a perennial object of comment. Several chapters of Huysmans' book are sensuous enumerations of the contents of des Esseintes' house and garden: the sumptuous fabrics and exotic plants, the pictures he collects and the books he reads. Des Esseintes' unsettling obsession with the biblical character of Salome, particularly as portrayed in the complex and symbolic paintings of Gustave Moreau, is dealt with at length, as is his drift from the lassitude of conventional heterosexual liaisons towards more stimulating and amoral manipulations of young men. *A rebours* shook Wilde to the core, profoundly influencing not only his own forthcoming novel,

The Picture of Dorian Gray, but also the direction in which his own tastes and interests developed. Not least, the book reinforced Wilde's growing susceptibility to the allure of evil, and the seductiveness of the unknown.

On the second day of the Wildes' honeymoon, Oscar went out, alone, with Robert Sherard, whom Constance, when she set eyes on him, found as romantically beguiling as the young eighteenth-century English poet Thomas Chatterton. The two men's promenade was not a success. Sherard was non-plussed by Oscar's description of the pleasures of deflowering a virgin on one's wedding night; the young man was dismayed by the sharing of such intimacy, yet also felt excluded from this important new dimension to Oscar's life. Constance, still full of romantic illusions about her husband, happily accompanied him to the Salon to view two of Whistler's new paintings; earlier banished and ridiculed by the French artistic establishment, the American painter was now finding greater acceptability there.

Constance enthused about Sarah Bernhardt as Lady Macbeth in the Shakespearean production she and Oscar saw together. Oscar, who had paid court to Sarah Bernhardt in Paris the previous year (as earlier in London he had paid court to Lillie Langtry), needed no convincing on that score. Bernhardt was symbolic of what Oscar was increasingly seeing as France's superiority to perfidious Albion, in theatre, in art, in poetry and in prose. As he announced pompously at a breakfast with the critic Catulle Mendès, 'There is no modern literature outside France.'

Accordingly, by the time Oscar returned to Paris in February 1891, staying at the Hôtel de l'Athénée in rue Scribe, near the Opéra, and taking daily drives in the Bois de Boulogne, the city had a familiarity which made it feel like a comfortable spiritual home. Furthermore, this time Oscar was bringing with him much more substantial achievements. Although his two early plays, *Vera* and *The Duchess of Padua*, had made little impact, even in New York (where at least they had been staged), Wilde had received considerable praise for his volume of children's stories *The Happy Prince and Other Tales*. He had also, to the dismay of some of his friends, aroused considerable controversy with his speculative fiction based on Shakespeare's supposed love for a boy actor, Will Hughes, *The Portrait of Mr W.H.*, published in *Blackwood's* magazine. Most significantly, in June 1890, *Lippincott's Monthly Magazine* had published the first version of *The Picture of Dorian Gray*, which would shortly appear in book form. Full of echoes of Huysmans' *A rebours* and of other French nineteenth-century literature, *Dorian Gray* was nonetheless a great breakthrough for Oscar – and indeed for English literature – combining a sophisticated expression of the author's aesthetic concerns with a blatant disregard for society's values and a taste for criminality, thus providing a distorted reflection of the author's own real and fantasy lives.

Oscar had long been an expert self-publicist. Now he had real reason to promote himself, and he was determined to conquer Paris as well as London. Partly this was an act of homage, for, as he acknowledged in the preface to *Dorian Gray*, he had learnt from the French Symbolists, centred on the poet Stéphane Mallarmé, that 'all Art is at once surface and symbol. Those who go beneath the surface do so at their peril. Those who read the symbol do so at their peril.' Having adopted this new credo, Wilde now needed to be accepted by Mallarmé and others as a colleague and a brother. He attended one of Mallarmé's open houses on Tuesday 24 February 1891, when the two men spoke of Edgar Allan Poe; Mallarmé presented Oscar with a copy of his translation of Poe's *The Raven*. In a rather gushing letter of thanks, addressed to 'Cher Maître', Wilde told Mallarmé that 'in England we have prose and we have poetry, but French prose and poetry, in the hands of a master such as yourself, become one and the same thing'. A week later, he was welcomed back to Mallarmé's salon; he could feel he had been accepted.

Mallarmé's modest little fourth-floor apartment in the unfashionable rue de Rome, near the St Lazare railway station, hardly corresponded to most people's idea of the perfect setting for one of the most celebrated literary and artistic salons in *fin-de-siècle* Paris. The rooms were cramped. A narrow hallway led to a living-room that doubled up as the dining-room; the Louis XVI dining-table had to be folded away when visitors came, so they had enough space to move around. Japanese crêpe paper covered the lights, to soften their glare. The family cat, Lilith, stared nonchalantly down at visitors from her favourite spot on top of the sideboard. The most prominent feature was a positively Germanic porcelain stove. The walnut furniture was nondescript and sparse.

To the right of the stove, however, hung Edouard Manet's fine, small oil portrait of Mallarmé. An informed eye, panning across the walls, would pick out a river scene by Claude Monet and a pastel of flowers by Odilon Redon. In later years, on the sideboard, alongside the cat, there was a statue by Auguste Rodin of a naked nymph caught by a faun, in recognition of Mallarmé as the author of *L'Après-midi d'un faune*. The wooden profile of a Maori was by Paul Gauguin. This was clearly no ordinary lower-middle-class household, nor was the host an ordinary secondary school English master, though that was how he subsidised his literary activities.

The fare on offer on Mallarmé's legendary Tuesday evenings was meagre to the point of insolence. A Chinese bowl of tobacco and cigarette papers were laid out for people – predominantly but not exclusively men – to help themselves. Regulars, dubbed the *mardistes* or the Tuesday crowd, knew not to turn up before 10 p.m., having fortified themselves with dinner beforehand. New invitees might be summoned an hour earlier, so Mallarmé could engage them in one-to-one conversation. Later, as the assembled company grew, he discoursed to an eager audience. His topics ranged from the latest trends in poetry – his own most-favoured field of literary expression – to wild, light-hearted speculations about what the urban planners would dream up next further to transform the face of Paris.

German bombardments during the Franco-Prussian War in

1870–71 and the excesses of the short-lived Paris Commune had acted as temporary brakes on the capital's drive to modernity. But by the time of the World Exhibition of 1889, dominated by Gustave Eiffel's startling metal tower, confidence in the future and in France's greatness had returned. The scramble for colonial possessions in Africa and Asia had been taking place, from which France was emerging with satisfyingly copious spoils. But few of the *mardistes* at Stéphane Mallarmé's found all this a cause for the swelling pride that infected so many of their bourgeois countrymen.

Mallarmé himself – short, bearded and by 1891 prematurely aged beyond his forty-nine years – held court, as his daughter Geneviève emptied ashtrays or answered knocks at the door. His German wife Marie, who suffered poor health, stayed largely in the background. Less famous guests rarely dared interrupt the Master's flow. But few people mocked. On the contrary, as the young poet and novelist Henri de Régnier noted in his diary in December 1890, 'Nothing could replace these evenings at Mallarmé's where, in addition to the exquisitely perfect presence of the host, you have the good fortune to encounter an intelligent group of people.'

Officials in the Ministry of Education, as well as many of Mallarmé's pupils, had a much lower estimation of the man's abilities. More painfully, even his own relatives considered his work highly distasteful. It is a wonder that they believed they understood it; many more qualified critics claimed they themselves did not. For Stéphane Mallarmé had broken away from the more accessible so-called Parnassian group of poets, with their scientific, impersonal representations of nature and their evocations of the ages of antiquity. Rejecting a descriptive style, Mallarmé wrote poems which suggested rather than stated. He employed elaborate metaphors and symbols; hence the sobriquet 'Symbolist' accorded to the school of poetry which he was seen to lead. Words, rhythm and syntax were given shocking freedom to convey the musicality of the poet's thoughts, which were deliberately not made transparent. More conservative publishers baulked at the apparent impenetrability of Mallarmé's more radical work. But to a growing band of fellow writers, the little schoolmaster was helping lead them into a brave new world, just as electricity and other inventions and discoveries were transforming life outside.

When Mallarmé's Tuesday soirées began the *mardistes* were limited to a tight-knit group of his friends and colleagues, mainly poets, of whom by far the most esteemed was Paul Verlaine. Not that Verlaine's behaviour was always estimable. He drank to excess, notably poisonous absinthe, which led to violent outbursts, even against his devoted mother. He had treated his wife abominably and his tempestuous relationship with his young protégé and lover Arthur Rimbaud, acted out in Paris, London and Brussels, had scandalised conservative opinion on both sides of the English Channel, just as Oscar Wilde's with Lord Alfred Douglas later would. Verlaine was sent to prison in Belgium in 1873 for shooting and wounding Rimbaud. Back in France, after his liberation, Verlaine became progressively more seedy; he struck Oscar as being depressingly dilapidated when the Irishman met him for the first time in 1883. By 1891, if anything, Verlaine was worse, though he did have his little periods of lucidity. And by then, his reputation as a poet was immense. Far from shunning him on account of his physical and moral sordidness, many Parisians would salute his genius.

Verlaine was largely responsible for boosting Mallarmé's standing through a series of three laudatory articles on Les Poètes Maudits (Accursed Poets) published in the magazine *Lutèce* in late 1883 – namely Rimbaud, Mallarmé and the now largely forgotten Breton chronicler of the seafaring life Tristan Corbière. Mallarmé suddenly found himself the object of attention of a generation of young poets and would-be writers, all clamouring for invitations to his Tuesdays.

Among these were the appealingly extrovert young poet, future novelist and practical joker Pierre Louÿs (born more prosaically Pierre Louis, to French parents in Ghent) and his much shyer former schoolfriend André Gide. The two had attended the Ecole Alsacienne in Paris, where both had shown precocious literary talent. This could easily have led to bitter rivalry, as André feared would happen the first time he displaced Pierre as top of the class in French composition. However, when Pierre found André reading Heine's poems in the original German, he offered the hand of friendship.

In André's case, the precocity was evident in his sexual development, too. Entering the school at the age of eight, he was soon sent away after a master discovered him masturbating. In his memoirs, Gide also confessed to experimenting sexually with the concièrge's son under the dining-room table at home. However, a few months under the watchful eyes of his parents seem to have curbed this activity, or at least made him more discreet, enabling him to return to school.

André was the only child of Protestant parents: a scholarly and kindly law professor at the Sorbonne, Paul, and his pious, forceful heiress wife, Juliette (née Rondeaux). Paul Gide was originally from Uzès, in the south of France, while Juliette's family was in Normandy. This geographical contrast of parental origin provided one of several influential polarities in André's nature. Although Paul Gide died, of intestinal tuberculosis, when André was not yet eleven, the boy continued to visit his paternal grandmother at Uzès, savouring the region's sunny weather. There was something oddly reassuring about his mildly eccentric grandmother, who spent her days knitting socks, leaving them unfinished around the house.

In Normandy, Juliette Gide had inherited an historic moated country house, the Château de La Roque-Baignard, which was surrounded by woods and fields. These became the young André's playground and scientific observatory. He developed a particular passion for beetles, and his mother noted in her diary that he would be a perfectly nice boy were it not for his habit of standing for hours on end, motionless, under a tree, watching insects. Despite such outdoor pursuits, André's health was poor. This was aggravated by his propensity for working himself up into a cataleptic state when he was mentally agitated or felt thwarted.

When not at school, the teenage André lived largely in a world of women. His mother had a Scottish governess-turned-companion called Anna Shackleton, an amateur botanist who nurtured André's interest in the natural sciences. Miss Shackleton also had a great love for German literature, introducing André to the works of Goethe, Heine and others, both in the original and in her own translations (though strangely she did not teach him English). Books became central to André's life, especially after he was given free run of his late father's extensive library in Paris. During term-time, he could compare notes with Pierre Louÿs on what the two of them were reading; in the holidays, at La Roque, he found a literary soul-mate in the eldest of three girl cousins who lived nearby: Madeleine Rondeaux, a confidante who would one day become his wife.

Two years André's senior, Madeleine emanated an appealing purity and modesty, tinged with sadness. The reason for the sadness, as André discovered one day, was that Madeleine had learnt of her mother's infidelity – a scandal about which local society was laughing behind the family's back. Madeleine's resultant distress, compounded when her mother went off with her lover, touched André to the core. He became extremely protective towards her and determined that he would make himself worthy of her own purity, to expiate her mother's carnal sins.

This new mission in André's life involved an extended period of puritanical religious fervour, bordering on asceticism. Despite her wealth, Juliette Gide ran a rather parsimonious household regime as a matter of religious principle. But for a while André went much further. Monk-like, he slept on boards, took cold baths and rose in the middle of the night to pray. The New Testament was his constant companion (though this immersion in biblical texts was occasionally alleviated by the counterpoint of stories from *The Thousand and One Nights*).

André's moral welfare was put in the hands of a young pastor, Elie Allégret, who took him on his first visit abroad, shortly before his nineteenth birthday, to London. Conventional sightseeing there was supplemented by more religiously oriented activities, including a visit to a revivalist meeting where the preacher baptised people *en masse*. On the way out, André was approached by an attractive young woman, who smiled at him and asked him something in the softest of voices. He did not understand exactly what she said, but assuming he was being propositioned, returned the smile while saying firmly: 'No, thank you'. He was astonished by the acute look of dismay that this provoked, until Elie Allégret explained that what the girl had actually asked was whether André wanted to be 'saved'.

By the time he had turned twenty-one in 1890, André had focussed his mind clearly on how to persuade Madeleine to become his wife. It would not be an easy task, as Madeleine, doubtless affected by her parents' uninspiring example, was appalled by the very idea of marriage, even to him. André's courtship – which was observed and strongly disapproved of by his mother – was mainly through the medium of a highly self-indulgent first book, *Les Cahiers d'André Walter* (*The Notebooks of André Walter*). Most of this was written in a chalet by Lake Annecy, to which he had retreated alone, largely to get away from his friend Pierre Louÿs, who was displaying an irritatingly zealous interest in the project. André showed the finished work to his beloved Madeleine before publishing it privately in 1891. By then, Madeleine had become so alarmed by the way things were developing that she had turned down the young author's first proposal of marriage in January 1891 and broken off communication.

In Gide's first book, the hero André goes mad through renunciation; no wonder the manuscript had made Madeleine panic. In real life, the author André certainly went through mental agonies. The anguish was largely caused by his hyper-sensitivity and the uncomfortable balance in his make-up between the spiritual and the sensual. In the book, the spiritual is predominant and Gide seems to have wished to convince Madeleine that the same was true in his life. However, Madeleine's rejection enabled Gide to push aside his *alter ego* André Walter; he was on the verge of discovering life, not abandoning it. Paris offered a whole new existence, and the more outgoing Pierre Louÿs and Henri de Régnier offered him the entrée. Pierre took André off to see Verlaine, and encouraged him to promote himself by contacting other eminent writers.

Emboldened by his correct perception that André Walter was a Symbolist figure, Gide accordingly delivered an advance copy of his little book to Mallarmé's home at the rue de Rome. Mallarmé was impressed and invited the young man to come to a Tuesday gathering, on 10 February, a whole two hours before the crowd. In many ways, the atheist Mallarmé was the ideal person to lead Gide gently away from the religious mysticism of André Walter towards an aesthetic mysticism; as Gide's biographer Jean Delay astutely noted, through Mallarmé's patient and courteous instruction, Gide was taught to substitute the religion of poetry for the poetry of religion. Captivated, Gide would become a regular attender at Mallarmé's.

However, Gide was absent when Oscar Wilde turned up at the rue de Rome, just a fortnight after André's own initiation into the Symbolist coterie. Their first meeting would have to wait until Oscar's return to Paris that autumn. By then, mainly at Mallarmé's, André had heard a great deal about Oscar, for whom 1891 had proved an *annus mirabilis*. There was not just the impact of the publication of *The Picture of Dorian Gray*. Oscar had completed the first of his four great comedies, *Lady Windermere's Fan*, and he was busy composing his play *Salomé* – in French. Furthermore, he had met his 'darling boy', Lord Alfred Douglas, thereby sowing the seeds of his own destruction and that of the literary pre-eminence he so craved.

From Mallarmé, André would have heard the story of Oscar's return to Paris at the end of October and of the jealous tantrum this provoked in James McNeill Whistler, who happened to be in Paris at the time. Wilde had written to Mallarmé, saying he would attend the soirée on 3 November. This news prompted Whistler to write to Mallarmé to excuse himself for *not* attending that evening, 'to denounce Oscar in front of your disciples'. A self-confessed expert in the art of making enemies, Whistler had decided that Wilde was an aesthetic plagiarist, a shameless self-publicist and a sham. Mallarmé, who liked both men, was amused. He must have laughed (as Whistler half intended him to) when, on the day in question, he received the following telegram from Whistler, apropos Wilde:

Preface propositions; forewarn disciples; precaution: familiarity fatal. Hide the pearls. Have a good evening. Whistler.

Mallarmé left the telegram on the table for his guests to enjoy. Wilde could only admire how Whistler had guaranteed that he would be a central topic of conversation in his absence; the painter's works were indeed much discussed, and Wilde joined in the praise.

André Gide finally set eyes on Oscar towards the end of the month, at an unspecified literary gathering, not necessarily at Mallarmé's. Gide recalled in his short memoir of Wilde, published over a decade later, that Wilde had in 1891:

what Thackeray calls the 'chief gift of great men': success. His gestures and his look triumphed. His success was so sure that it seemed as if it preceded Wilde and that he merely had to come forward after it. His books astonished and charmed. His plays were to be the talk of London. He was rich; he was tall; he was handsome. He was full of good fortune and honours. Some people likened him to an Asian Bacchus; others to some Roman Emperor; others, to Apollo himself. And the fact is, he shone.

Oscar would have been flattered had he been told this description to his face. At thirty-seven, beginning to be bloated with good living as well as with success, he was not most people's idea of handsome. Indeed, the journalist and art critic Lady Colin Campbell went so far as to describe him as a 'great white caterpillar'. Various Paris acquaintances of Wilde's were similarly taken aback, yet fascinated, by the man's appearance. Catulle Mendès' young secretary Marcel Schwob – a good friend of Gide's – noted that Oscar was 'a big man, with a large pasty face, red cheeks, an ironic eye, bad and protruding teeth, a vicious childlike mouth with lips soft with milk ready to suck some more ... A terrible absinthe drinker, through which he got his visions and his desires.' The young American-born Symbolist poet Stuart Merrill, who lived in Paris and wrote in French, was a little more complimentary, acknowledging the powerful effect that Wilde could have on those around him, being 'gigantic, smooth-shaven and rosy, like a great priest of the moon in the time of Heliogabalus. At the Moulin Rouge, the habitués took him for the prince of some fabulous realm of the North.'

André Gide himself was star-struck. Oscar was the brightest planet in the new literary firmament that had revealed itself to André (the newspaper *L'Echo de Paris* endorsed Wilde's special status, calling him 'the great event of the season in literary salons'). As André enthused to his young friend Paul Valéry, with whom Pierre Louÿs and he were working on an ambitious little literary review, *La Conque*:

> [28 November 1891]
> A few lines from someone dazed, who no longer reads, who no longer writes, who no longer sleeps, nor eats, nor thinks – but runs around, with or without Louÿs, in cafés or in salons, shaking hands and smiling at people. [José-Maria de] Heredia, Régnier, Merrill, the aesthete Oscar Wilde – oh, *he* is admirable, admirable!

André's first impressions of Oscar were reinforced at a brief encounter at José-Maria de Heredia's a day or so later. Like Mallarmé, the Cuban-born Parnassian poet Heredia held open house to like-minded individuals, but on Saturday afternoons, at his home in the rue Balzac off the Champs Elysées. Henri de Régnier had first taken André there, in March; at first André had been dismayed by the contrast between the Parnassians he met there and the Symbolists with whom he felt so much more akin at Mallarmé's. But that did not stop him becoming a regular visitor to Heredia's salon as well. Oscar Wilde was similarly catholic in his acceptance of invitations (though he did run away from Marcel Proust's, allegedly offended by the décor and the presence of Proust's parents).

At Heredia's, Oscar sidled up to André conspiratorially – perhaps provoked as much by the young man's earnest mien as by alcohol – and whispered to him: 'Shall I tell you a secret? But promise me you won't pass it on to anyone else. Do you know why Christ did not love his mother? [*Pause for dramatic effect.*] Because she was a virgin!'

This unsettling approach gave André the courage to ask Pierre Louÿs to arrange a small dinner party for Wilde, which Louÿs did, at the Café d'Harcourt in the Place de la Sorbonne – the scene of many famous literary dinners. There were just four of them in the party that evening (the fourth was probably Stuart Merrill) and Oscar dominated the talk over dinner. André had the impression that some of the stories were confused and not of Oscar's best, as if he were not quite sure of his audience. André had quickly realised that the Irishman's repartee was rarely spontaneous, that his conversation was practised and contrived. But after dinner, out in the street, Oscar took André aside, and recounted a story about Narcissus. As Gide had just finished writing a short book based on the Narcissus legend, *Le Traité du Narcisse* (*The Treatise of Narcissus*), it was a topic that was bound to interest the young man. Besides, both Oscar and André were rather narcissistic themselves; both were obsessed with how they reflected themselves in public, though Oscar had already discovered something which André had not: the passion of physical desire for another human being.

According to Wilde's tale, the flowers of the field asked the river for some drops of water to weep for Narcissus after his death. The river surprised the flowers by asking whether Narcissus was beautiful. Surely, the flowers protested, the river must have noticed, as each day Narcissus leant over its banks to behold his own beauty in its water? But the river replied that any love it had for Narcissus was because when Narcissus had leant over it, the river saw the reflection of its own waters in the boy's eyes.

It is clear that Oscar was out to startle and impress André. He was not physically attracted to the young man in the way that he was to Pierre Louÿs (a red-blooded youth who would go on to become one of the most successful erotic writers of his generation); André was far too mousey, for all his romantic long locks of hair, his hallmark cape and studied literary air. The novelist Maurice Barrès, seven years André's senior, provided a glimpse of André at this time: 'He had created a literary personality for himself, shivery yet uptight, child-like, a little crazy, but highly cultured and charming as well.' His eyes were slightly oriental and he often frowned. Oscar stared hard at André's mouth and declared disconcertingly: 'I don't like your lips. They are straight like those of someone who has never lied. I want to teach you how to lie, so your lips become beautiful and twisted like those of an antique mask.' In fact, André's lips were not particularly straight, but Oscar was not one to let the truth get in the way of a good story.

Oscar was amused by the young man's gravity and piety, which he was determined to puncture. Cruelly, with the wisdom of years and his understanding of the Protestant's reverence for Truth and propensity for guilt, Oscar knew exactly where to put in the knife. Many of the shocking stories he told André at this time were perversions of biblical tales, turning the morals of Christ's parables on their head, and employing paradox to put accepted ideas under scrutiny. When Gide wrote his memoirs of Wilde, he decided that the Gospels disturbed and tormented the pagan playwright. Yet at times in his life, Oscar himself was receptive to some Christian teaching. People who knew Wilde well often spoke of his immense goodness and charity, however hard he might try to conceal it behind his façade of super-ficiality, bombast and immorality. The eccentric, not to say slightly deranged, amateur musician and society hostess Princess Ouroussof, who entertained Wilde and Gide simultaneously several times during November and December 1891, claimed even to have seen a halo round Oscar's head. But André began to wonder whether Oscar was the devil in disguise, determined in his conversational assault to authorise evil.

Oscar's preoccupation at the time with religious themes, as well as the interplay of good and evil, can partly be explained by the fact that he was working on *Salomé* – a theme which had also been taxing Mallarmé. Yet undoubtedly there was an element in Oscar's didacti-cism of wanting to goad André into re-evaluating the rigid religious convictions he supposedly still shared with his mother and Madeleine. Even if Wilde had not appeared on the scene, it is likely that Gide would have carried out such a re-evaluation as he savoured the intellectual challenges of Parisian society. But Oscar pushed him so hard and so relentlessly that the young man became frightened of the possible consequences.

Oscar particularly chided André about his addiction to truth and his belief in its high moral value. Each time they met, Oscar would ask André what he had done in the intervening hours and often the young man's answer would disappoint Oscar, prompting him to encourage André to fantasise, as Gide recounted in his Wilde memoirs:

'Is that really what you've done?' [Oscar would ask.]
'Yes,' I would answer.
'And what you say is true?'
'Yes, quite true.'
'But then why repeat it? You do see that it's not at all interesting? You have to understand that there are two worlds: one of them *is*,

without people speaking about it. We call that *the real world*, because there is no need to speak about it in order to see it. And the other is the world of Art. That's the one you do have to speak about, because otherwise it wouldn't exist.'

Equally, Oscar pontificated, there are two types of artist: one brings answers, the other brings questions; one needs to decide which one is, because one cannot be both. Some works of art are not understood for years, Oscar continued, because they are answering questions that have yet to be put. In such cases, the question often arrives long after the answer.

As if that were not enough to disorient his young interlocutor, Oscar unveiled to André his now familiar thesis that people should try in their lives to imitate art; one's life can thus become a work of art in itself. Such a proposition was of course completely at odds with the sort of thing Gide had been learning at Mallarmé's feet, notably the idea that one should scorn life in order to devote oneself to the Symbolist work of art.

Over a period of about three weeks, Oscar saw André every day, playing with him rather as he had played with the far less intelligent Robert Sherard eight years previously. He bombarded the poor boy with his parables and paradoxes, André becoming increasingly confused. Stuart Merrill noted that at one dinner, André just stared dumbly down at his plate as Oscar entertained the party with outrageous stories (though Oscar himself observed that André was often listening to him 'with his eyes'). After about a fortnight, several of André's friends independently arrived at the conclusion that André had fallen in love with this devil's advocate from the other side of the Channel.

It is impossible to know exactly what was going through André's mind at the time, as he ripped out the pages of his journal covering the relevant weeks in an effort to banish some of his current thoughts. But on 11 and 12 December he wrote in huge letters across the pages of his engagement diary the single word WILDE! Even without those destroyed journal pages, however, there is no doubt that the emotions Oscar stirred in André were churning him up almost to the point of a nervous breakdown. Little of this appears in Gide's published memoirs of Wilde; but more can be found in notes he made and kept. And much can be gleaned from his correspondence and from later entries in his journal. It is clear that shortly after meeting Oscar, André plunged into the depths of misery. It was as if his whole world had collapsed around him, as he wrote to the young poet Paul Valéry (yet another literary contact gained through Pierre Louÿs):

> [Friday 4 or 11 December 1891]
> De Profundis . . . Wilde is piously setting about killing what remained of my soul, because he says that in order to know the essence of something, one has to suppress it. He wants me to deplore my soul. The effort to destroy it is to be the measure of it. Everything is made up only of its emptiness, etc.

It was if André were battling with Mephistopheles, and losing. By the time Wilde left Paris to return to his family in time for Christmas, André felt he had been spiritually raped. He was anxious to get together with Paul Valéry at the earliest opportunity, in the belief that his friend could help him recover, as he wrote to Valéry on Christmas Eve:

> I shall come soon. Forgive me for remaining silent: since Wilde, I hardly exist at all. I'll tell you all about it . . . After all this squirming around, I hope to find a tranquil oasis for myself near to your quiet soul.

His grandmother's comforting home at Uzès meanwhile provided some respite. It was there that André decided to renounce Wilde and

the doctrines with which he had been tempted and instead turn back
to God, as he confided in his journal:

[Uzès, 29 December]
O Lord, I return to thee as I believe all is vanity save knowing thee.
Guide me in thy paths of light. I have followed tortuous routes
and thought I was enriching myself with false goods. Lord, have
pity on me: the only true goods are those thou givest. I wanted to
enrich myself, and I impoverished myself. After all this turmoil, I
have again found myself very poor. I remember days gone by, my
prayers. Lord, lead me as before along thy paths of light. Oh Lord,
keep me from evil. May my soul once more be able to be proud;
my soul was becoming just an ordinary soul. Oh! May my strug-
gles of long ago and my prayers not be in vain!

André needed strength through prayer to help him win his internal
spiritual battle and to make him worthy to woo Madeleine once
more. He began 1892 with a firm New Year's resolution to restart his
life, to put it back on track:

[1 January]
Wilde did me nothing but harm, I believe. With him, I had forgotten how to think. I had more varied emotions, but I no longer
knew how to keep them in order. Above all, I was no longer able
to follow other people's conclusions. A few thoughts, sometimes;
but my clumsiness in handling them made me abandon them.
Now I am taking up again – with difficulty but great joy – my
history of philosophy, in which I am studying the problem of language . . .

Still anxious to share his recent anguish, André wrote to Paul Valéry
on 5 January: 'I have so many impure things to tell you, a deadly cold,
a silence of a frozen lake to recount.'

However, Oscar Wilde could not be driven out of André Gide's life, even with the help of prayer. They would meet repeatedly over the next ten years. Moreover, the personality, words and actions of Oscar Wilde would haunt Gide for the rest of his days.

CHAPTER TWO

Robbie

AMONG Oscar's London friends, few could have been more eagerly awaiting Wilde's West End theatrical début, with *Lady Windermere's Fan*, than young Robert Ross, aspiring man of letters and art critic.

Just six months older than André Gide, Robbie or Bobbie, as he was generally called, was also born in France, in Tours. His Canadian parents had hoped that the Loire Valley's relatively mild climate would ease the ailments of Robbie's father, the Hon. John Ross, who had been Canada's Attorney-General. However, fate was unkind, as indeed it so often was to be during Robbie's eventful life. The family's sojourn in France was cut short by the looming Franco-Prussian War; back in Canada, within a matter of months John Ross was dead. Trunks and cases were packed again, as Mrs Ross once more crossed the Atlantic with her young family, this time settling in London.

Fortunately, she had been left quite comfortably off financially, which enabled her to maintain a series of appropriately genteel households in Chelsea and South Kensington, as well as assisting her children with their advancement in the world. Robbie was the most problematic, mainly because of his own delicate health. Much of his education was entrusted to a private tutor, with whom he travelled on the Continent. Between 1884 and 1886 Mrs Ross also took the boy travelling herself, notably to Switzerland and Austria, in the firm belief that a wider cognisance of European civilisation would do him a power of good.

By the spring of 1886 Robbie was back in London, studying at a well-known 'crammer's' in Covent Garden, W.B. Scoones, in the hope of obtaining a place at King's College, Cambridge. But it was probably on a visit to Oxford that he first met Oscar Wilde, with whose poems he was already familiar (he claimed to have been beaten for reading them). Oscar's good friend the sensational journalist Frank Harris (an entertaining but notoriously unreliable authority) maintained that Oscar and Robbie picked each other up in a public lavatory, but it is far more likely that they were introduced by a mutual undergraduate friend. Although Oscar had no nostalgic hankerings to be back at university himself – an affliction suffered by many lesser minds, which have found everything after Oxbridge to be an anticlimax – he was addicted to the presence of intelligent but preferably adoring youth, who were as much an intellectual as a physical stimulation. As he wrote in *The Picture of Dorian Gray*: 'The only people to whose opinion I listen now with any respect are people much younger than myself.'

Oscar was intrigued and attracted by the seventeen-year-old Robbie, with his Puck-like features, lively personality and precocious knowledge of the world. That knowledge extended to the art of homosexual love; Robbie had no doubts about where his proclivities lay, and he proceeded to seduce the fascinated Oscar, who was nearly twice his age. This was almost certainly Oscar's initiation into the physical side of homosexuality, however often in the past he might have been stirred by the sight or idea of beautiful youths. It is unlikely that it was Robbie's deflowerment.

Mrs Ross and Constance Wilde must both have been unaware of the sexual relationship that existed between Robbie and Oscar, as the following year, 1887, Robbie moved into the Wildes' home at 16 Tite

Street, Chelsea – the 'House Beautiful' so much written about in fashionable papers – as a paying guest. He stayed for three months, while his mother was away on yet more foreign travels. In view of the fact that homosexuality between men had been made illegal in England through the Labouchere Amendment just over twelve months previously, and that Robbie was still a minor, Oscar's recklessness in arranging for his young lover to move in is breath-taking. Perhaps he felt that such an inadvisable liaison was best kept hidden from public view within the sanctuary of his household – a precaution he would have been well advised to take in the future. But it seems that already Oscar enjoyed dicing with danger. At the same time, the arrangement demonstrated an extraordinary lack of concern for his wife's feelings. One can imagine Robbie and Oscar rather enjoying the situation, like naughty schoolboys, exchanging knowing looks across the dinner-table. But for Constance, it was a humiliation that would soon be compounded by others.

The Wildes had been married for only two years, but with the onset of Constance's pregnancy with their second son, Vyvyan (who was born in November 1886), Oscar was no longer physically attracted to her. On the contrary, he found her disfigured and disgusting. Lithe young Robbie was a most palatable alternative, not just physically, but also in the lightness of his being, his youth, his vivacity and his ability to converse on a wide range of literary and social topics while being more than willing to play the role of disciple. Oscar undoubtedly found adulation an aphrodysiac, especially when it came from young men who fell within his preferred age range of approximately seventeen to twenty-five.

Having Robbie in the house probably prevented Oscar from looking for commercial sex from the numerous rent-boys who plied their trade in Victorian London, operating openly around Piccadilly Circus, inside several theatres and pubs and on other cruising grounds. Given widespread poverty, prostitution of all kinds was rife in the great metropolis, despite all the legal and social constraints.

There were even brothels with boys, as the scandalised newspaper-reading public was to discover in 1889 when the Cleveland Street scandal broke; telegraph boys operating out of that West End location were delivering more than just urgent messages to their clients. A number of prominent personalities were implicated, including the aristocrat Lord Arthur Somerset; many thought it prudent to flee to France (which had a more relaxed attitude to people's private lives) rather than face the consequences.

However, it would be only a matter of time before Oscar would succumb to the temptation of male whores, nearly all of whom came from the 'lower orders', to use then current terminology. About the time Robbie came to stay with the Wildes, Oscar noticed some of them, with their painted faces, hanging around Piccadilly Circus. Oscar had been shopping with Constance at Swan & Edgar's. As he came out of the department store building, his eye caught that of a boy who had registered Oscar's interest and leered back, laughing. Years later Oscar recalled to his friend Reggie Turner that at that moment 'something clutched at my heart like ice'. It was the nervous reaction of one looking forward to the pleasure of a forbidden yet irresistible encounter.

Robbie Ross clearly profited from his time at the crammer's and at the Wildes', as he was indeed accepted for King's College, Cambridge. He went up to the university in the autumn of 1888, though his stay there was both short and unhappy. He was unpopular among his fellow undergraduates, being too urbane and self-confident. Perhaps subconsciously influenced by Oscar, he also took on poses which irritated his peers when they were shown to be false. For example, he claimed to be a Roman Catholic, though his conversion was not formalised for a further seven years. Even more foolishly, he said he was a member of the Savile Club, one of the most literary of London's gentlemen's clubs (of which Oscar also aspired, unsuccessfully, to become a member); Robbie was not in fact elected to membership of the Savile until 1893.

The nadir of Robbie's Cambridge University experience was a dunking in the college fountain by a group of fellow students (including E.F. 'Fred' Benson, who was to become a prolific novelist), who felt he needed to be taught a lesson. This was no spur-of-the-moment drunken prank by sporty 'hearties', but a carefully planned assault, carried out on a cold March night, for which Robbie tried to get the perpetrators suitably punished – in vain. After considerable pressure on the college authorities, the ringleader of the assailants was forced to make a public apology to Robbie, but the damage had been done, not just to his dignity, but also to his health. The onset of measles later in 1889 was the final blow to his chances of carrying on with his university studies. He retired to London, joining his mother and sister Lizzie, who were then living in Onslow Square. During his convalescence he appears to have 'come out' as a homosexual to his family (a most unusual and brave thing to have done in that day and age). This caused considerable strains in his relationship with some of Robbie's relatives, though his eldest brother Alex stood by him admirably for the rest of his life.

It is tempting to speculate on the extent to which Robbie's bravado rubbed off on Oscar. They undoubtedly influenced each other. Probably after two or three years of relative bourgeois respectability as a married man, Oscar would anyway have sought more adventurous entertainments, even if he had not chanced on Robbie. He had had romantic attachments to other young men before, without developing them into physical relationships. Moreover, despite his ungainly appearance, Oscar had boundless charm and a way with words that could sweep many young men off their feet. Partly thanks to Robbie, this became a technique Oscar learnt to perfect in dealing with undergraduates and youths with literary aspirations, several of whom were further wooed by Oscar's fatal generosity as a host in restaurants and hotels. This became a habit also extended to boys of much humbler origins and destinies. They were at least as much dazzled by the luxury of such unaccustomed surroundings as they were by Oscar's wit, happily offering their bodies in exchange. As Oscar became more prosperous, his entertaining became more lavish, including dinners at the Savoy and the hiring of private rooms at Kettner's restaurant in Soho, where a cuddle could be indulged in between courses. He began to distribute inscribed silver cigarette cases to particular favourites as liberally as a more cautious man might hand out cigarettes.

Oscar found nothing strange about his thirst for new encounters, despite his marriage and his parallel relationship with Robbie. Years later he joked that he had been married three times in his life, once to a woman (Constance) and twice to men (Robbie and Lord Alfred Douglas), but these core relationships did not deter an accelerating interest in promiscuous sex with youths, several of whom became objects of infatuation, at least for a day. He became adept at seducing them in the most unlikely, and inappropriate, places, including his own publishers' offices. For it was on the premises of the publishers Elkin Mathews & John Lane that Oscar fell for an eighteen-year-old clerk, Edward Shelley, who would feature prominently in the trials that brought about Wilde's downfall.

Edward Shelley was flattered by the attention and was among other youthful admirers of Wilde's to be sent complimentary tickets for the opening night of *Lady Windermere's Fan*, at the (now demolished) St James's Theatre, on 20 February 1892. Oscar had had a series of spats with the actor-manager George Alexander (who cast himself as Lord Windermere) over various suggested changes to the play. These disagreements almost tempted the playwright to boycott the opening and go off for some relaxation on the Riviera instead. But his mother, Lady Wilde, urged him not to do anything so foolish. 'Do try to be present yourself at the first performance,' she wrote. 'It would be right and proper and Constance would like it. Do not leave her all alone.'

Oscar made sure he would be surrounded and cushioned by loyal friends, as well as his wife, to soften any possible hostile reception from the critics or the rest of the audience. These friends included leading figures in the theatre world, such as Lillie Langtry, Florence Terry and Norman Forbes-Robertson. But there was also a claque of Oscar's young males, including Robbie Ross and two other stalwarts of the Wilde camp, More Adey and Reginald Turner. Pierre Louÿs came over from Paris at Oscar's urging, and found himself sitting next to Edward Shelley in the stalls. André Gide was unavailable, as he was busy preparing himself to go to Munich for private studies in the German language, music and art, in the hope of rebuilding his shattered morale with some Teutonic logic and sobriety.

One of the first things that Pierre Louÿs and other observant members of the audience would have noticed was that Robbie Ross and a number of Oscar's other special friends were sporting green carnations, as was Wilde himself. Purchased at Goodyear's florists in the Royal Arcade, these unnatural blooms would become as much associated with Wilde's *fin-de-siècle* aura of decadence as sunflowers and lilies had been with his earlier aesthetic pose. When asked if the green carnation had any special significance, Oscar laughed and replied that the whole point was that it had none, though people would think that it did. But wearing these perverse buttonholes doubtless made Robbie and Reggie Turner and other homosexuals in Wilde's coterie feel part of a select and secret fraternity. They met in the bar during the first interval, and found Oscar buoyant about the audience's reception so far. Some professional critics, like Frank Harris, were equally enthusiastic, but others were much less so. Notwithstanding the conflicting verdicts being voiced in the crush, Robbie Ross was convinced that Oscar had found his true vocation.

At the end of the play – a piece as full of intriguing deceit and illusion as it is of humour and ingenuity – the author was called for loudly; his appearance on stage made as much impact as the drama that preceded it. Bulky but languid, Wilde nonchalantly held a lighted cigarette in his hand, cocking a snook at convention in a way that was calculated to outrage propriety but charm the more unconventional members of the audience. According to George Alexander, Wilde addressed the predominantly admiring auditorium with the words:

> Ladies and Gentlemen, I have enjoyed this evening immensely. The actors have given us a charming rendering of a delightful play, and your appreciation has been most intelligent. I congratulate you on the great success of your performance, which persuades me that you think almost as highly of the play as I do myself.

Other people present, such as Marie de Mensiaux, who wrote about the occasion for the *Boston Evening Transcript*, gave a markedly different version of the playwright's speech. But that was of no importance. What mattered was what people believed Oscar had said; with every word, real or imagined, his legend grew.

Pierre Louÿs was charmed by the elegant anarchy of it all. Later he would report to his elder brother Georges and to André Gide his pleasure at the liberating customs of Robbie Ross and his friends. When one asked the other for a cigarette, for example, rather than just present an open cigarette case to the supplicant, the donor would extract a cigarette himself, put it into his own mouth, light it, draw on it, and then hand it over. The camp affectation and sexual innuendo of this seemingly trivial act were for the time being masked from Pierre by its attractive daringness. But not for long.

Constance was pleased and relieved by the first-night success of her husband's play, but she was anxious to get back home to the children, knowing full well that Oscar would not accompany her. It had become his custom to sup late at Willis's rooms, a favourite haunt of theatre-goers, socialites and insomniacs. Flushed by the reception of *Lady Windermere's Fan*, Oscar went there that evening with a small, noisy group of his green carnation coterie. As the party broke up, Oscar was left alone with Edward Shelley, as he had planned, to end the night of celebration together in bed at the Albemarle Hotel.

This was no one-night stand; for over the next two years, Oscar

wined and dined the young man intermittently at the Café Royal and
at Kettner's, took him to exhibitions, gave him books and money and
tried to help him in other ways (to the growing dismay of Shelley's
father, not to mention the publishers). As was emphasised in the
trials in 1895, such conduct by a thirty-eight-year-old dramatist and
an office boy half his age was considered most unbecoming. The
rumours and the disapproval began to ferment.

Yet Robbie Ross, who perhaps had more legitimate reason to be
offended by Oscar's new associations, seems to have taken a very
tolerant, philosophical view of his lover's philandering, at least when
youths of a lower social and intellectual standing were involved.
Robbie set no great store by physical fidelity; sex was fun. He even
seems to have accepted Wilde's relationship with a handsome young
poet of some talent, John Gray, who liked to style himself 'Dorian',
with Oscar's indulgence. But it was a different matter when a serious
rival came on the scene, in the form of Lord Alfred Douglas, the
glamorous and brilliantly connected third son of the mad and bad
Marquess of Queensberry, pugilist, atheist and fanatic.

We cannot be certain exactly when Oscar first met 'Bosie' (a
corruption of his childhood nickname 'Boysie'). Douglas's own
voluminous autobiographical writings are both unreliable and
contradictory, and Wilde was hopeless about dates and ages. But it
was probably in the summer of 1891, between Oscar's two important visits to Paris that year. It was certainly after the publication of
The Picture of Dorian Gray, as Douglas, then reading Greats at
Magdalen College, Oxford, had been given a copy of the novel by his
cousin, the poet Lionel Johnson. Douglas had purportedly read the
book nine times over and expressed a keen interest to meet the
author. Johnson accordingly took Lord Alfred up to London to effect
the introduction, at Wilde's home in Tite Street.

As a connoisseur of ethereal male beauty, as well as an unrepentant snob, Wilde could hardly fail to find the twenty-two-year-old
Lord Alfred appealing. Blond, fine-boned and looking younger than

his age, Alfred could deploy all the poise and charm of good breeding and fine education when he wanted to. Yet this was not love at first sight on Oscar's part, however much he appreciated his new acquaintance. He politely offered to be of assistance, presumably having the young man's academic concerns in mind. But when Lord Alfred did come seeking Oscar's help, a few weeks after the opening of *Lady Windermere's Fan*, the need for assistance was of an entirely different and more urgent kind. Douglas was being blackmailed.

Both at Oxford and for several years after coming down from university, Alfred Douglas was a shamelessly promiscuous homosexual. Moreover, he had a taste for rough trade: servants, grooms, street-boys and others whose services could be cheaply bought. His disdainful treatment of some of the boys left them feeling resentful, and he was extremely careless in his behaviour, not least in the way he handled incriminating material, such as letters. This was particularly unwise in the wake of the Labouchere Amendment, which had made homosexuality a criminal act; not for nothing was it known as the 'blackmailers' charter'. Unscrupulous youths on the game could, by accident or design, often 'rent' their clients twice over, first being paid for sex, and then extracting further payment from them under the threat of public exposure.

Alfred Douglas found himself in exactly that position in the spring of 1892. Unable to turn for help to his detested father, who would have been far from sympathetic, Douglas appealed to Wilde. Although their acquaintance was then still slight, Oscar responded magnificently. He had a long-standing fascination in the activities and psychology of the criminal classes, and the prospect of rescuing a young lord from disaster was as romantic as some of the plots of his own fairy tales. Oscar travelled to Oxford to reassure Lord Alfred that everything would be all right, spending the weekend with him to emphasise the point. Fortuitously flush with money from the success of his play, Oscar arranged through his solicitor George Lewis to buy the blackmailer off with the not inconsiderable sum of £100. Alfred

Douglas was effusive in his thanks, and Oscar's heart was touched by
the young man's gratitude.

Preposterously, later in life Lord Alfred Douglas maintained in
print that he never had sexual relations with Wilde, though he
exploded his own lie by describing elsewhere what happened
between them, if not exactly when and where. One has to treat all
related material with a degree of scepticism. Nonetheless, the evidence seems overwhelming that Oscar's physical relations with his
'golden boy', whether they started that weekend in Oxford or not,
remained on what Douglas himself called a schoolboy level; in other
words, mutual masturbation and what is rather prissily referred to as
'inter-crural intercourse', which means non-penetrative sex, rubbing
the penis through one's partner's legs until orgasm is achieved.
Douglas was an active sodomite, who practised buggery with rent-
boys; Oscar was not. Nothing of that kind appears to have taken
place between the two of them. The issue is of more than prurient
concern, as it helps explain why Wilde was so angered by the
Marquess of Queensberry's later allegation that he was 'posing as a
sodomite'. Also, one needs to appreciate that Oscar was determined
to protect Lord Alfred Douglas from provable charges of sodomy,
for which the penalties were far heavier than those relating to gross
indecency or non-penetrative homosexual activity.

Such concerns were far from the minds of Oscar and Bosie when,
in that spring and summer of 1892, they set about falling in love, as
both undeniably did. Robbie Ross, who had graduated from lover to
confidant, without ever fully dropping his claim to Oscar's emotional
commitment, became the recipient of effusive expressions of
Oscar's enchantment for the Scottish Lord. For example, an undated
note from the Royal Palace Hotel in Kensington (probably written in
June 1892), informs him:

My dearest Bobbie, Bosie has insisted on stopping here for sand-
wiches. He is quite like a narcissus – so white and gold. I will come

either Wednesday or Thursday night to your rooms. Send me a line. Bosie is so tired: he lies like a hyacinth on the sofa, and I worship him.

You dear boy. Ever yours.

Oscar

Magnanimously, Robbie decided that he had to accept Bosie's appearance in Oscar's firmament, not just as a shooting star, but as a planet that was likely to stay in orbit for some time. But he had no intention of being entirely displaced from Oscar's affections himself. Over the coming years, Robbie and Bosie would maintain a veneer of camaraderie, which barely concealed the mutual distrust and jealousy that lay underneath, leading eventually to outright enmity. Meanwhile Robbie neatly reversed the roles that might normally have been played by Oscar and himself. As Oscar became increasingly obsessed with Bosie, so Robbie, like some benign uncle, urged caution and restraint. This was not just in regard to passion, to which, as an Irishman, Oscar was predictably not immune. Robbie's cautionary advice also touched on more practical matters, including expense. Thanks to an advantageous percentage deal on theatre takings that Wilde had signed with George Alexander, he was now more affluent than he had ever been. But Bosie, with the insouciance of the true aristocrat, was an effortless spender of other people's money. A bon viveur and inveterate gambler, he demanded – and received – entertainment in London and Oxford: the best food, the best wines and champagne, frequent presents, even boys. Oscar had tended towards profligacy himself while at university, but at that time did not have the means to indulge himself properly; he more than made up for that now. In his long and bitter open letter to Douglas written in prison, *De Profundis*, Wilde chides Douglas for the way he supposedly obliged Wilde to overspend in those three mad years before the catastrophe.

But that criticism was to a degree unfair. For it was an obligation which Oscar fulfilled with love.

Robbie Ross was not alone in finding this largesse disturbing at the time. Pierre Louÿs was back in London in June, shortly before Oscar and Bosie went off to the spa of Bad Homburg in Germany for a cure. Louÿs got caught up in the whirlwind of Wilde's progression round fashionable London venues, with or without Bosie. Although Oscar more often than not picked up the bill, Pierre Louÿs (unlike Bosie) felt morally obliged sometimes to return the hospitality, at the same sophisticated level. Consequently, his funds were rapidly running out, as he complained to his brother Georges and André Gide. André did not approve; he was still puritan enough to regard conspicuous consumption with disdain. But Oscar mocked the disapproval he knew was emanating from his young friend on the other side of the Channel. As he explained to Bosie, this all stemmed from the fact that André Gide was a French Protestant, 'the worst kind, except of course for the Irish Protestant'. Even when criticising, Oscar could not resist a joke and some self-deprecation.

CHAPTER THREE

Salomé

THE THREE WEEKS Oscar and Bosie spent together in Bad Homburg ought in principle to have been their 'honeymoon', but the opportunities for intimacy were considerably limited by the fact that Bosie's mother, Lady Queensberry, and his maternal grandfather, Alfred Montgomery, were there with them. They lodged in the fashionable Kaiser Friedrich Promenade, within easy walking distance of the Kurhaus, where Oscar took the waters and was pummelled by masseurs. To the considerable amusement of Constance, who had stayed in London, he was obliged to rise at 7.30 – several hours earlier than his usual practice – and had to be in bed by 10.30. He was subjected to a strict diet and was forbidden to smoke, which did little to improve his humour. But he did lose weight, and his skin took on a somewhat healthier aspect; that pleased Bosie, who normally found Oscar physically rather repugnant, which put a dampener on their sexual relationship. Besides being with Bosie, Oscar's main consolation was to be seen by European high society not only in the company of but on familiar terms with members of the nobility.

Bosie had suggested the trip to Bad Homburg so that Oscar could leave his professional worries behind in London, but it is clear from letters Wilde wrote between sessions at the baths that the visit was a failure in that respect. The main annoyance was that a play he had written, in French, based loosely on the scriptural story of Salome, had been banned by the Lord Chamberlain's office. The Lord Chamberlain could then veto productions, on the recommendation of the Examiner of Plays, Edward Smyth Piggott, who was memorably described by George Bernard Shaw as a 'walking compendium of vulgar, insular prejudice'. The objection was to the portrayal of biblical characters on stage. *Salome* had already gone into rehearsal at the Palace Theatre in London, with Sarah Bernhardt in the title role, when the censor's axe fell. As Wilde wrote bitterly from Homburg to the artist William Rothenstein:

> [Early July 1892]
> The curious thing is this: all the arts are free in England, except the actor's art; it is held by the Censor that the stage degrades and that actors desecrate fine subjects, so the Censor prohibits not the publication of *Salome* but its production. Yet not one single actor has protested against this insult to the stage – not even [Henry] Irving, who is always prating about the Art of the Actor. This shows how few actors are artists. All the *dramatic* critics, except [William] Archer of the *World*, agree with the Censor that there should be censorship over actors and acting! This shows how bad our stage must be, and also shows how Philistine the English journalists are.

The theme of the Jewish princess Salome – who fails to seduce John the Baptist, and then manoeuvres her stepfather Herod into serving up the prophet's head to her on a silver dish – had excited Oscar's imagination for years. While still a student at Oxford, he had toyed with the troubling images conjured up in his mind by John the Baptist's stubborn martyrdom and Salome's depravity. The figure of Salome had continued to impinge on his consciousness, clamouring for attention. As we have seen, while in Paris on honeymoon with Constance in 1884, he had been particularly struck by the descriptions of Moreau's two paintings of Salome contained in Huysmans' *A rebours*, as well as by the quotation from Mallarmé's epic *Hérodiade*, in which the poet sees Salome's mother, Herodias, as the key figure. Oscar had spoken at length to Mallarmé and many other Paris friends about the whole legend. He shared Huysmans' view that Salome was a personality of supreme fascination, being, as Huysmans put it, 'the symbolic incarnation of undying lust'.

It was probably largely because *A rebours* had made such an impact on Oscar that he visualised his Salome in French. At the same time, the Belgian playwright Maurice Maeterlinck unwittingly influenced him in his choice of language. Wilde, like André Gide, had an immense admiration for Maeterlinck's work. Gide was even claiming at this time that whereas Mallarmé was *the* poet of prime importance, Maeterlinck was *the* playwright and himself *the* novelist, on the strength of *André Walter*!

Maeterlinck's appeal to both Gide and Wilde can be explained largely by the fact that he managed to bring to the stage suggestions of emotions and sensations in the same way that Mallarmé and other Symbolist poets did in verse. That is considerably more difficult to do convincingly in drama than in poetry; Maeterlinck succeeded through the beauty of the rhythm and cadence of his language, as well as by his deceptive simplicity. Those characteristics were already visible in Maeterlinck's first published play, *La Princesse Maleine*, which came out in 1889; Wilde was invited to write the introduction to the English translation. Maeterlinck's style all too readily lends itself to parody, however, so when Oscar first read some early drafts of speeches from his *Salomé* to one friend, his listener howled with laughter, thinking it was a rather clever pastiche. Oscar was not amused.

Salome was rarely far from Oscar's mind during his two sojourns in Paris in 1891. He saw her everywhere, not just in paintings, but in the faces of women in the streets. He would stand immobile in front of the windows of jewellery shops, imagining the stones and baubles displayed there draped across her naked form, or swaying lasciviously as she danced. One evening when Oscar went with Stuart Merrill to the Moulin Rouge, the playwright was transfixed by a Romanian acrobat who danced on her hands. Instantly he wanted her to star in his *Salomé*, dancing just like that. He scribbled a note to that effect to her on a visiting card, which she ignored, doubtless assuming that this was just another ploy to get to meet her on the part of some lecherous old man.

According to an account Oscar gave several years later to the young writer Vincent O'Sullivan, the decisive moment in the formulation of his play came when he had been discussing the theme with a group of young French devotees in a café, and then returned to his lodgings in the boulevard des Capucines. There was a blank notebook on the table, prompting him to write down what he had just been saying. He wrote for hours, until he felt the need to go out for refreshment and to clear his head, installing himself in the Grand Café on the corner of the boulevard des Capucines and the rue Scribe. A gypsy orchestra was playing and Oscar called its leader over to his table, informing him: 'I am writing a play about a woman dancing with her bare feet in the blood of a man she has craved for and slain. I want you to play something in harmony with my thoughts.' The gypsies then played such wild and terrible music that the people in the café stopped talking and looked at each other with blanched faces. Then Oscar got up, returned to his rooms and finished *Salomé* in a frenzy.

Like many of Oscar's stories, this is entertaining nonsense. He did indeed write most of *Salomé* in Paris, but he finished it more prosaically in Torquay, at Babbacombe Cliff, the comfortable home of one of Constance's grander relatives, Lady Mount-Temple. While he was in Paris, however, Oscar took the opportunity of getting some advice from young friends about the acceptability of his French. Various drafts seem to have passed through the hands of people such as Stuart Merrill, the young Symbolist poet Adolphe Retté and Pierre Louÿs. Stuart Merrill persuaded Wilde that it was not a good idea for so many of the speeches in the play to begin with the word 'Enfin', a convenient colloquial term with a host of meanings, more or less equivalent to the English 'Well . . .'. And Adolphe Retté managed to expunge some of the more glaring anglicisms from the text, as well as several lines of a speech by Herod which were little more than a catalogue of fabulous jewels; the speech would have slowed the impetus of the play and was anyway too blatantly reminiscent of Huysmans. However, Merrill and Retté found that Wilde ignored many of their other suggestions and even seemed resentful about them. Pierre Louÿs fared a little better, mainly because he limited himself to grammatical points, such as the correct use of the subjunctive. His most important role was as intermediary between Wilde and the printers.

Because of his visits to London in 1892, Pierre was also witness to Sarah Bernhardt's involvement in the enterprise. In the spring of that year the forty-seven-year-old actress was at the height of her career. Among her most slavish admirers in Paris was the novelist Anatole France (her exact contemporary), who drooled: 'She is poetry itself. She bears upon her face that afterglow of stained glass which the visitations of the saints have left on Joan of Arc, the fanatical visionary of Domremy. She is legend come to life.' So powerful was Bernhardt's presence on stage that only two years previously, when she played Joan of Arc and defiantly spoke the line 'I am nineteen years old!', the audience cheered to the rafters.

Not all of Bernhardt's roles were so heroic. In fact, her greatest successes were often when she was interpreting on stage characters of brazen lasciviousness. Such was her repertoire that fifty respectable Parisians signed a letter to the newspaper *Le Gaulois* asking its theatre critic to persuade her to accept roles that women and young girls could safely see. 'Sometimes she plays a vicious queen, sometimes a strumpet,' the letter ran, 'sometimes a great lady of doubtful morality. How many of us would acclaim her with enthusiasm if she were to play a pure heroine in a moral work!' In Britain there were similar reservations about some of her performances. In the middle of one particularly steamy rendering of Cleopatra, an elderly lady in the audience exclaimed loudly: 'How unlike, how *very* unlike, the home life of our own dear Queen!'

Bernhardt's total lack of inhibition in tackling risqué subjects in many ways made her the obvious choice for the role of Salome, though her being offered it seems to have owed much to chance. She was in the middle of a three-year world tour (during which she stormed cities as disparate and difficult as Melbourne and Bucharest) when she appeared in London for a mixed and not particularly successful season in the spring of 1892. Henry Irving gave a party for her at his home, which Oscar attended, taking a star-struck Pierre Louÿs with him. Sarah Bernhardt had heard of the continuing success of *Lady Windermere's Fan* and told Oscar he should write a play for her. He replied that he already had, later presenting her with a manuscript copy of *Salomé*. Pierre Louÿs, who had earlier boasted to Paul Valéry that he had in his possession back in Paris two great literary manuscripts, namely Wilde's *Salomé* and Gide's *André Walter*, could hardly contain his excitement at being at the centre of what he thought was literary history in the making.

Bernhardt threw herself into the project with gusto. Oscar had met his match when it came to flights of fancy about how the production would be made unforgettable. It would assault all of the audience's senses. Oscar had decided that the Jewish characters in the play would be dressed in yellow, the Romans in purple and John the Baptist in white. But Bernhardt coveted the blue-powdered hair that Wilde had envisaged for Herodias, insisting that Salome should have it instead. She also declared that she herself would do the dance of the seven veils – with which Salome bewitches Herod into granting her any wish that she might have – rather than employing a more nubile stand-in. When pressed on exactly how she intended to execute the dance, she answered coyly that people would have to wait and see. No wonder Oscar called her 'the serpent of Old Nile'.

Oscar asked the gay artist and stage-designer Charles Ricketts to devise the sets. Ricketts proposed that the floor should be black, which would show up Salome's white feet; the sky should be turquoise green, 'cut by the perpendicular fall of strips of Japanese matting, forming an aerial tent above the terraces'. Braziers of incense and oils would send exotic perfumes wafting in clouds across the stage, to intoxicate the auditorium. However, as Bernhardt would be paying the production costs, she sabotaged many of Oscar's and Ricketts's more expensive fantasies. She discovered that she could borrow a more-or-less appropriate set from Henry Irving, and she decided to use many of the costumes from *Cleopatra*. However, Ricketts did design a magnificent new gold robe for Salome, as well as a triple crown of gold and jewels.

It is as well that Bernhardt did not commit herself for further expense, given the way the production was aborted by the censor. She was understandably furious, largely blaming Oscar himself for not realising that the play would fall foul of the ancient law against the portrayal of biblical characters on stage. He protested rather feebly that he thought it would not apply, as the play was in French. But his own wrath was considerable. He gave a series of bitter interviews to newspapers and magazines, in several of which he declared that he was so disgusted with English small-mindedness that he intended to emigrate to France. Robbie Ross interviewed him for the *Pall Mall Budget*, eliciting the comment from him that he would take out letters of French naturalisation. 'I will not consent to call myself a citizen of a country that shows such narrowness in artistic judgement,' Oscar thundered. 'I am not English. I am Irish, which is quite different.'

The British satirical press had a field day. The cartoonist Bernard Partridge produced a splendid drawing of Oscar as a French army conscript (a copy of the script of *Salomé* poking out of his kit-bag), on the fanciful notion that Oscar would have to do military service if he did acquire French nationality. The caricature appeared in *Punch*, which had long considered Oscar to be an object of ridicule. Even in America, his response to the Lord Chamberlain's action was greeted with scorn. The *New York Times*, in its issue of 3 July, gleefully reported that 'All London is laughing at Oscar Wilde's threat to become a Frenchman.'

In France, though, he received a much more sympathetic response, as in his anger he pandered to traditional cross-Channel rivalry. As he gravely informed a correspondent from *Le Gaulois*:

> For me, there are only two languages in the world: French and Greek. Here [in England] people are essentially anti-artistic and narrow-minded. Though I have English friends, I do not like the English in general. There is a great deal of hypocrisy in England which you in France very justly find fault with. The typical Briton is Tartuffe,[1] seated in his shop behind the counter. There are numerous exceptions, but they only prove the rule.

This was strong stuff, which inevitably filtered back to some of his enemies in London, who were only too pleased to have ammunition to employ against him on some future occasion.

The three weeks Oscar spent with Bosie in Bad Homburg provided a welcome respite from the furore in London, though Oscar could not get the banning of *Salomé* off his mind. As he wrote plaintively to Pierre Louÿs, although physically he was undeniably well, he was feeling terribly sad and bored. Loyally, Pierre came to see him, *en route* for Bayreuth, where he planned to wallow in the Wagner

---

1. The absurd anti-hero of Molière's eponymous comedy (1664), which, as Wilde may have conveniently chosen to forget, was itself banned in France when it was first produced.

Festival. Oscar said he would join him in Bayreuth, but failed to keep his promise.

Oscar's disenchantment with England quickly subsided when he realised how much work there was for him to do there. He had signed a contract with Elkin Mathews's partner John Lane to bring out in book form his long poem *The Sphinx*, and even if *Salomé* could not be performed, the text could at least be published. Technically, it was to be a joint publication, printed in Paris, under the auspices of André Gide's publishers, the Librairie de l'Art Indépendant, and Elkin Mathews & John Lane. Oscar was still taking advice from French friends about the text and he made extensive corrections to the proofs, before returning them to the Librairie de l'Art Indépendant in early December, with the request that the reset corrected proofs then be sent not only to himself, but also to Marcel Schwob and Pierre Louÿs.

When *Salomé* came out, in February 1893 – in an ordinary edition of just six hundred copies, plus a *de luxe* edition of fifty larger copies on finer paper – it was dedicated 'to my friend Pierre Louÿs'. Pierre, who had been doing a few months of military service near Abbeville, on the Somme, acknowledged the dedication with a short and apparently sarcastic telegram (which is not extant). This mortified Oscar, who wrote to him in protest from Babbacombe Cliff, where he was working on *A Woman of No Importance*. For once, the letter was not in French, but in English:

[27 February 1893]

My dear Pierre, Is this really all that you have to say to me in return for choosing you out of all my friends to whom to dedicate *Salomé*? I cannot tell you how hurt I am.

Those to whom I merely gave copies have written me charming letters coloured with delicate appreciation of my work. You alone – you whose name I have written in gold on purple – you say nothing, and I don't understand what your telegram means;

some trivial jest I suppose; a drop of froth without wine. How you disappoint me! Had you wired 'Je vous remercie', it would have been enough.

It is new to me to think that friendship is more brittle than love is.

Suitably chastened, Pierre sent Oscar a new work of his own, a sonnet entitled *La Danseuse* (*The Dancer*), as a peace offering. Oscar, never one in his pre-prison days to nurse a grudge, quickly forgave him.

Besides, the response to *Salomé* from many of Oscar's other French and Belgian friends and literary acquaintances was gratifyingly enthusiastic. Stéphane Mallarmé, in true Symbolist fashion, wrote to him to say that from each page 'there arises the unutterable and the Dream', while Maurice Maeterlinck described the play as 'mysterious, strange and admirable'. The popular novelist Pierre Loti, to whom Wilde had also despatched a copy, commented: 'it is beautiful and dark, like a chapter from the Apocalypse.'

Wilde was highly selective in his choice of people in England to whom he sent complimentary copies: mainly those few critics and writers who had deplored the block on the play's production, such as William Archer and Bernard Shaw. However, a review appeared in *The Times*, which irritated Oscar greatly, partly because it claimed that the play had been written specifically for Sarah Bernhardt, but mainly because of its patronising tone. 'As a whole, it does credit to Mr Wilde's command of the French language,' the review read, 'but we must say that the opening scene reads very much like a page from one of Ollendorf's [language] exercises.'

Undeterred, Oscar decided that an English-language version should be prepared for publication. Too busy to do the translation himself, he had what he thought was the inspired idea of commissioning Lord Alfred Douglas instead. Love blinded him to the fact that Lord Alfred's French was not up to scratch, as later would become embarrassingly evident. However, in posterity's view, Oscar's choice of illustrator for the English-language *Salomé* playscript was more felicitous: the iconoclastic young Aubrey Beardsley. Oscar had been impressed with Beardsley's precocious talent ever since their first meeting at the home of Edward Burne-Jones in July 1891, when Beardsley was just eighteen. Both Oscar and Constance gave him encouragement. But what clinched the commission of the illustrations for *Salomé* was the appearance in a magazine called *The Studio* of a recent work the artist had done depicting Salome staring at the severed head of John the Baptist; one of her hands held a lock of his hair, while the other trailed in blood. It was a shocking image that was a foretaste of what was to come, not all of it by any means relevant to the plot. Beardsley used the opportunity of the *Salomé* commission to pursue his own artistic agenda, combining aestheticism with eroticism, beauty with horror. Cruelty infuses many of the illustrations. One of Herodias was deemed too obscene to use. Even the playwright was not safe from the artist's perverse brilliance; Oscar appeared unmistakably as a chubby-faced, fatuous-looking moon. Many of the images were not at all what Oscar had had in mind, but he recognised their originality and power and let them go ahead.

Cruelty was something Oscar was increasingly encountering in his private life as well, not least at Bosie's hands. Oscar had become hopelessly enamoured of the young man, whose own feelings were far more fickle. When Lord Alfred was petulant, cross or more than usually selfish, Oscar was driven to despair. But when things were going well between the two of them, he enjoyed degrees of happiness that he never achieved with anyone else. While staying at Babbacombe Cliff, working on *A Woman of No Importance*, Oscar received a sonnet from Bosie, who was in his last year at university. Oscar acknowledged it ecstatically:

[? January 1893]
My Own Boy, Your sonnet is quite lovely, and it is a marvel that those rose-leaf lips of yours should have been made no less for

music of song than for madness of kisses. Your slim gilt soul walks between passion and poetry. I know Hyacinthus, whom Apollo loved so madly, was you in Greek days.

Bosie was so nonchalant about Oscar's adoration that he simply stuffed this remarkable love-letter and several others into the pocket of a jacket and forgot all about them. Worse still, a couple of months later, he gave the coat to a seventeen-year-old rent-boy called Alfred Wood, without checking first that there was nothing in the pockets. When he discovered the letters, Wood knew exactly who they were from; in February, Bosie had passed the boy on to Oscar with his personal recommendation, the first of several sexual encounters between Oscar and Wood, both at Tite Street (when no-one else was at home) or in hotel rooms. Despite his passion for Bosie, and his mini-affair with Edward Shelley – who was anxious to bring his own relationship with the playwright to a close – Oscar was now definitely in the market for likely lads. Bosie was more than happy with this situation, as it relieved the pressure on him to allow Oscar to make love to him.

Wood saw no reason to show loyalty either to Bosie or to Oscar, between whom he was now being passed like a shuttlecock. He showed Oscar's letters to two friends, William Allen and Robert Clibborn, who were professional blackmailers. They realised that the letter about Bosie's 'rose-leaf lips' was every renter's dream, and assured Alfred Wood that it would prove his passport to a better life by providing him with the funds to go off to America, which was then widely seen by impoverished and unemployed Europeans as the great land of opportunity. Together, the unsavoury trio hatched a plan.

Rather than approach Oscar directly, Wood sent a copy of the 'rose-leaf' letter to the actor-manager Herbert Beerbohm Tree, who was then rehearsing *A Woman of No Importance* at the Haymarket Theatre in London. Tree drew the matter to Oscar's attention and warned him that the letter could easily be construed as evidence of a homosexual relationship. Oscar bluffed successfully by saying that the letter was really a poem in prose, an extravagant artistic conceit which merited being published in a literary magazine. Oscar maintained his bravado when Alfred Wood turned up at the theatre's stage door to see him. According to Wilde's testimony in 1895, during his libel case against the Marquess of Queensberry (not all of which should be taken at face-value), the boy claimed that Oscar's letters had been stolen from him by William Allen and that he had had to go to great trouble and expense to get them back. He said he was afraid of Allen and wanted to escape London for America. He handed a bundle of letters over to Oscar, who gave him enough money for the boat fare across the Atlantic.

When Oscar checked the bundle, however, he discovered that the 'rose-leaf' letter was missing. There then followed a series of visits to Tite Street by the blackmailers that would have been farcical had the situation not been so serious. William Allen brought up the matter of the 'rose-leaf' letter, saying a man had offered him £60 for it; doubtless he expected Oscar to give him at least as much to get it back. But instead, Oscar declared that no-one had ever paid him so much money for such a short piece of work and he therefore recommended that Allen accept the offer he said he had received. Nonplussed by this development, Allen then changed tack, whining that he was in a desperate situation, in need of financial help. Wilde claimed later that he gave Allen half a sovereign out of charity (in reality it was probably more) and Allen left.

Clibborn then turned up and handed over to Oscar the by now very crumpled 'rose-leaf' letter, saying that Allen and he had decided that there was no point trying to blackmail him, as he just laughed at them. Again according to his testimony in the Queensberry libel trial, Wilde said he gave Clibborn half a sovereign and sent him on his way, with the tongue-in-cheek admonition: 'I am afraid you are leading a wonderfully wicked life.'

It is doubtful that this brush with blackmailers went anything like as smoothly as Wilde made out. Although he was probably able to limit his financial outlay in the affair to about £35, and he managed to get these particular criminals off his back, he had had a very nasty exposure to the risks that his new lifestyle entailed. Alfred Wood did indeed go off to America, but not for long; he would be back in England the following year, to join the growing pool of youths who could be drawn on by those who wanted to bring about Oscar's downfall.

Meanwhile Oscar thought it prudent to try to have the 'rose-leaf' letter formally converted into a work of art. He realised that there was no point trying to get a mainstream British magazine to print it, as its meaning was all too clear and (to public opinion of the era) offensive. So instead, Oscar hit on the idea of having it translated into French and published in a small Oxford magazine called the *Spirit Lamp*, which Alfred Douglas edited. Rather than choosing one of his homosexual friends for the translation, Oscar approached Pierre Louÿs. Still embarrassed by the episode of the *Salomé* dedication, Louÿs obliged, and the 'poem' duly appeared. Only gradually did it dawn on Pierre that he had been involved in what amounted to an attempt at a cover-up.

CHAPTER FOUR

Pierre

AVAILABLE photographs of Pierre Louÿs do not do full justice to his looks. Combined with his out-going personality, these were sufficiently striking to appeal to both Oscar Wilde and André Gide. Oscar was quite open in his admiration. Early on in their friendship, he presented Pierre with a copy of his children's book *The House of Pomegranates*, with the inscription (in French): 'To the young man who adores Beauty; to the young man whom Beauty adores; to the young man I adore.' Pierre was too flattered to be unnerved by this. Besides, Oscar never seems to have tried to convert their friendship into a physical relationship; he knew he would be on a hiding to nothing.

André was more circumspect about his feelings for Pierre, which were genuinely confused and fluctuated in intensity. Their intimacy began when they were schoolmates with common literary interests that set them apart from their fellows; they were outsiders thrown together into necessary solidarity in the cause of Art. The intimacy developed as they set about launching their own literary careers, often as collaborators, sometimes as rivals. Their mutual passion for poetry encouraged their use of emotive and romantic language when they communicated with each other, especially in writing. As the relationship developed, they sometimes described themselves not as 'friends' but as 'lovers'.

There is no reason to assume that this relationship between 'lovers' was ever consummated. But on André's part, at least, the emotional involvement was as deep and as painful as if it had been. As early as June 1891, for example, after Pierre had failed to keep an appointment to listen to André reading some of his work in progress, instead sending a note saying he preferred to have dinner elsewhere, André wrote in distress to their mutual friend Paul Valéry:

> [17 June 1891]
>
> Louis [*sic*] killed me cruelly yesterday . . . The desire I had to see him again really burned my heart; I give myself to friendship as I would to a lover (we spoke of these things, you know) . . . I couldn't sleep all night: such things upset me, as if they were done by a lover.

The fact that in this instance André used the feminine form of 'lover', as if talking about a girl, did not conceal the strength of his feeling for Pierre. Nor could he hide his jealousy when Pierre spent time with other people. When Louÿs enthused about a young new discovery, the future novelist and poet Camille Mauclair (the pen-name of Séverin Faust), André complained to Valéry that he felt jilted. Valéry urged Gide to love Louÿs for what he was, rather than trying to make him into something else. It was sound advice, but André found it impossible to follow; he was too enamoured to be able to view the relationship objectively. As a result he was on a seemingly unending roller-coaster, one moment living with a sense of heightened reality because of his proximity to Pierre, the next plunging into disillusionment and pain. Separations – some unavoidable, others self-imposed – provided an opportunity to try to put things in perspective. Gide's sojourn in Munich in 1892 was as much to escape from Pierre Louÿs as it was to recover from the spiritual battering André had received from Oscar.

Pierre never loved André in the way that André loved him, but the relationship did provide him with a kind of moral support that he craved. After a night on the tiles with Robert Sherard, for example, Pierre wrote to André:

[6 October 1892]
Come back quickly, or you won't find me alive. I've just spent twenty-four hours without sleeping, wandering day and night in Paris . . . I feel rather ashamed of what I'm doing, and for the first time in my life, I am horribly disgusted with myself this morning. Come quickly and tell me that you respect me, and that I am Pierre Louÿs.

While Pierre was doing his military service at Abbeville, André was working on a new book, *Le Voyage d'Urien* (*Urien's Journey*), in which the hero is tempted by both women and boys, but succumbs to neither. One of the women he encounters on his travels, Ellis, is clearly based on André's cousin Madeleine, though in a different guise from the beloved girl of *André Walter*; Madeleine was fated to reappear in other forms in several more of Gide's books. Urien's psychological condition remains unresolved at the end of the story, which is a fairly accurate reflection of the author's own state. Carried away by the tide of his own writing, André decided that he must leave on a journey of self-discovery himself, preferably to Italy. Pierre was the only conceivable companion. André wrote eagerly to him in January 1893, urging him to come to see him as soon as his military service was over, to plan the journey. But Pierre turned him down flat. André's mother stepped into the breach and took him to Seville in Spain instead.

Although Pierre spent only four months in uniform, the experience seems to have hardened his attitude to male friendship, particularly when there were intrinsic ambiguities. Military service also coarsened his humour and increased his delight in practical jokes. As we have noted, his heavy-handed telegram to Oscar Wilde about the

Salomé dedication in February 1893 shocked its recipient. Equally, André was distressed to start receiving letters from Pierre addressed to *Miss* Andrée Gide. He decided it might be wise to back off a little from his handsome but unpredictable friend.

Pierre went to London again in April 1893 for the première of *A Woman of No Importance*; Oscar allocated him a fine seat in the stalls, next to the publisher John Lane. Pierre stayed in London just three days, and Oscar invited him to lunch each day. Far from being charmed by the company Oscar was keeping, as he had been only the year before, this time Pierre felt deeply uncomfortable, not least with the overt intimacy between Oscar and Bosie. One morning he called on Oscar at the Savoy Hotel, where the playwright was staying with Lord Alfred. Pierre noted that there was just one double bed with two pillows. To make matters worse, Constance Wilde called by while Pierre was there, bringing Oscar his post from Tite Street. She begged her husband to come home with her, but Oscar quipped cruelly that it was so long since he had been there that he could not remember the number of the house. Constance smiled despite the tears that had started trickling down her face; Pierre was disgusted.

Back in Paris, he recounted what he had seen to several friends, including Henri de Régnier, which led to the following entry in Edmond de Goncourt's diary:

> [30 April 1893]
> On hearing the name 'Oscar Wilde', Henri de Régnier, who has come to see me, starts smiling. I ask why. 'Ah you don't know! Well, he's not hiding it himself. Yes, he has come out as a pederast . . . You don't know that following the success of his play in London, he left his wife and his three [*sic*] children and set himself up in a hotel, where he is living conjugally with a young English Lord.'

This situation became the talk of the town, in both Paris and London. After consultations with his brother Georges, Pierre decided that he could not remain a friend of Oscar's unless Oscar admitted the folly of his ways. Accordingly, when Oscar was in Paris briefly that May, Pierre visited him in his hotel and told him that he would have to choose between leaving Bosie or maintaining their friendship. As Oscar later recounted to André, he looked at Pierre sadly, as he liked him a lot, and for that reason Pierre's reproaches hurt him. But there was no question which choice Oscar would make. 'Farewell, Pierre Louÿs,' Oscar said, 'I wanted to have a friend; in future I shall just have lovers.'

It was not homosexuality *per se* to which Pierre objected; he maintained good relations with a number of gay friends. What bothered him was its public manifestation. He was particularly offended by the way Oscar was vaunting his relationship with Bosie while neglecting his duty to his family, without a care for what other people might think. Many of Wilde's former admirers in London took a similar view. A little discretion would have kept the wolfhounds at bay. But as a libertarian who had no patience with cant and hypocrisy, Oscar believed that it was his right to behave as he pleased, and to give his natural desires full rein. Moreover, Bosie goaded him on, insisting, for example, that when they entered the Savoy Hotel they did so together, through the front door, arm-in-arm, heads held high. Such defiance was intensely provocative.

Pierre stood by his decision to stay away from Oscar. As he wrote to their mutual friend (and Oscar's former lover) John Gray: 'I would very much like to see you for a while, but I cannot come to London. You know I have fallen out completely with Oscar Wilde, and can never see him again, anywhere.' Nor did he.

André continued to meet up with Pierre through the spring and summer of 1893, sometimes entertaining him by playing Chopin or Schumann on the piano. Yet much of André's confidence in the friendship had been destroyed. It was not to Pierre but to his own

diary – hesitantly restarted after a long lapse – that André confessed:
'[March 1893] I have lived to the age of twenty-three, completely
virgin and depraved, so crazed that I ended up looking everywhere
for a piece of flesh on which to plant my lips.' During his own brief
and miserable military service at Nancy the previous winter, he had
failed to follow the lead of some of his comrades-at-arms, who
patronised the local brothels. And in Spain, despite all the inflammatory colour and passion of Holy Week, he had been under the
watchful eye of his mother. This did not prevent him working out
his frustrations in his writing; he managed to produce another short
book for publication, rather poignantly titled *La Tentative amoureuse*
(*The Attempt at Love*).

The southern sun had rekindled André's wanderlust. Pierre had
turned down the opportunity to discover Italy with him; that did not
mean he could not find a replacement companion. For once, luck
was with him. Among his old schoolmates from the Ecole
Alsacienne was one Paul-Albert Laurens (usually just called Paul), the
son of a celebrated artist, Jean-Paul Laurens. The Laurens family had
a house at Yport, on the coast west of Dieppe. It was an oasis of calm
and creative sensibility where André spent several happy weeks that
summer. Then he learnt that Paul, who was following in his father's
footsteps by training to become a painter, had been awarded a travelling scholarship by the Ecole des Beaux-Arts. Italy beckoned, but
with the adventurous illogic of youth they decided to go there via
North Africa. Paul hoped to find the light and Arab folklore that had
inspired Ferdinand Delacroix, whose work he greatly admired.
André hoped to find himself. While doing his packing, he picked up
the Bible that usually accompanied him everywhere, then put it
firmly to one side, leaving it behind.

The two friends set sail from Marseilles to Tunis in the third week
of October. They had barely arrived at that then still charming and
exotic city before a lively and amusing fourteen-year-old Arab boy
called Cécy attached himself to them, proposing himself as their

guide and servant. As André wrote to his mother, in the first of dozens of long letters that he sent her from North Africa, 'we have at our command a joker of a slave, who will be devoted to us.' With Cécy's help, they found amusing places to eat and have tea; they hired a piano and haggled with Jewish and Arab merchants in the souk. André watched in wonderment as their adolescent companion unselfconsciously stripped off his clothes to show his employers how to put on the native burnous. Apart from a social call on some courteous army officers at Carthage, for most of the time André and Paul stayed clear of other Frenchmen, revelling in the sights and sounds and smells of the Arab town. One of André's favourite cafés was frequented by tall, jet-black Sudanese, some of whom had severed toes as a sign of their servitude. Camel-drivers gathered silently in otherwise deserted squares with their charges at night; other Arabs slept like corpses on piles of stones.

André was in heaven. The letters to his mother radiated joy and excitement. For the first fortnight or so, even the weather was fine; André could wander the narrow streets of the medina late at night, under the light of the moon. But he was increasingly incapacitated by a cold that had been bugging him since he left France. One of the friendly French officers urged Paul and him to move south before the winter winds and rains arrived, when they would find Tunis far less pleasant. Their plan was to travel down to Sousse, then along the coast to Sfax and Gabès, with a detour to the island of Jerba, before heading inland and crossing into Algeria. They would stop at various oases in the desert; André instructed his mother to consult an atlas when she read his letters, to monitor their progress. The two friends then planned to settle at Biskra for the worst of the winter. Little Cécy would accompany them as far as Jerba, whence he would be despatched back home to Tunis. In his letters, André kept reassuring his mother that she had nothing to fear for his safety or for his health. Reports of cholera in Sousse were dismissed as alarmism.

André and Paul duly set off, in an elegant landau drawn by four horses, the carriage piled high with books and provisions; like Sarah Bernhardt, they did not believe in travelling light. They had hired two Maltese, one to drive the landau, the other to act as interpreter. Their route took them through Kairouan, one of the holy cities of Islam. The caliph there invited them to a sumptuous feast, consisting of thirty-two different dishes. The following day, at a mosque, frenetic dancers entered into a trance, insensibly swallowing nails, pieces of glass and live scorpions, or pushing long skewers through their own flesh.

Sousse was inevitably something of an anticlimax after such devotional fervour; André thought the town dull. Worse, he immediately went down with bronchitis. Although he initially kept this a secret from his mother, he foolishly confided his lamentable state in a letter to a cousin of his, Albert Démarest. According to André, one of his lungs was out of action, and the other was almost as bad. He was feverish and was sweating; a French army medical officer who had been summoned declared solemnly that it might be tuberculosis and that he could expect to be spitting blood within a few days if he did not leave for a warmer and drier clime. Not surprisingly, Albert passed this disturbing news on to Mme Gide, who began to fret about her son's well-being. André's father had died of the dreaded disease, and he himself had been invalided out of military service because of chest problems. If things got worse, André rashly informed his cousin, he would suggest that his mother meet him in Algeria.

Yet André's illness did not prevent his going out to sit with Paul Laurens, as his friend painted local scenes, or persuaded local children to pose for him. The children fascinated André. Groups of boys would gather outside the hotel where the two friends were staying, out of curiosity or a wish to earn a few coins through some trivial service. André's attention had been particularly caught by one brown-skinned lad called Ali, who one day suggested that he should carry André's overcoat and invalid's rug to the dunes, where André could enjoy some of the weak autumn sun. Paul stopped to paint a group of dark-skinned girls who had gathered by a stream to do their washing, but Ali continue walking up the dunes to a kind of crater whose rim was just high enough to hide someone from view, while also offering a commanding view of the countryside and the opportunity of seeing anyone approach. André followed.

As soon as they got into the crater, the boy threw the coat and rug to the ground, then flung himself down, stretched out on his back, his arms spread out, all the while laughing. André sat down primly at a distance, well aware of what was on offer, but not quite ready to accept. Ali's face clouded; his smile disappeared. 'Goodbye then,' he said, rising to his feet. But André seized the hand that the boy held out and pulled him to the ground. Giggling, the boy started trying to undo the knots that held up his trousers, then impatiently drew out a knife and cut the cord. The garment fell, revealing him naked. 'His body may have been red-hot,' Gide recalled over thirty years later in his autobiographical volume *Si le grain ne meurt* (*If It Die . . .*), 'but it seemed to my hands to be as refreshing as a shadow. How beautiful the sand was! In the wonderful splendour of that evening, what radiance clothed my joy!' André had indeed found himself.

Despite this restorative treatment, André realised that it would be sheer folly to go through with the desert safari Paul and he had planned; instead, they took a boat back to Tunis. From there, they travelled by train to Constantine in Algeria and on to Biskra. There they found admirable first-floor lodgings in a hotel that had been converted from an old Whitefriars' monastic community. André had the grandest room, which had been furnished for a cardinal, no less; it had a balcony that looked out over a palm grove. Paul had the mud-brick equivalent of an ivory tower, a pavilion up a flight of steps at the end of the terrace. They had their own dining-room, and Paul had thoughtfully employed a boy to look after them: a tall fifteen-year-old called Athman, 'as black as the ace of spades', as André informed his mother, 'with fuzzy hair'. The boy was tall for his age, and a little ungainly. But he had a natural authority. In fact, he swaggered around, full of self-importance at being responsible for waiting on the needs of the two French gentlemen. Unlike Cécy in Tunis, who had proved adept at profiting from his position, Athman was, so André had decided, the best and most honest boy in the world, incapable of taking advantage of anyone. Far from grasping whatever he could get, he had a tendency to give away what he had.

Athman's turn of phrase enchanted André. Like Oscar Wilde, Athman spoke French fluently, but with an unconventionality that would have been insufferable in a native speaker; this had all the charm of exoticism when uttered by a foreigner. Athman admired André's literary vocation and intended to emulate it. In the mean time he made André smile with his innocent pretensions. When André had bought some fine lamps and hung them on the balcony, he was amused to see Athman peering over the edge, waiting for someone to pass in the street below. Then he would exclaim 'Ah, what beautiful lamps!', positively swooning with pleasure if the passer-by then looked up in appreciation. Athman had his own little room, beyond the dining-room. There he would sit cross-legged, earnestly cleaning André's and Paul's shoes. André once surprised him at this task, singing to himself, surrounded by lighted candles in dishes and little vases full of flowers.

Confined to the terrace by his continuing ill-health, André would watch wistfully as Paul set off on his artistic forays into the surrounding countryside, Athman trudging behind carrying his easel and folding chair. But André would laugh when the pair returned in the evening, and Paul complained good-naturedly that as Athman hated going far, he had tried to persuade Paul to stop and paint at the first moderately attractive site, praising its beauty to the skies.

Consciously or unconsciously, André began to get emotionally, though not physically, involved with Athman. All the while he told himself that his heart was true to Madeleine, still an angelic and asexual presence at the back of his mind. The fact that Athman's prime loyalty was to Paul, who had hired him, may partly explain why the relationship between Athman and André did not develop further at this stage. In addition, André was not in the mood to fix his attentions on one sole boy. He was captivated by many. Biskra was the perfect place in which to indulge this new passion, and children became his obsession. Some little boys came of their own volition attracted like bees to the perfume of the kind foreigner, who would watch benignly as they played marbles on the terrace outside his room; they in turn would then introduce brothers, cousins or visitors from their home village. Others André met outside the gates of the French school and enticed into the hotel compound, on the pretext that Paul needed models for his work. Paul, in his naivety, was delighted by André's cooperation in this matter, as a series of pretty or striking local children – usually, but not always, boys – turned up to sit for him, at André's invitation.

In *Si le grain ne meurt*, Gide analysed his own behaviour by declaring that the sight of the health of youth sustained him in his illness: 'It was not with any one of them in particular that I fell in love, but with their youth indiscriminately.' From a late twentieth-century viewpoint, 'youth' seems a glaring euphemism. Most of André's and Paul's little visitors were on the wrong side of puberty, as moralists these days would view it. Not that Andre's paedophilia seems to have taken on any physical dimension. Many of his future sexual partners would range between the ages of fourteen to seventeen, with the initiative coming from the adolescent himself. But it was their younger brothers whom André liked to watch playing. In observations not incorporated into the final version of *Si le grain ne meurt*, André discourses at length on the characters of numerous little Alis, Mohammeds, Larbis, Bashirs, Lashmis, Achanis, Telis, Madanis, Noouis, Hammas, Mhamharrs and Sadecks, including several brothers and cousins of Athman. His notes on their personality traits and mannerisms are as detailed as a trainspotter's jottings on locomotives. In that era of Charles Dodgson (alias Lewis Carroll), such

interests were not taken amiss and there is no evidence that André
ever interfered with any of the pre-pubescent children. But it is interesting to reflect that a century later it would have been André Gide,
not Oscar Wilde, who risked prison as a result of his lifestyle.

André himself saw no reason for guilt or even embarrassment.
Paul seems to have thought there was nothing odd about his friend's
devotion to children. And Mme Gide was happy to oblige when
André wrote asking her to send not only the books and sheet music
he habitually requested but also a box of toys.

Besides, Paul knew nothing of André's romp with Ali in the sand
dunes of Sousse. He assumed André was 'straight', if a little inhib-
ited. Furthermore, when Paul became involved with a sixteen-year-
old girl called Mériem from the Oulad Naïl tribe, and generously
offered to share her, André seemed only too pleased to comply.
Having spent some time with Paul, Mériem came to André's room,
let her clothes fall around her feet and stood, naked but for her jan-
gling bracelets. To André's surprise, the union was a success. As he
explained in *Si le grain ne meurt*, however, Mériem had an adorable,
dark-skinned younger brother called Mohammed, and the first time
André made love to her, he imagined that it was Mohammed that he
held in his arms. Nevertheless, as Mériem spent part of each night in
Paul's room at the hotel before moving down to André's, André
began to feel real pleasure from their love-making. Meriém was like
a sturdy young animal, totally without shame, in that way more like a
boy than a girl. It was a tradition in her tribe for poor girls to accu-
mulate a dowry by prostituting themselves, after which they got
respectably married. Paul and André must have seemed like a
godsend. Within a matter of weeks, they had settled into a cosy nocturnal *ménage-à-trois*, with Athman gravely tending to their needs for
refreshments as required. When Pierre Louÿs sent André a copy of
his latest production, a long poem entitled *Chrysis*, about a young
courtesan, André was able to respond smugly that he knew exactly
the sentiments Pierre was describing, as Chrysis's real name was

Mériem, and was currently visiting him nightly. Pierre was astonished and impressed.

It was at this rather inconvenient moment that André's mother announced that she was coming to stay. This intrusion was largely André's fault, as he had first raised the possibility of her visiting Algeria. He found himself torn between the pleasurable prospect of a little maternal coddling and dismay at the prospect of his Biskra idyll being disrupted.

Mme Gide duly arrived, by train, on 7 February 1894, accompanied by her faithful maid Marie, who had long been a forceful presence in the Gide household. The woman who ran the hotel where André and Paul were staying had prepared suitable rooms for the new arrivals. Athman had been running round for days in a state of near hystéria, determined that everything should be perfect for Monsieur Gide's mother. However, André and Paul had omitted to tell Mériem that it might be advisable to make herself scarce for a while. She therefore turned up as usual that night, after Mme Gide and Marie had gone to bed. As inevitably as in a Feydeau farce, just as Mériem was coming down the steps from Paul's tower at dawn, Mme Gide threw open the shutters of her own room, spotted the girl and let out a scream of indignation. André, emboldened by nearly six months away from home, calmly informed her that not only was he aware that Paul was having a sexual relationship with a native girl, but also that Mériem was, as had become the custom, on her way to him. Mme Gide broke down in tears.

In the cold light of morning, the crisis was smoothed over; André and Paul agreed not to allow Mériem on the premises again. As André entertained his little friends from the nearby school, Mme Gide looked on happily, believing that her son had driven all sensual concerns from his mind. The truth was not quite so simple. Having had his libido unleashed by Mériem, Paul Laurens was in no mood to engage in abstinence in order to humour André's mother. He had discovered where the Oulad Nail community lived, fortunately sufficiently far from the hotel to be safe from Mme Gide's dis-approving gaze; André felt he could hardly refuse to accompany him there. The girl they both patronised that evening was a cousin of Mériem's, called En Barka. En Barka was older than Mériem, and far more beautiful. But perhaps her resemblance to the young Mohammed was insufficient; whatever the reason, André failed to get an erection, despite the girl's caresses and cajoling. It was both a humiliation and a disappointment. André paid his money and left, wondering if this failure meant that he would henceforth be impo-tent. Then he reasoned that the real problem was the presence of his mother in the town. He decided it would be better to abstain from any sexual activity during her visit.

Mme Gide and Marie stayed six weeks in Biskra, supervising André's return to health. His strength gradually increased, enabling him to take walks into the countryside with his little Arab compan-ions. He carried a notebook and pencil with him, as he was working on a new book, which would become *Les Nourritures terrestres* (*Fruits of the Earth*). Far from distracting him, the boys who accompanied him inspired him, with their games and moods and their gossip about their friends. Occasionally, among the palm trees, André would chance upon young goatherds, playing on their flutes, putting him in mind of Virgil. The lyricism of such scenes penetrated the marrow of his bones; for the rest of his life, he would look back on those moments with painful nostalgia, shivering over the loss of times past.

Paul Laurens stayed loyally by André's side during his period of convalescence. By the end of the March, however, both felt it was time to move on to Italy; Mme Gide and Marie would return to France. Paul and André retraced their steps to Tunis, which now seemed a dismal town in contrast to the Biskra they had left behind; the cheap lodgings they took were depressing and the fact that Ramadan was in progress made things worse, as the locals strictly observed the fast, staying indoors for most of the day. On 2 April the two friends embarked for Malta. True to their liking for adventurous routes, they then intended to sail to Italy by way of Libya.

Three months later two other young Frenchmen arrived in Algeria in search of artistic and sexual excitement: Pierre Louÿs and his fellow Wagner enthusiast, André-Ferdinand Hérold. Stirred by André Gide's account of the charms and skills of Mériem, the pair had abandoned earlier plans to spend their summer at the Wagner Festival in Bayreuth and instead made their way quickly to Biskra, barely stopping at Algiers *en route*. As Pierre wrote to his brother Georges, the heat at Biskra was infernal; even at night, the temperature was seldom less than 35 degrees. But Mériem was everything that André had said. Pierre had brought her a silk handkerchief from André, as a memento and a form of introduction. For Athman, André had sent a small barrel organ, which the boy soon sold for a few francs.

Mériem entertained Pierre and André-Ferdinand, just as earlier she had entertained Paul and André. They took her off to Constantine, where the heat was less ferocious. There she became Pierre's erotic muse. Her personality and the Algerian environment pervade much of the book of poems he was then writing and which helped make his literary reputation, *Les Chansons de Bilitis*. Few of the early readers of that volume could have realised what lay behind its laconic dedication: 'For André Gide and Mériem B.A., 11 July 1894.'

Through Pierre's letters, Mériem asked André what present he would like from her. Jokingly, he replied: André-Ferdinand Hérold's beard. This was exactly the sort of challenge that appealed to Pierre's taste for pranks. One night, while Hérold was sleeping, Mériem cut off his beard with a pair of scissors, gathered up the hair and put it in an envelope, which Pierre triumphantly sent off in the post.

CHAPTER FIVE

Florence 1894

THE crossing to Valletta was so rough that André Gide and Paul Laurens agreed that they could not face a similar boat journey to Tripoli. They spent a couple of days recovering from their sea-sickness in Malta, which was described by Paul in a letter to André's mother as a 'vast rock which has been made even harder by the British occupation'; the villages all seemed to have cathedrals instead of churches. From Malta they headed for Naples, by way of Syracuse and Messina. Paul was keen to spend a few days examining the ruins of Pompeii. But André felt so ill again, shivering and wheezing, that he decided to press on alone to Rome, where he would be able to consult a decent doctor. The doctor's verdict was fairly reassuring; what André needed was rest. By the time Paul rejoined him, he had settled into a gentle routine of carriage rides to some of Rome's more attractive gardens, where he could sit in the warm sunshine, reading. He had also been to St Peter's in the Vatican, where he saw the Pope, carried resplendently on a throne through the crowds of pilgrims. Despite his Protestant faith, the spectacle brought a lump to André's throat.

André rented a comfortable ground-floor room in the via

Gregoriana, not far from the Villa Medici; Paul found lodgings almost opposite. Between them, they had three pianos and a harmonium, giving them ample opportunity to indulge their shared passion for music. Nonetheless, both of them felt acutely bored and unimpressed with Rome. André told his mother that he would happily exchange both the Colosseum and the Forum for a single Beethoven symphony. The problem was that the two young travellers were missing North Africa. At times they tried to make light of this. Their lunch was brought in from the Villa Medici in a stacked heating device that they dubbed 'Athman'. This did not alter the fact that André, in particular, was unable to get Athman and all the other juvenile inhabitants of Biskra out of his mind. One morning he woke up crying, having dreamt of Algeria during the night. When a letter from the real-life Athman arrived, complaining that his new employers made him get up too early in the morning, André kept rereading it, masochistically nurturing his melancholy. Working on another new book, entitled *Paludes* (*Marshlands*), was one of André's few consolations. However, the book's slow progress became a standing joke with Paul and other close friends.

Meanwhile Paul found a substitute for Mériem, in the form of a high-class Italian tart, whom he entertained in André's room. Later Gide claimed that he could not remember whether he had attempted to make love to her himself; all that remained was a recollection of disgust at the lady's elegance and affectation, so different from the wildness and cynicism of the Oulad Nail.

The doctor wanted André to stay in Rome until the end of June, arguing that the hot, dry weather would do him good. But André was determined to get out of the city before the end of May; he was feeling completely stifled. Florence seemed the most suitable destination. The idea was that Paul would go on ahead, first spending a few days travelling in Umbria; then he would try to find suitable accommodation in or around Florence. But André's dissatisfaction with Rome reached such a pitch after Paul had left that he set off for

Florence himself on 23 May, wrapped up in rugs, and supervising the transfer of a considerable amount of baggage. André arrived in the city before his friend. Almost instantly he felt better than he had for many months, which suggests that his recent poor health was as much psychological as physical.

He found an attractive room in a rather smart family *pensione* which had a view over the Arno. The bridges over the river enchanted him. Even though it was raining, his spirits soared. Paul arrived shortly afterwards and moved into the same lodgings; together, they started to explore. Everything seemed so beautiful, from the historic build-ings of the town centre to the tree-covered hills around. As Francis King has pointed out, in his *Literary Companion: Florence:*

> With rare exceptions – Byron was one – the love which nineteenth century expatriate writers felt for Florence was passionate and unqualified. Of all the cities of Italy, it was the one which, lacking the religious oppressiveness of Rome and the hedonistic frivolity of Venice, they most favoured.

One long-term foreign resident was the then popular Anglo-French novelist Ouïda (pen-name of Marie Louise Ramé), who was just coming to the end of a twenty-three-year stay in Florence when André and Paul arrived. In one of her books, *Pascarel,* she summed up what for her was the special magic of the place:

> The beauty of the past goes with you at every step in Florence. Buy eggs in the market, and you buy them where Donatello bought those which fell down in a broken heap before the wonder of the crucifix. Pause in a narrow street and it shall be that Borgio Allegri, which the people so baptised for the love of the old painter [Cimabue] and the new-born art. Stray into a great dark church at evening-time, where peasants tell their beads in the marble silence, and you are where the whole city flocked, weeping,

at midnight, to look their last upon the dead face of their Michelangelo.

André and Paul concurred. They even found their fellow guests at the *pensione* agreeable. It was quite unusual for André to be civil to adult strangers; frequently, he would ignore people, his forehead creased in an intimidating frown, his nose deep in a book. But in Florence, he was alert to the people and places around him. He scanned the faces of customers in cafés, and of passers-by. One made him sit up with a jolt. The man's features were heavier and uglier than he remembered. But there was no mistaking Oscar Wilde.

Oscar did not seem pleased to see him. André suspected that the playwright, who was accompanied by Lord Alfred Douglas, had hoped to remain incognito in Florence, though that would hardly have been possible considering the number of British expatriates and tourists there. Oscar quickly regained his composure and they sat down together for a couple of vermouths. It was two-and-a-half years since their encounters in Paris, when Oscar had so upset André's equilibrium. André was now more resilient and mature. He still found Oscar a fascinating raconteur – rather as Baudelaire must have been (so André informed his mother), 'but maybe less sharp and more charming'. Oscar had been in Paris with Bosie before they had moved on to Florence, so he was able to give André the latest gossip from literary circles there. He had also written another play, *An Ideal Husband*, guaranteeing that his name would continue to feature prominently in London's West End.

Bosie had spent most of the winter in Egypt, staying at the British Residency in Cairo, as the guest of Lord Cromer, the British Agent and Consul-General there. Lady Cromer was a friend of Bosie's mother, Lady Queensberry, who had been given the idea of sending Bosie to Egypt by Oscar. The two lovers had fallen out dreadfully over Bosie's woefully inadequate translation of *Salomé* and Oscar decided it would be better for both of them if they separated. Bosie was making his life a misery. Having left Oxford that summer, without taking a degree, Lord Alfred had embarked on a course of such self-indulgence that even Oscar's liberal standards were tested beyond endurance. It was as if the young man were actively courting disaster. In particular, in the summer of 1893, there was a most inadvisable affair with a sixteen-year-old schoolboy, Philip Danney, who was the son of a colonel in the British army. This very nearly turned into a dreadful scandal. According to a gleeful and rather malicious account provided to Reggie Turner by the writer and caricaturist Max Beerbohm, Robbie Ross had first become sexually involved with the boy, who was a boarder at a school in Bruges in Belgium. Robbie brought the lad over to London, foolishly boasting of his conquest to Oscar and Bosie, who were then staying at Goring-on-Thames. With typical impulsiveness, Bosie rushed up to London, virtually stole young Philip from Robbie (or so said Beerbohm), installing him in the Albemarle Hotel. Bosie later took the boy to Goring, where – according to corroborating evidence contained in a letter to Frank Harris from the homosexual public schoolmaster Oscar Browning – 'on Saturday, the boy slept with Douglas; on Sunday he slept with Oscar. On Monday, he slept with a woman at Douglas's expense.' The following day, Philip Danney returned to Bruges, three days late for the school term. Questioned by a teacher, the boy revealed what had delayed him.

Colonel Danney wanted to put the matter into the hands of the police. But he was warned by a solicitor that although the men involved would undoubtedly get two years in jail for gross indecency, Philip himself ran the risk of being locked up for six months, as well as having his future prospects ruined. The colonel reluctantly agreed to drop the matter, while Robbie Ross and Lord Alfred Douglas travelled over to Bruges to ensure the destruction of incriminating letters. Robbie's family were aghast at this near miss with total disgrace; he agreed with their verdict that it would be a good idea to stay out of England for a few months. Lady Queensberry was blissfully unaware of the details of this affair, but readily agreed with Oscar that it was wise to get Bosie out of the country for a while as well, in the hope of calming his reckless Douglas temperament.

Bosie enjoyed himself enormously in Egypt. While André Gide and Paul Laurens were savouring the low-life native delights of Biskra, Bosie was cavorting with high society in and around Cairo and up the Nile. A devotee of opera and horse-racing, he was able to indulge both passions fully in Egypt, often accompanied by Lord Cromer. A young British journalist called Robert Hichens was in the crowd at the Cairo races one day when Cromer and Lord Alfred drove by in the Residency carriage; he thought the young man sitting next to the Consul-General looked strikingly aristocratic and poetic. Not long after, Hichens ran into Bosie at a hotel in Luxor. They then teamed up with Reggie Turner and E.F. Benson, who were also cruising the Nile, in order to visit Aswan. Benson was flushed with the success of his recently published novel *Dodo*; not to be outdone, Lord Alfred produced a sonnet he had just written, entitled, *The Sphinx*.

Bosie and E.F. Benson goaded each other into ever-more brilliant repartee and wit; Hichens thought their conversation on the voyage was the most entertaining he had ever heard. Moreover, he was not just listening. He was surreptitiously taking notes, not least when the subject turned to Oscar Wilde. With the material he gathered, Robert Hichens was able to write an anonymous caricature of Oscar's and Bosie's relationship in a novel called *The Green Carnation*, which was to provide yet more ammunition for Wilde's enemies.

Douglas claimed to have written to Oscar every day while he was in Egypt; determined to shake off Bosie's spell, Oscar tore up the letters and threw them away. Oscar knew that in trying to disentangle himself from Bosie, he had an ally in Lady Queensberry, who was quite convinced that her son would be doomed if he continued to be influenced by Oscar's 'eccentricities and peculiar views of morality'. It was a strange alliance between a mother and her son's older homosexual lover, but for a while it seemed to be working rather well. Oscar was relieved to learn that Bosie had been offered an honorary position with the diplomatic service in Constantinople (now Istanbul); again, the main motive was to keep him out of harm's way.

The logical assumption was that Bosie would make his way to Turkey from Egypt when his stay with the Cromers came to an end. But Bosie had other ideas. He chose to go to Athens, to stay with E.F. Benson, who was doing some archaeological research there. At the same time Bosie was bombarding Lady Queensberry with letters threatening that he would do something rash if he was prevented from seeing Oscar. 'There is nothing I would not do for him,' Bosie told his mother in one letter, 'and if he dies before I do I shall not care to live any longer.' Bosie even sent a telegram to Constance Wilde begging her to persuade Oscar to write to him. Otherwise, he intimated, he might kill himself. Unable to resist such emotional blackmail, Oscar agreed to meet Bosie in Paris. He was still determined to formalise a break in their relations, but when he was face-to-face with his beloved, he succumbed to Bosie's entreaties to give him another chance. As Wilde later recalled in *De Profundis*: 'The unfeigned joy you evinced at seeing me, holding my hand whenever you could, as though you were a gentle and penitent child: your contrition so simple and sincere at the moment made me consent to renew our friendship.' Characteristically, Bosie celebrated their reconciliation by running up a vast bill at their Paris hotel.

They returned to London briefly, before Bosie withdrew to Florence, supposedly out of Oscar's orbit; Oscar then went to Paris for a few days, before discreetly joining his lover. They rented a lovely apartment by the river for a month, but had been there only a fortnight when they ran into André Gide. Things were not going well between Oscar and Bosie once again, as was evident from the expression on Oscar's face. Then Oscar startled André by informing him that he had decided to leave Florence the following day, and won-

dered whether André and Paul Laurens would like to take the apartment over for the rest of the month. André went to have a look at
the premises, which were indeed very fine, so initially he accepted the
offer. But later, after discussion with Paul, he changed his mind,
ostensibly because neither of them wanted the bother of having to
arrange for meals to be cooked; at the *pensione* where they were
staying, they could eat in.

That may indeed have been one reason for not taking over Oscar's
and Bosie's lodgings. But circumstantial evidence suggests that there
was also a reluctance on André's part to be publicly associated –
however marginally – with a couple whose behaviour had become so
notorious. Significantly, although André did say in a letter to his
mother that he had encountered Oscar Wilde in Florence, he made
no mention of Lord Alfred Douglas. Even more importantly, André
did not inform his regular correspondent and confidant Paul Valéry
about the meeting with Wilde until several weeks later; by that time
Valéry was on a visit to London, and might therefore have conceiv-
ably found out himself. In a letter dated July 1894, Gide explained
that he had not mentioned Wilde in his letters to Paris, because he
feared Valéry would pass the news on to mutual friends. Even now,
he urged Valéry to keep the information to himself. Clearly André
was worried about being compromised by being thought of as an
intimate of Wilde's. But there might also have been an element of
guilt at play. Robert Hichens was not the only person writing a fictionalised portrait of Wilde behind his back; a key character called
'Ménalque' in one of the two books on which André was then
working, *Les Nourritures terrestres*, was largely based on Wilde.

After Oscar and Bosie had left Florence, André got into the habit
of rising early, leaving the *pensione* straight after breakfast. He turned
his back on the museums and churches of Florence (where Paul
spent long hours copying the works of Italian masters) and set off
for long walks into the countryside, often spending the whole day
out. As he wrote to his mother:

[9 June 1894]

The country round Florence is beautiful, with its pine-trees and cypresses, which give it a funereal and tragic aspect which appeals to me . . . From all the hills over which I walk one looks down on dark Florence, which always seems to be in a state of meditation. Of course, this is not one of those great visions, such as we knew in sun-filled Kairouan; on the contrary, there is a great sadness – yet noble, energetic and constantly protesting. As I walk, I read, I think, I feel myself alive, I am very happy.

One day, Paul accompanied André on his perambulations and was equally seduced by the physical surroundings. He too decided to relinquish the more crowded beauties of the city for the calm of the villages and woods. The two young men struck up a friendship with a group of stone-cutters, who had a shack where Paul could leave his box of artist's materials when he and André went for lunch at what became a favourite trattoria in Fiesole. Usually, there were no other customers eating there, though sometimes André and Paul would invite one of André's few Italian acquaintances, Roberto Gatteschi.

Gatteschi was an extremely erudite and fanatical twenty-six-year-old, who was writing two weighty theses concurrently: one on Sidonius Apollinaris, Bishop of Clermont, and the other on the musical instruments of ancient Rome. He had a very broad range of aesthetic interests, including music, painting, literature and archaeology, and was constantly scribbling notes and thoughts all over little bits of paper. André was amused by Gatteschi's obsessive nature and found him intellectually stimulating. The trattoria in Fiesole became the scene of lengthy and impassioned lunch-time discussions about the relative merits of writers and painters, past and present. Even during the months he had spent in North Africa, André had managed to keep abreast of the French literary scene, largely thanks to his mother, who sent him regular packages of books, as well as cuttings from newspapers and magazines.

Yet after a week or so of gentle walks and pleasurable discourse in the hills, André started to feel dissatisfied once more. The bubbling enthusiasm of the early letters he had sent his mother from Florence evaporated, to be replaced by the same complaint he had communicated from Rome: he was bored. It was not as if he did not have enough to keep him occupied: when he tired of expeditions in the countryside, there was all the art to absorb him in the city; when his eyes demanded a rest from reading, he could sit down at the piano in the *pensione*, where the other guests were only too pleased to enjoy an impromptu musical entertainment. And like Roberto Gatteschi, André had two manuscripts in progress, albeit of a very different kind.

The real problem, as André realised, was that he was on the wrong continent. However European he might be in appearance, education and habits, Africa had awakened something in him which would keep nagging him until he returned there. As he wrote to his mother: '[17 June 1894] Florence bores me . . . *Europe bores me*. I find it hard not to keep thinking all the time about Cairo.' It was presumably Bosie who had put Egypt into André's mind, with his stories of life with the Cromers and his trip up the Nile. André was convinced that people and places in Egypt would be of a totally different order to those he would inevitably encounter anywhere in Europe. Mme Gide was not the only correspondent who was informed of this new obsession. André wrote to Paul Valéry:

[? June 1894]
I dream only of leaving for Cairo; if I were healthier, I would go to Batavia [Indonesia]. Houses with windows, men wearing hats, women with their confessors, bore me. I dream of Africa, where I enjoyed myself tremendously. I will go back there as soon as the temperature is suitable.

The reference to Batavia suggests that it was not just North Africa that was exerting such a powerful pull on André, but exotic travel itself. An intense curiosity about other peoples and their ways of life partly accounts for this. But André's ambivalence to what awaited him in France also contributed to his sense of malaise. André was deeply fond of his mother, but at the same time he often found her overbearing. He was – or believed he was – still in love with Madeleine, yet he was nervous about the possible consequences of renewed intimacy with his cousin, whether or not she continued to reject his proposal of marriage. Travel was a useful means of escape from his responsibilities and difficult decisions, and would remain so for the rest of his life.

The impetus to leave Florence came when Paul Laurens announced that he needed to get back to Paris. His funds were running out, and he wanted to prepare himself for resuming his formal art studies. But even after eight months of travel, André could not yet face going home. Besides, his health had taken a turn for the worse again; he was breathing with difficulty and feared that bronchitis was setting in. The doctor he consulted expressed concern not only about the state of his lungs, but also about his heart. Accordingly, Mme Gide endorsed André's plan to go to Switzerland, though she was becoming impatient with the way his travels kept being prolonged and with his repeated requests for more money. In Switzerland he could benefit from a healthy climate and the best medical attention, notably from a specialist in Geneva who had been highly recommended by André's uncle Charles.

On 23 June André and Paul had a farewell lunch at the little trattoria in Fiesole. Summer had arrived in full force. The heat was intense and the air vibrated with the noise of the cicadas in the grass; the two friends experienced a great sense of well-being. Their friendship had survived the stringent test of such a long time in close proximity and they both felt they had learnt an immense amount. As they reminisced on that last day in Fiesole, André's breathing eased considerably. In fact, by the time he left Florence the following morning, he was in high spirits.

The journey to Geneva did not go entirely smoothly, however, even though he took it in easy stages. At Pisa he considered the Leaning Tower too straight and the Campo Santo too small, or so he told his mother; he did not spend long there as he found the town suffocating. Much more to his taste was the coastal route from La Spezia to Genoa. However, he was dirty and dishevelled when he arrived in Genoa and looked even worse by the time he left; his hotel room was infested with fleas, and he spent much of a sleepless night fighting them off. The only consolation was that at dawn the view from his bedroom window, overlooking the tiled roofs of villas along the coast, reminded him of Zaghouan in Tunisia. As if by magic, this association brought him immediate joy and repose.

In Turin the heat was so infernal that André was revolted by the very idea of food; he craved endless glasses of lemonade and 'iced oxygen'. The museum his mother had recommended he visit was closed that day. He dreaded spending another sweaty night in an Italian hotel, tossing and turning with insomnia. So he decided to get the night train to Geneva, which left Turin shortly before midnight. There was nowhere for him to rest properly beforehand, so he measured out the hours with ice-creams at the station restaurant, going out for a walk between each one. Even on the train, he did not sleep and he could see almost nothing of the Alps in the dark. But as the train climbed up the valleys, the temperature started to fall and André began to savour the breeze through the open carriage window and the smell of the mountains outside.

He arrived at Geneva at 9 o'clock the following morning. 'The weather is splendid,' he informed his mother, 'the air just a tiny bit cooler. A placid and pure serenity over all the town. And the feeling that I am going to get well.'

CHAPTER SIX

Bosie

WHEN OSCAR WILDE sought to excuse, or at least explain, Lord Alfred Douglas's erratic and selfish behaviour, he usually put it down to the young man's genes (of which Bosie himself was immensely proud). The Douglases were one of the most ancient and noble of Scotland's families, but their history includes more than its fair share of derangement and disaster. The most alarming of Bosie's ancestors was James, the 3rd Marquess of Queensberry, who was not inaccurately dubbed the 'cannibalistic idiot'. Mentally disturbed from birth, he was so violent that he had to be confined to a cell at Holyrood Palace in Edinburgh, under permanent supervision. One day in 1707, when there were riots in the streets of the city in protest at the Act of Union between Scotland and England, servants in the palace left him unguarded, as they went out to watch what was happening. The Marquess escaped from his prison and found his way to the palace kitchens, where a young cook's assistant was turning a roast on the spit. The Marquess attacked and killed the boy, then skewered him with the spit and proceeded to roast him over the fire.

An earlier forebear, Sir James Douglas, was a fourteenth-century warrior of formidable bravery who fought in no fewer than seventy battles, mostly against the English; he very nearly captured the English King Edward III on one occasion. Sir James was given the nickname 'Black Douglas', who features not only in several of Sir Walter Scott's heroic novels and stories, but also in the chronicles of his own French contemporary Jean Froissart. Black Douglas's disposition to fight was so notorious that, according to Sir Walter Scott, writing five centuries later, his name was used by 'women in the northern counties to still their forward children by threatening them with the Black Douglas'. Later Douglases concentrated their pugnacity in the boxing-ring. The 6th Marquess of Queensberry, Charles, was a well-known prize fighter. And Bosie's own father, the 9th Marquess, John Sholto, devised the rules which still largely govern the sport, not least adopting the then innovatory principle of pitting fighters against opponents of similar weight.

There was as much tragedy as glory in the Douglas family line, including a suspiciously large number of deaths by misadventure. Some casualties were the victims of genuine accidents; one such was John Sholto's beloved brother, Lord Francis Douglas, who died as a result of a fall while climbing the Matterhorn, causing Queen Victoria to propose that mountaineering should be banned. But several other Douglases undoubtedly took their own lives, usually by a single, well-aimed shot, though the truth of their end was invariably concealed, as suicide was then considered not only a crime but a sin.

Francis Douglas's death probably encouraged John Sholto's agnosticism. At a time when church-going was an important social as well as religious obligation, the 9th Marquess's publicly vaunted lack of conventional Christian faith helped make him unpopular with the Scottish gentry and directly led to his being removed from the list of nominated representative Scottish peers who had the right to sit in the House of Lords in London. To make matters worse, he liked to create scenes, such as interrupting theatre performances when he thought the play or its author was unworthy. He was fond of firing off vituperative letters to the press and he did not shirk from taking real or imagined enemies to court, in a series of legal actions.

The impression has often been given that the 9th Marquess of Queensberry and Lord Alfred Douglas regarded each other with undiluted loathing. The reality was much more complex. In his own gauche way, the Marquess loved his youngest son. He was proud when Bosie got to Oxford University and sincerely thought it was his duty to try to protect Bosie from bad influences both there and in London. Similarly, Bosie would at times make gestures of filial loyalty and respect, such as publishing in the Oxford magazine the *Spirit Lamp* one of the few poems that his father wrote. But such was Bosie's temperament that when he felt his father was rejecting his love, or behaving in some particularly piggish fashion, he turned on him with vehemence. Sharing a hot temper that was often fired by a sense of grievance, the two of them spurred each other on in their vindictiveness.

A central cause of Bosie's ambivalent attitude to his father was the way the Marquess treated Bosie's mother, whom the young man adored. The Marquess's furies and condescension were almost more than anyone could be expected to endure, but when he flaunted his sexual infidelities as well, Lady Queensberry felt she had to escape. She divorced him in 1887, on the grounds of adultery. Her three sons all took her side in the matter, which only heightened John Sholto's bitterness. Bosie in particular became very protective of Lady Queensberry, at times behaving towards her more like a surrogate husband than a son. In letters he would refer to her affectionately as 'my pretty' and 'my darling', endearments that would have been more usual between coevals.

Such closeness did not prevent Lord Alfred exploiting his mother's kind heart and generosity. Relieved to have someone on whom she could focus her love, Lady Queensberry lavished Bosie with spoils. In his autobiography (published in 1929), Lord Alfred attributes many of the follies of his youth to that spoiling:

What was lacking in my home was a father. My mother's spoiling would not have harmed me if my father had been a real father, and had he ever taken half as much interest in his children as he did in his dogs and horses. As it was, I scarcely ever saw him.

All through my childhood and youth the shadow of my father lay over me, for although I loved him, and had indeed a quite absurd admiration for his supposed heroic qualities, I could not be blind to his infamous treatment of my mother, even long before she was driven to divorce him, which took place when I was sixteen.

Lady Queensberry brought Bosie up to love purity, truth and beauty, but going to public school put paid to most of that. Bosie had wanted to go to Eton, which was also his mother's choice; however, the Marquess had put him down for Winchester, and to Winchester he went. The school was going through a difficult period. Indeed, as Lord Alfred recalled in his autobiography, it was 'a sink of iniquity', in which the boys displayed contempt for all religious or ethical standards. He was miserable for the first year or so, until he adapted himself to the immorality of the place, after which he enjoyed himself hugely. 'I left Winchester neither better nor worse than my contemporaries – that is to say, a finished young blackguard, ripe for any kind of wickedness.' Oxford did the rest.

It is tempting to see the undergraduate Bosie's interest in Oscar as a form of recompense for not having a 'real' father. In many ways Oscar played that paternal role splendidly. He gave Bosie admiration as well as love, encouragement as well as indulgence. Oscar did many of the things a doting father would have done, such as taking Bosie to smart restaurants and introducing him to prominent figures in London's literary world. In return Oscar hoped for a reciprocity of attention and consideration; but in father–son relationships (at least in Western countries), that is rarely the case. Bosie expected warmth and support – moral as well as financial – from Oscar, but without the obligation of dependency. Not surprisingly, from time to time, Oscar felt he was being used.

To complicate matters further, Bosie consciously or unconsciously played Oscar and the Marquess of Queensberry off against each other, manoeuvring Oscar into situations which would rile his father. For example, at the beginning of April 1894, when Oscar and Bosie had just arrived from Paris, but before Bosie set off for Florence, the two of them took lunch together at the Café Royal, in open defiance of the Marquess's expressed wish that they should stay apart. As luck would have it, the Marquess was at the Café Royal himself that day; with growing anger, he spied on their animated and intimate conversation. His wrath was temporarily defused when they invited him over to join them for a drink. Oscar turned on all his Irish charm, so much so that as the Marquess left the table after a short while in their company, he told Bosie he could quite undersand why he was so fond of Wilde, saying 'He is a wonderful man.'

Within a matter of hours, though, Oscar's spell had worn off and the Marquess despatched a stern letter to his son which spelt out in no uncertain terms his outrage and his determination to use any means in his power to force Bosie to end his intimacy with Oscar:

It must either cease or I will disown you and stop all money supplies. I am not going to try and analyse this intimacy, and I shall make no charge; but to my mind to pose as a thing is as bad as to be it. With my own eyes I saw you both in a most loathsome and disgusting relationship as expressed by your manner and expression. Never in my experience have I ever seen such a sight as that in your horrible features. No wonder people are talking as they are. Also I now hear on good authority, but this may be false, that his wife is petitioning to divorce him for sodomy and other crimes. Is this true, or do you know of it? If I thought the actual thing was true, and it became public property, I should be quite justified in shooting him at sight. These Christian English cowards and men, as they call themselves, want waking up.

Your disgusted so-called father,

Queensberry.

Far from being intimidated by this blast from his father, Bosie responded with a short and insolent telegram, which he knew would enrage the recipient: 'What a funny little man you are.'

Bosie thought this was a clever and sophisticated riposte; certainly it was the sort of thing that would have gone down well among Oxbridge undergraduates. However, Oscar was horrified. He rightly feared that the Marquess would receive this latest act of contempt by his youngest son as a challenge. Sure enough, Queensberry reacted by sending Bosie a letter in which he repeated his threat to cut off his allowance if he continued to see Oscar, adding the warning that if 'I catch you again with that man I will make a public scandal in a way you little dream of.'

Hence Bosie's departure for Florence, Oscar's ploy of going there later by way of Paris, rather than risk being seen travelling together – and Oscar's dismay at the chance encounter with André Gide. It is possible that Oscar left Florence precipitously partly because the relationship with Bosie was uncomfortable but also because he was worried that he would meet people who might relay the news back to London, where Queensberry could hear of it. Oscar wanted to avert any provocation that could lead to the Marquess ending his allowance to Lord Alfred, as that would make Bosie even more of a financial burden than he was already. More importantly, Oscar took very seriously Queensberry's threats of violence or of creating a terrible scandal. The unfounded allegations in Queensberry's letter to Bosie about Constance wanting to divorce Oscar on grounds of sodomy could be extremely damaging if they were made public.

Oscar therefore decided it was time he consulted a lawyer. He returned to London in early June, and would have liked to have hired

Sir George Lewis, the solicitor who had so skilfully arranged to pay off the youth who had tried to blackmail Bosie at Oxford two years previously. This time, unfortunately, Lewis was unavailable; Queensberry had got there first, and hired Lewis himself. At Robbie Ross's suggestion, Oscar turned to his solicitor, Charles Humphreys, whose firm specialised in criminal law, but was far less knowledgeable and adroit than Lewis's regarding the special considerations necessary in delicate cases such as this.

Under Oscar's instructions, Humphreys sent off a solicitor's letter to the Marquess of Queensberry demanding an apology for the way that he had 'most foully and infamously' libelled Wilde in letters to Bosie. Queensberry parried by refusing to tender any apology, arguing that he had made no direct accusation against Oscar and was merely trying to bring an end to the playwright's undesirable association with his son. Queensberry followed this letter with a visit to Humphreys's office, where he threatened that if Oscar and Bosie continued to defy him by behaving scandalously in public, then he would take the matter up with the police at Scotland Yard.

Presumably Humphreys advised Wilde to take no action for the time being, but the Marquess had no intention of letting things rest there. On 30 June he turned up unannounced at Oscar's house in Tite Street, accompanied by one of the intimidating 'heavies' he used to employ on occasions when he wanted to frighten his adversaries. The Wildes' young servant nervously showed the visitors into Oscar's library; what happened next is unclear. According to Queensberry, Oscar capitulated and agreed to terminate his relationship with Bosie. However, Oscar's version was quite different. He told Robbie and other close friends that he bravely stood up to Queensberry and his bully-boy and drove them out of the house, informing the servant that the Marquess should never be admitted again.

Meanwhile, Bosie had returned to London; the honorary diplomatic appointment in Constantinople had fallen through, and he had no wish to linger on the Continent in pointless exile. Partly to spite his father, he intended to resume his regular meetings with Wilde. And it is clear from Oscar's letters to Bosie that summer that despite the dangers, on his side the passion had not waned:

[? July 1894]

It is really absurd. *I can't live without you.* You are so dear, so wonderful. I think of you all day long, and miss your grace, your boyish beauty, the bright sword-play of your wit, the delicate fancy of your genius, so surprising always in its sudden swallow-flights towards north or south, towards sun or moon – and, above all, you yourself.

Somehow, even with such troubling preoccupations, Oscar was managing to keep working. He had to, as he was living above his means. His long poem *The Sphinx* was published in a limited edition, though little financial benefit could be expected from that. Casting for *An Ideal Husband* had begun, and Oscar had been commissioned to write a fourth comedy, which would become *The Importance of Being Earnest.* Oscar realised that he needed to get out of London if he was to be able to write the play. Unable to afford a hotel in one of the more fashionable seaside resorts, he rented a rather small house suitably called The Haven, on the Esplanade at Worthing on the Sussex coast, taking Constance, their two little boys Cyril and Vyvyan, and their rather horrid, ugly Swiss governess with him.

Oscar made good progress with *The Importance of Being Earnest* and even drafted a rough scenario for a fifth comedy, which he never wrote (though it was eventually turned by Frank Harris into *Mr and Mrs Daventry*). He tried to dissuade Bosie from coming down to Worthing to visit him, knowing this would interrupt his work, though the excuse he gave for putting Bosie off was that he feared Lord Alfred would be bored. However, Bosie was not someone who could be put off easily. To Constance's dismay, he came to stay for a few days at a nearby hotel, and immediately monopolised Oscar's company. Together they became friendly with three young boys whom they met on the beach; one, Alfonso Conway, a newspaper-seller, became Oscar's favourite. Oscar took him on an outing to Brighton and bought him a new suit of clothes.

Oscar was as addicted to such casual juvenile company as he was to Bosie's, even if his love for Lord Alfred was on a very different plane. Sex was not always involved, but it was a welcome bonus if the boy who had caught Oscar's fancy was willing. Such compliant youths would often be passed round networks of homosexual friends, which in principle made such liaisons less risky. Yet for some people, the inherent danger of illegal sex gave it an added appeal; that was certainly the case for Oscar, who derived great pleasure from 'feasting with panthers', as he described his courting of working-class youths, any one of whom was a potentially dangerous animal who could do him great harm.

As a timely reminder of the hazards to which he was exposing himself, one morning in Worthing Oscar read in the newspaper of a police raid on a club in Fitzroy Street in London, during which eighteen men had been arrested, including two in drag. One of the men taken into custody was Alfred Taylor, who was well known to Wilde. A former pupil of the reputable public school at Marlborough, Alfred Taylor was the scion of an affluent family of cocoa-manufacturers. He frittered away a comfortable inheritance, entertaining generously at his home in Westminster, which became a meeting-place for well-connected homosexuals who liked rough trade. Taylor even went through a form of marriage ceremony with one young man, Charles Mason – a detail Pierre Louÿs was quick to circulate in Paris. Through Alfred Taylor, Oscar met a series of boys, such as Charles Parker and Sidney Mavor (whom Oscar took off to Paris for a classic dirty weekend). Some of these boys would later be brought into court to give evidence against him. Typically, when Oscar heard of Alfred Taylor's arrest, his first reaction was compassion. He wrote to Charles Mason expressing the hope that Taylor's family, from whom he was estranged, would rally round him. He deplored the fact that he himself was in such straitened circumstances that he could not send any money to assist Alfred Taylor.

In addition to growing financial worries, Oscar was beset by other irritations which with hindsight one feels he should have recognised as danger signals. His publishers, John Lane and Elkin Mathews, threatened to renege on the contract to bring out a book version of Wilde's earlier speculative fiction on the supposed homosexual inspiration of Shakespeare's sonnets, *The Portrait of Mr W.H.*, despite the fact that they had been advertising its forthcoming appearance for many months. John Lane seems to have got cold feet about being associated with such a controversial subject, given the swelling gossip about Oscar and Bosie. In revenge, Oscar gave Lane's name to the unctuous manservant who appears in the first scene of *The Importance of Being Earnest.*

In September Robert Hichens's anonymous satire of Wilde and Douglas, *The Green Carnation*, was published; Oscar and Bosie were instantly recognisable as the characters Esme Amarinth and Lord Reginald Hastings. Such was Oscar's reputation for self-publicity that even some of his friends wondered whether he had written the novel himself. Oscar and Bosie both made light of the book, but they must have known that it served to intensify the spotlight on their relationship. The Marquess of Queensberry was so incensed by it that he took to touring the Café Royal and other London restaurants regularly patronised by Wilde and Douglas in the past, in the hope of catching them together and making a scene. In fact, Oscar was still in Worthing, though Constance and the children had returned to London. Bosie came to visit him again, and Oscar suggested they go off for a few days to Dieppe. Instead, at the beginning of October, Bosie persuaded him to book them both into the elegant Hotel Metropole in Brighton, a move that was guaranteed to exacerbate Oscar's financial problems and to put the two of them even more into the public gaze.

In Brighton Bosie soon went down with 'flu, so for four or five days Oscar found himself playing the role of nursemaid. He faithfully sat by Bosie's bed, feeding him and giving him medicine, reading to him and generally keeping him amused. When Bosie felt better, they moved into lodgings in the town, so Oscar could get on with writing his play. But then he succumbed to Bosie's virus and had to take to bed himself. Bosie had no aptitude for looking after invalids, and quickly left Oscar to his own devices, on one occasion abandoning him without even a glass of water to drink. When Oscar remonstrated about this negligence, Bosie threw such a violent tantrum that Oscar dragged himself out of bed and down the stairs, to try to call for help. In response, Bosie simply packed his bags and returned to the hotel.

On 16 October, Oscar's fortieth birthday, he received a poisonous note from Bosie, bragging about the fact that he had charged his hotel bill to Oscar's account and ending: 'When you are not on your pedestal you are not interesting. The next time you are ill I will go away at once.' There may well have been a masochistic element in Oscar's relationship with Bosie, but this was going too far. He was so hurt that he determined that this time he really was going to bring their affair to an end.

By 19 October Oscar had recovered sufficiently to travel up to London. He had decided that when he got there he would instruct the solicitor Charles Humphreys to inform the Marquess of Queensberry that he was ready to give an undertaking never to see Bosie again. But as he perused the morning paper at Brighton railway station, his eye was caught by a report of the death of Bosie's eldest brother Francis, Viscount Drumlanrig, who had been killed in what purported to be a shooting accident the day before. Though the newspaper made no mention of any doubts about this version of events, not for the first time in the Douglas family the more likely explanation was suicide. Rumours had been circulating – some of them probably originating from the Marquess of Queensberry – that

Drumlanrig was involved in a homosexual relationship with the Foreign Secretary, Lord Rosebery, for whom he worked as a private secretary. Queensberry had even travelled to Bad Homburg the previous year to confront Rosebery with this allegation; the Prince of Wales, later Edward VII, had had to intervene to get the police to send Queensberry away.

Obviously, Drumlanrig's death meant this was not the moment for Oscar to cut off all contact with Bosie. On the contrary, he telegraphed to his lover, making himself available as a shoulder for Lord Alfred to cry on. As Oscar wrote to the author and criminologist George Ives: '[22 October 1894] It is a great blow to Bosie: the first noble sorrow of his boyish life: the wings of the angel of Death have almost touched him: their purple shadow lies across his way, for the moment: I am perforce the sharer of his pain.'

Lord Queensberry did not attend his eldest son's funeral. Instead, by cruel coincidence, he was hearing the annulment proceedings brought against him by his second wife, Ethel, an attractive young woman whom he had met in Eastbourne. They had been married only since the previous November, but she had already decided she could not bear him any longer. The grounds for the annulment were non-consummation of the marriage, due to alleged 'genital malformation' on his part. This humiliating turn of events did nothing to improve Queensberry's mood. Having (so he reasoned) lost his heir Lord Drumlanrig because of homosexuality, the Marquess was even more determined to save his youngest son from the same fate.

As so often, Bosie reacted with defiance. Largely under his influence, the *Spirit Lamp* had provided a platform for those who wished to express discreet homosexual sentiments. Now, with Bosie's encouragement, an undergraduate at Exeter College, Oxford, Jack Bloxam, wanted to go further by launching a new literary review, called *The Chameleon*, which would publish some overtly homo-erotic pieces. Oscar was introduced to Bloxam by George Ives. Ives had himself just come under fierce attack in the *Review of Reviews* for an article he had published in *Humanitarianism*, lamenting the absence of a discussion of homosexuality in a recent essay by Grant Allen. The *Review of Reviews* denounced Ives's piece as a 'dissertation in praise of unnatural vice', adding that 'the New Morality which is seeking for a new heaven and a new earth might . . . have gone elsewhere for its ideal than Sodom and Gomorrah.'

Oscar congratulated Ives on being the object of this attack. 'When the prurient and the impotent attack you,' he wrote, 'be sure you are right.' Oscar was therefore favourably disposed when, at Ives's rooms in the Albany, Jack Bloxam asked if he could publish some of Wilde's epigrams in the first issue of *The Chameleon*. The fact that Oscar considered Bloxam to be 'an undergraduate of strange beauty', as he informed his friend the journalist and parodist Ada Leverson, provided a further incentive. Accordingly, Oscar supplied *Phrases and Philosophies for the Young*, which began with the exhortation: 'The first duty in life is to be as artificial as possible. What the second duty of life is no-one has yet discovered.'

Doubtless Jack Bloxam saw the Wilde aphorisms as the new magazine's greatest selling-point (though its circulation was restricted to 100 copies by subscription, partly because of its controversial content). But other items in the magazine's first and only number caused more of a stir than Wilde's contribution. There were two poems with obvious homosexual overtones written by Bosie: *In Praise of Shame* and *Two Loves*. The latter ended with the now celebrated lines:

> 'I am true Love, I fill
> The hearts of boy and girl with mutual flame.'
> Then sighing said the other, 'Have thy will,
> I am the love that dare not speak its name.'

Even more provocatively, *The Chameleon* printed an anonymous story, written by Bloxam himself, called *The Priest and the Acolyte*, about a priest who falls in love with an altar-boy. The story makes a plea for people not to judge others by their own conventional – and hetero-sexual – standards and practices:

> To think that we are all the same is impossible; our natures, our temperaments are utterly unlike. But this is what people will never see; they found all their opinions on a wrong basis. How can their deductions be just if their premises are wrong? One law laid down by the majority, who happen to be of one disposition, is only binding on the minority legally, not morally. What right have you, or anyone, to tell me that such-and-such a thing is sinful for me? Oh, why cannot I explain to you and force you to see . . .

Oscar instinctively sympathised with the idealism of those senti-ments, even if he had a low opinion of the literary qualities of the story itself. On the publication of *The Chameleon*, in December, he confided in a letter to Ada Leverson that *The Priest and the Acolyte* was 'to my ears, too direct: there is no nuance: it profanes a little by revela-tion: God and other artists are always a little obscure. Still, it has inter-esting qualities, and is at moments poisonous: which is something.'

Other, less indulgent critics, also thought the story was 'poison-ous', but in a dangerous way. In an editorial in his journal *To-Day* the comic novelist Jerome K. Jerome fulminated against *The Chameleon* for 'the undesirable nature of some of its contents' – a blast which helped to hasten its demise. Later Oscar berated Alfred Douglas for allegedly getting him involved with such a notorious publishing venture. But at the time he seems to have been more amused than alarmed. Furthermore, as a camp in-joke to be savoured by Bosie and other close friends, Oscar even gave the name 'Lady Bloxham' [*sic*] to a character in *The Importance of Being Earnest* (to which play he was then putting the final touches): she was supposed to be the tenant in Jack Worthing's London house in Belgrave Square.

The New Year 1895 opened in triumph, with the première of *An*

Ideal Husband at the Theatre Royal, Haymarket. The Prince of Wales was among the glittering audience and enthusiastically commanded Oscar not to change a word of the text. Also present were several Cabinet Ministers, including Arthur Balfour and Joseph Chamberlain. The play was of particular interest to politicians, as it dealt with the moral dilemma of a talented man, Sir Robert Chiltern, who had committed a dishonourable act to advance his political career. Chiltern's past comes to haunt him in the form of the blackmailing Mrs Cheveley, who warns:

> Nowadays, with our modern mania for morality, everyone has to pose as a paragon of purity, incorruptibility, and the other seven deadly virtues — and what is the result? You all go over like ninepins — one after the other. Not a year passes in England without somebody disappearing. Scandals used to lend charm, or at least interest to a man — now they crush him. And yours is a very nasty scandal. You couldn't survive it.

At the end of the play, there was sustained applause and loud calls for the author. But Oscar had already left the theatre, unwilling to confront his public as self-confidently as he had at the opening of *Lady Windermere's Fan* three years earlier. Instead, he repaired to the Albemarle Club for supper with Bosie and a few close theatrical colleagues. Oscar knew he had another assured success on his hands (though some critics, such as Bernard Shaw, were less enthusiastic than the first-night audience). Yet his mind was far from being at rest. He was surely aware that the likelihood of scandal hung over his head just as perilously as it did over that of the fictitious Sir Robert Chiltern. Oscar might not be a politician, but he was in the public eye and therefore equally vulnerable to the 'modern mania for morality'.

Moreover, Oscar was worried about his next play, which was due to open in just six weeks' time. George Alexander, who had started rehearsing *The Importance of Being Earnest* at the St James's Theatre, had expressed the opinion that the play was too long; reluctantly, Oscar had cut it down from four acts to three. Alexander also made it plain that he would prefer that Oscar stay away from the rehearsals; there had been considerable acrimony between Wilde and some of the cast of *An Ideal Husband* because of the way he drove them on relentlessly in search of his idea of perfection, even over Christmas. Alexander was therefore relieved when Oscar informed him he was leaving London for a couple of weeks' holiday. The weather in London was particularly cold at the time, which made the lure of the Mediterranean considerable. Rather than head for the Riviera, however, Bosie persuaded Oscar that a jaunt to Algeria was exactly what both of them required. In mock despair, Oscar wrote to Ada Leverson: '[?16 January 1895] Yes: I fly to Algiers with Bosie tomorrow. I begged him to let me stay to rehearse, but so beautiful is his nature that he declined at once.'

A journalist from *The Era* caught Oscar on the eve of their departure. Obligingly, Oscar provided him with what the journalist called characteristic quips, duly reproduced in the paper's columns a few days later. 'The stage is the refuge of the too fascinating' was one; another was 'only mediocrities improve'. Tartly, *The Era* commented that these remarks were quite up to the 'Wildean standard of sententious statement'. In reality, they were damp squibs. Oscar was tired and uninspired; he was not feeling well. And at the back of his mind there was a nagging conviction that something terrible was going to happen.

CHAPTER SEVEN

Algeria 1895

BY 1895 Algeria had become such a fashionable winter destination for European travellers that the London publisher John Murray brought out a new edition of its travel guide to that country and neighbouring northern Tunisia, compiled by Sir Robert Lambert Playfair, a former diplomat who was the author of such evocative works as *The Scourge of Christendom*. In his preface to the 1895 edition, the compiler emphasised the importance of new facilities then on offer in Algeria, including enhanced accommodation at the increasingly popular oasis resort of Biskra, where André Gide and his friend Paul Laurens had spent the previous winter. Playfair noted approvingly that in front of Biskra's modern French fort there were well-tended public gardens that offered an agreeable and shady walk. He declared the marketplace also worthy of a visit, 'for the curious nature of the wares exposed for sale, and the picturesqueness of the vendors and the buyers'. He acknowledged that the street of the Oulad Nail (where Mériem and her cousin En Barka were based) was one of the curiosities of the town, adding primly that 'it is not a sight to be recommended to English ladies.'

What Playfair did not mention was that there were curiosities of a different kind in Algeria which had helped make the French-ruled territory a considerable draw to a certain kind of European male clientele: namely the beauty and availability of its Arab boys. Lord Alfred Douglas was well enmeshed in the late nineteenth-century international homosexual underground network – the precursor to what in the 1930s the poet W.H. Auden memorably dubbed the 'Homintern' – and so was well informed on the best places to go.

In particular, there was the walled town of Blidah, about fifty kilometres from Algiers – a prosperous place with a large French garrison, a cavalry barracks and a horse stud, as well as a sizeable native town. Outside the walls there were woods and extensive orange and lemon groves, where both visitors and local boys liked to go for walks. Oscar and Bosie went to stay there for several days, lodging at the Grand Hôtel d'Orient (described by Playfair as 'comfortable, well-managed and clean; Cook's coupons, Series A, B and C, accepted'). As Oscar reported back to Robbie Ross in a letter sent from Algiers:

> [late January 1895]
> There is a great deal of beauty here. The Kabyle boys are quite lovely. At first we had some difficulty in procuring a proper civilised guide. But now it is all right, and Bosie and I have taken to haschish: it is quite exquisite: three puffs of smoke and then peace and love. Bosie wakes up at night and cries like a child for the best haschish. We have been on an excursion into the mountains of Kabylia – full of villages peopled by fauns. Several shepherds fluted on reeds for us. We were followed by lovely brown things from forest to forest. The beggars here have profiles, so the problem of poverty is easily solved.

Interestingly, Oscar made no mention in this letter to Robbie that in Blidah, Bosie and he had also acquired an unpaid companion: André Gide.

André had been considerably reinvigorated by his health cure in

Switzerland the previous summer. For six weeks he had taken a pre-scribed series of cold baths and showers, as well as breathing in the clear mountain air. When he arrived back home in La Roque in Normandy in August, after an absence of ten months, he was far fitter than his mother had dared hope. A whole group of friends and relatives had gathered to welcome him, though it was his cousin Madeleine that he was particularly anxious to see. Yet even with her, he felt a disturbing sense of estrangement; his life and thinking had undergone radical changes during his travels in North Africa and Italy, whereas his family and friends seemed to have stayed exactly the same. He had so many new things that he wanted to say to them, but he felt unable to speak, convinced that they would not even begin to understand. Although he could forgive them for not realising how much he had changed, he looked on them as aliens. The prospect of Paris and the artificiality of the life of its literary salons was even more unpalatable. After barely a fortnight in France, he headed back to Switzerland.

André found accommodation in a temperance hotel at Neuchâtel, where he recovered hope in life. He strolled under the autumn-tinted trees, reading Gottfried Leibniz's philosophical work *Theodicée* (1710) as he walked. One wall of the hotel dining-room bore the huge inscription 'The Lord Is My Shepherd; I Shall Not Want', below which a smaller notice proclaimed more mundanely 'Raspberry Lemonade'. There André devoured even heavier intellectual fare: a huge manual of zoology, which unveiled a world that was even richer than the world of thought. He savoured the Latin names of previ-ously unimagined species and sub-species, several of which passed straight into the manuscript on which he was working, *Paludes*.

When the days grew shorter, André followed his doctor's orders and moved to a little village called La Brévine high up in the Jura, near the border with France. For weeks the temperature never rose above zero. André took three rooms in a farmhouse and slept there with the windows open, his body and head wrapped up in blankets and mufflers, his feet pressed against a stove that was built into the wall. The largest room he used as a study; he had had a piano sent up from Neuchâtel, so he was able to alternate beween playing that and standing at a tall writing-desk, where he worked on *Paludes*.

Most days he would hike in the frozen countryside, meeting the sullen and hostile stares of the few farmers he encountered along the way. For nearly three months, André stayed in La Brévine without talking to a soul, apart from the buxom local girl who came each day to clean his rooms. The girl often spoke of her fiancé, and one morning produced a photograph of him for André to admire. As she was bent over him, André impulsively tickled her neck with the feather of his quill-pen. To his acute embarrassment, she then collapsed into his arms. He lugged her over to a sofa, where she pulled him down on top of her. As his head was enveloped in her heaving bosom, a wave of nausea swept over him. He managed to pull himself away, telling the girl falsely that he heard voices approaching. Then he rushed out of the room, to wash his hands.

Once he had finished *Paludes*, André felt he could justifiably leave Switzerland, which he had grown to detest. His health was restored and he had promised himself that his reward for successfully completing his cure would be a return journey to North Africa. At Christmas he went briefly to Paris, where, somewhat half-heartedly, he asked his mother and Madeleine whether they would like to accompany him; he was relieved when they replied that they did not think that was a good idea, quite apart from the expense.

Accordingly, armed with several volumes of Dickens in French translation, André travelled back south and set sail for Algiers, intending to settle in that city, which he hardly knew. The crossing was so rough that he was laid out on his bunk with sea-sickness, unable to move. He had hoped to find a premature spring when he arrived in Algiers on 22 January, with the sun reflected off the city's whitewashed buildings. Instead, the weather was miserable. The sky was dark and the rain heavy. An icy wind was blowing from far inland. André was informed that it would be impossible to rent suitable lodgings in the Arab quarter, while the more elegant French district was not 'authentic' enough for his taste. He wandered the boulevards, feeling utterly depressed. He wrote a despairing letter to his mother, complaining that he had been plunged into a new mental crisis. Nothing in Algiers aroused his interest. He was sure he would not be able to write a word of the book he had begun on his previous visit to North Africa, *Les Nourritures terrestres*.

Yet forty-eight hours later, as soon as he had turned his back on the city, and the clouds cleared to reveal a weak but warm sun, his spirits soared. He headed for Blidah, hopeful that he would find there the exaltation that he had known at Biskra the winter before. He had heard Blidah romantically described as the 'desert rose'. But he was quickly disillusioned, his mood a barometer of forces beyond his control. The weather closed in again; under the overcast sky, the snow-topped mountains around Blidah seemed not beautiful but mournful. Arabs huddled in their robes, looking as uncomfortable and out of place as André felt. He locked himself away in his room at the Grand Hôtel d'Orient, and sent a telegram to his former landlady at Biskra, asking whether she had room for him there. She replied promptly, saying everything would be ready for him whenever he wanted to come. He envisaged shutting himself off from the world at Biskra, writing, studying and getting his mind in order.

On the afternoon of Sunday 27 January he locked his trunks and had them carried out to the hotel waggon, to be taken to the railway station. He went to the reception desk to settle his bill and idly looked at the slate on which the names of guests were written in chalk. His own was at the top, followed by those of several strangers. At the bottom of the list were written the names of the two latest arrivals: Oscar Wilde and Lord Alfred Douglas. André's heart missed a beat. He picked up the sponge that was sitting on the desk and wiped out his own name, paid his bill and set off slowly for the station on foot. Under his arm he carried a copy of the eighteenth-century German philosopher Johann Fichte's *The Destiny of the Scholar and of the Literary Man*.

On the way to the station André began to have second thoughts. What if Oscar had seen his name when he had checked into the hotel? Would he not think it unforgivably rude of André to leave without even acknowledging his presence? Might he not assume that André was deliberately trying to snub him, as some people in London were now reportedly starting to do, because of his flaunted association with Bosie? And was not André merely trying to escape human contact because of his low spirits? Was he not being cowardly as well as discourteous? By the time he reached the station his mind was made up; he ordered his trunks to be put back on the hotel waggon, and he returned. The hotel receptionist informed him that Oscar and Bosie were both out, so he sat down in the hall to wait.

According to various accounts Gide wrote of this Algerian sojourn (several details of which were hotly denied in later life by Lord Alfred Douglas), Oscar looked distinctly put out to find André sitting in the hotel lobby when he strolled in, alone (exactly as had happened in Florence). However, he quickly regained his composure and innate good manners and asked André what he was reading: André had been passing the time of his wait with *Barnaby Rudge*. Knowing of Wilde's professed dislike for Dickens, he felt a perverse pleasure in handing it over. Oscar pulled a face, and said it was no use reading Dickens. Pleased to have the opportunity for an intellectual argument, André stubbornly defended the novelist's worth. With a sigh, Oscar suddenly changed the subject, now rhapsodising about how 'divine' Bosie was. André was surprised, as in Paris and in Florence Oscar had made no direct reference to his homosexual passions; perhaps he was now beyond caring what people thought. Besides, he must have realised that André would have kept abreast of all the Paris gossip, as well as getting a first-hand account from Pierre Louÿs of Oscar's affair with the young Scottish lord.

Oscar proposed a walk in the town. He and André had not got

very far before they were approached by a hustler who offered to show them round and to procure whatever special services they might have in mind. To André's embarrassment, instead of shooing the man away, Oscar smiled broadly and declared with poetic extravagance that he wanted to see some Arab boys 'as beautiful as bronze statues'. The phrase struck André as ridiculous, but the pimp solemnly asked them to meet him again after dinner, when everything would be arranged.

Sure enough, when the trio emerged from the hotel after dinner, that rather unsavoury character was waiting outside. It was raining quite heavily, but Oscar was not going to let such a minor inconvenience spoil his plans. Normally reluctant to walk more than a few paces if he could avoid it, Oscar strode off with the guide, impatient to see what he could produce. Bosie took André affectionately by the arm and exclaimed breezily: 'All these guides are morons. It's no good trying to explain. They will always take one to cafés full of women. I hope you're like me. I have a horror of women. I only like boys. As you're coming along with us this evening, I think it is better to say so at once.' Stupefied by Lord Alfred's candour, André found himself unable to say a word.

This was the first opportunity André had had of observing Bosie closely. Although he did not share Oscar's unbounded admiration for Bosie's looks, he acknowledged the young man's grace, and could see how its combination with a despotic nature had turned Oscar into Bosie's slave, forever at his beck and call. André tagged along mutely as the guide led them into a *louche* café. Bosie's cynicism proved well founded. There were no particularly striking boys in the place. And the visitors had been there only a few minutes before a fight broke out among a group of Spanish customers and some Arabs. Several of the Spaniards pulled out knives, as most of the rest of the café's customers joined in the fray, or else cheered the combatants on from the sidelines. As soon as it looked as if blood was going to be spilt, Oscar's party decided it would be prudent to leave. In a letter to his mother, André said it was a scene worthy of one of Delacroix's paintings. But in his volume of memoirs *Si le grain ne meurt*, Gide recalled that actually he found the whole experience dismal.

Early the following morning he returned to Algiers, checked into a hotel and sat down to write a particularly long letter to his mother, to tell her about this latest coincidental encounter with Oscar Wilde:

[28 January 1895]

... this terrible man, the most dangerous product of modern civilisation – still, as in Florence, accompanied by the young Lord Douglas [*sic*], the two of them put on the Index in both London and Paris and, were one not so far away, the most compromising companions in the world. Moreover, as in Florence, despite the flood of smiles, seemingly very put out at our meeting. Charming, at the same time; unimaginable, and, above all, a very great personality.

I was very lucky to have seen so much of him and to have known him so well in Paris a few years ago; that was his prime, and he will never be as good again ...

It's impossible to gauge what is the young Lord's intrinsic worth; Wilde seems to have corrupted him to the very marrow of his bones, rather along the lines of a Vautrin,[1] but far more terrible (I find) than that in *Le Père Goriot*, because he does everything on the pretext of aestheticism. Douglas is meant to go on to Biskra, where I hope to see him a little more clearly, and to understand what is sincere and what is affected in his mad depravity. Otherwise, he does not interest me especially; he would interest me a lot more if I knew English society a little better, because he is representative of what is the most lordly, the most Brummelesque, the most Byronic.

1. The master criminal who appears in several of the novels of Honoré de Balzac's series *La Comédie humaine*, including *Le Père Goriot*.

Even if André – who had of course not yet seen or read any of Wilde's plays – believed that Oscar was past his best, his attitude to Oscar shows much of the same fascination and ambiguity that he had felt in Paris just over three years earlier. And even though André informed his mother that he had left Blidah almost surreptitiously, in order to escape Oscar, that was far from true. In fact he was delighted when Oscar had told him that he would be coming on to Algiers, alone, which meant that they could spend some time together. Bosie would follow a day later; he was courting a young Arab boy whom he had spotted pouring out coffee to customers in a café, and he wanted Oscar out of the way.

André was excited and charmed by the Oscar who now joined him in Algiers, for Oscar had suddenly let his disconcerting public mask fall. He no longer spoke in a series of finely tuned paradoxes, which left André wondering what he really believed. Instead he talked as a candid friend. The weather was still terrible, in fact it was getting worse, but even Algiers seemed wonderful in Oscar's company. This was a transformation which the astute Mme Gide must have noticed when André wrote to her ecstatically, beginning his letter in broken English, 'My swith [i.e. sweet] mother':

[30 January 1895]

Algiers is marvellous! And I was going to leave without really seeing it. At the moment, I just wish that Paul [Laurens] were here [to appreciate it]; its streets are enchanted, the shadows there are even more mysterious than in the souks or under leafy trees; and the walls that one touches, the houses that one sees always seem far away because of the blue glaze that covers them. Impossible, moreover, to say anything, because any description merely misleads . . .

Did I tell you that I skedaddled out of Blidah because that fearsome Wilde was there? Well, I've come across him again here. The first day, we dined together and spent the rest of the evening together; young Douglas had stayed on an extra day at Blidah. Prodigious! Prodigious, those two! That young Lord whom I'm beginning to see quite clearly, that future marquess, that royal son, that 25-year-old Scot, blackened, ruined, devoured by an unhealthy thirst for infamy, who seeks shame and finds it, and yet despite everything retains an ambiguous distinction . . . Oh, how badly I am describing all this – but what I couldn't recount about it all!! One sees characters like this in a Shakespeare play.

And Wilde! Wilde!! What more tragic life is there than his! If only he were more careful – if he were capable of being careful – he would be a genius, a great genius. But as he says himself, and knows: 'I have put my genius into my life; I have only put my talent into my works. I know it, and that is the great tragedy of my life.'

That is why those who have known him well will always have that shudder of terror when he is around, as I always do . . . I am happy to have met him in such a distant place, though even Algiers isn't far enough away for me to be able to see him without a certain fear; I told him so to his face. I told him that if I met him in London or in Paris, I would not acknowledge him – and that would be so we could protect our friendship, and so that I would be able to defend him against those who attack him . . .

He leaves tomorrow; I am pleased. If he came to Biskra, I would have to leave myself. Lord Douglas is staying on. He will come to Biskra, where I will be able to watch him at my leisure. If Wilde's plays in London didn't run for three hundred performances, and if the Prince of Wales didn't attend his first nights, he would be in prison, and Lord Douglas as well.

André may have been unclear about British usage and the intricacies of British aristocratic titles and the rules of succession, but his perception of the dangers Oscar was courting was faultless. However, André was not being honest with his mother. Much happened during the two or three days that Oscar and André spent together in Algiers

that accounts for André's sudden euphoria – and for his conviction
that Oscar was doomed. In *Si le grain ne meurt* Gide described at length
what he believed was the turning-point in his life, thanks to Oscar
Wilde.

According to that account (some aspects of which have been
questioned by several Wildean scholars as being so far-fetched that
they might be a product of Gide's over-fertile imagination), André
joined Oscar in a bar on one of the afternoons in Algiers. The playwright had a glass of sherry in front of him, and his table was strewn
with letters that had arrived from England. He chuckled as he
opened them, quickly glancing at their contents, before putting each
aside. He said that a friend in London (Robbie Ross?) opened all his
letters for him there, kept back the bills and the business letters and
forwarded only 'the really important letters – the love letters . . . Oh!
this one is from a young – what does one call them? – acrobat? Yes,
acrobat. Absolutely *delicious*!'

At that moment, Lord Alfred came in, wrapped up in a large fur
coat, the collar of which was turned up so that one could only see his
nose and his eyes; it was snowing outside. Bosie brushed past André
as if he had not seen him, and began to berate Oscar in a withering,
hissing, savage voice, before turning on his heels and storming out.
André had not understood a single word. Oscar had not responded
verbally to Bosie's tirade, but he had turned completely pale. 'He does
nothing but make scenes like that,' Oscar confided to André. 'Isn't
he terrible?'

André was beginning to think that Bosie was indeed terrible, particularly after the young Lord spoke to him about the beauty of
Oscar's two young sons, especially the elder one, Cyril, then still only
nine years old. 'He will be for me,' Bosie whispered to André, with a
conspiratorial and self-satisfied smile. André decided that Bosie was
himself like a spoilt young child, possessed by a perverse instinct
which was driving it to smash its favourite toy. Nothing and no-one
could ever satisfy him completely.

Douglas abandoned Oscar at this point, in order to return to Blidah, where he wanted to make arrangements to elope to Biskra with Ali, the young *caouadji* or coffee-server to whom he had taken such a fancy. André felt obliged now to keep Oscar company; this was hardly an onerous task, as Oscar was now talking freely and fascinatingly. He insisted on taking André to a Moorish café where, he said, extraordinary music could be heard. They went part of the way by carriage, as Oscar was having trouble walking. But at the edge of the kasbah, the old Arab town, they had to get down from the vehicle and follow a guide, who led them through a labyrinth of winding alleyways.

The café was up a particularly steep alley; as they climbed, Oscar expounded on his theory of guides. It was, he said, essential to choose the ugliest, as they were invariably the most intelligent. The reason the pimp in Blidah had failed to deliver the goods, Oscar said, was because he was not ugly enough. André noted that their guide this time was an absolute horror.

They stopped outside a half-open door; there was nothing to show on the outside that it was a café at all. Inside, a few elderly Arab men sat cross-legged on mats, smoking *kief*; none of them stirred as Oscar and André found somewhere to sit. The café features prominently in Gide's book *Amyntas*, written well after he had become an habitué. But he recalled his impressions of that first evening there in *Si le grain ne meurt*:

> At first I did not understand what it was about the café that could have attracted Wilde; but then I noticed in the shadows, by a hearth full of embers, a *caouadji*, still quite young, who was making us two glasses of mint tea, which Wilde preferred to coffee. I was half dozing off in the strange torpor of the place, when a marvellous youth appeared at the half-opened door. He remained there quite a while, one raised elbow propped up against the door-jamb, outlined against the blackness of the night. He seemed unsure

whether he should come in or not and I was worried that he would leave, but then he smiled when Wilde beckoned to him. He came and sat down opposite us on a stool, a little lower than the mat-covered dais on which we were squatting Arab-style. He pulled a reed flute from his Tunisian waistcoat and began to play exquisitely.

A little later, Wilde told me that his name was Mohammed, and that he was 'Bosie's boy'. The reason he had hesitated before coming in earlier was because he had not seen Lord Alfred. His large black eyes had that languorous look given by hashish. He had an olive complexion; I admired the way his fingers held his flute, the slimness of his boyish figure, the slenderness of the bare legs that protruded from his billowing white shorts, one of the legs folded back and resting on the other knee . . .

We stayed like that, without stirring, for what seemed to me to be eternity, and I would happily have stayed even longer, had not Wilde, all of a sudden, taken me by the arm, breaking the spell. 'Come,' he said.

The hideous guide was patiently waiting for them outside and André assumed that he would now lead them back to the way home. But Oscar placed one of his huge hands on André's shoulder, bent down and whispered into his ear: 'My dear, would you like the little musician?' Nearly choking with nervousness, André croaked back: 'Yes!'

Oscar had a few words with the guide who took them to the place where their carriage was waiting, then he left. Hardly had the two newly bonded friends climbed into the carriage than Oscar burst out laughing. The more André fidgeted in embarrassment, the more Oscar roared. Until that moment outside the café in the alley, André had not let on that he shared Oscar's sexual tastes. Oscar was overjoyed and triumphant by the confirmation of his suspicions; like a child, but also like the devil. In *Si le grain ne meurt* Gide analysed what was going on in Oscar's mind:

The great pleasure of the debauched is to lead others to debauchery. Given my adventure [with the Tunisian Ali in the sand dunes] at Sousse, doubtless there was not much of a victory left for the Devil to have over me, but Wilde was not to know that. Nor did he know that I was already conquered, or, rather, should I say (considering that the word 'defeat' seems inappropriate when one carries one's head so high) that I had, in my imagination, in my thoughts, overcome all my scruples. To be truthful, I did not realise this myself; it was only when I replied 'Yes!' to him that I suddenly became aware of it.

Oscar got the carriage-driver to drop them at a humble café in the centre of town; from there they walked to the Oasis Hotel, where they had a drink in the bar; or to be more accurate, André had one and Oscar had several. André realised that this subterfuge was an attempt to protect them from the prying eyes of other Europeans, who might wonder where they had been – or where they were going. André was itching to ask Oscar what he had arranged, but followed the older man's lead in limiting their conversation to trivialities. Then Oscar pulled out his watch and announced: 'It is time.' They set off again, this time for a more densely inhabited part of the city, where Oscar led the way into a large house that served as a short-stay hotel. No sooner had they crossed the threshold than two enormous policemen appeared out of the shadows.

Oscar laughed at André's alarm, reassuring him that the police were there to protect foreigners, not arrest them. The policeman led the way up the stairs to the second floor, where Oscar produced a key that let them in to a small, two-roomed apartment. The policemen left, soon to be replaced by the hideous guide, accompanied by the little flute player, Mohammed, and another young musician from the café. Both boys were swathed in large burnouses, so that their faces were completely hidden. Oscar despatched André and Mohammed to the further room, and took the other boy into the one he had chosen for himself.

Five times that night, so Gide boasted in his memoirs, he had his pleasure with Mohammed; he was surprised that the boy found this surprising. The floodgates of desire had opened, so much so that André was still full of energy and passion hours after separating from Mohammed and returning to the hotel where he was staying. He was up again at the crack of dawn, and ran through the streets, overcome with joyfulness and a lightness of body and spirit that did not leave him all day long. Hence the marked change of tone in his letters to his mother.

The following morning André headed for Biskra (intrigued to discover what Bosie's Ali would be like) and Wilde started his wearisome journey back to London, where he needed to prepare for the opening of *The Importance of Being Earnest*. André felt deeply sorry for him, not just because Bosie had selfishly not stayed to see him off. There was snow on the ground and a storm out at sea; the voyage across the Mediterranean would be rough. The incoming ferry had arrived twenty hours late, and in a battered state.

Even more disturbing was the uncertainty of what awaited Oscar in London as a result of his ongoing liaison with Bosie. It was almost as if he knew that he was going to meet his fate. He repeated to André something he had already said in Blidah: 'I have been as far as I can in my own direction. I can't go any further. Now *something* must happen.' Oscar was not just the protagonist of his Greek tragedy, but the chorus as well.

CHAPTER EIGHT

Speranza

SCANDAL was no stranger to the prominent but unconventional Irish Protestant family of the Wildes. Oscar's father, Sir William Wilde, was a most distinguished eye and ear surgeon who wrote several of the standard nineteenth-century reference books on those specialities. In 1863 he was appointed Surgeon Occulist in Ireland to Queen Victoria, receiving a knighthood the following year. His amateur scholastic interests were prodigious, ranging from the topography and archaeology of his homeland to its customs and myths, as well as the civilisations of the Mediterranean. He was a brilliant conversationalist, though he could be intimidating, as he did not suffer fools gladly.

Sir William took no care in his personal appearance; his clothes and hair were often dishevelled and his skin was of that unfortunate complexion that looks dirty, even when it is not. The poet W.B. Yeats helped circulate the mischievous riddle: 'Why are Sir William Wilde's nails so black?' to which the answer was 'because he has scratched himself.'

Far more damaging to Sir William's public reputation was his philandering. He had sired three illegitimate children before his marriage; the eldest, Henry, worked for him in his surgery. Sir William's elder brother, a clergyman, adopted the other two, both girls, who died in a terrible accident when their ball-gowns caught fire. Sir William made no effort to hide his past from his legitimate family, nor his grief when his daughters perished. His wife Francesca manifested a defiantly liberal attitude to her husband's peccadilloes, even after their marriage. She abhorred bourgeois conventionality and small-mindedness; to her mind, passion added interest to a man, and indeed to a woman. When she was in her sixties, she informed one young visitor: 'When you are as old as I, young man, you will know that there is only one thing worth living for, and that is sin.'

Lady Wilde attributed her romantic and flamboyant nature to her supposed Italian ancestry. Several of the claims she made about her purported forebears were spurious; even her Christian name was in reality plain Jane. But she thought Francesca was more becoming. When she took up her pen to defend the cause of Irish nationalism that was so dear to her heart, she adopted the pseudonym 'Speranza', which was singularly appropriate for her particular brand of spirited hope. She published numerous rousing poems and articles which struck a chord with Irish men and women who resented the continuing, heavy-handed rule from London; though today they must strike many readers as clumsy and emotional, Speranza's verses won her an enthusiastic following.

Unlike many of her female contemporaries, Speranza was prepared to show her mettle not just in print but also in the flesh, as witnessed by some of her appearances in lawcourts. She had written numerous articles for the nationalist newspaper the *Nation* when, in 1848 – the year of revolutionary turmoil on the Continent – the paper's editor, Charles Duffy, was put on trial for a variety of supposed crimes, including treason. While Mr Duffy was in prison, waiting for his case to be heard, she wrote a powerful, anonymous leader in the paper, calling on the men of Ireland to rise against the English oppressors. When Charles Duffy's case finally came to court, in February 1849, the prosecution emphasised the charge of sedi-tious libel, citing the offending leader in the *Nation* as evidence of his insurrectionary intent. According to heroic accounts that might owe more to Irish nationalist folklore than historical truth, when the Solicitor-General read out the offending article in court, Jane Wilde rose from her seat in the public gallery and declared 'I am the culprit, if culprit there be.'

Lady Wilde was happy for that version of events to be passed down to posterity, telling one friend that she would be imortalised by this act of addressing the court. In the cause of the liberation of a nation, what relevance did anything as banal as accuracy have? However, there is no doubt of the veracity of what she said in another case sixteen years later, in 1864, when she was the defendant in a libel case brought by a young woman who claimed to have been raped by Sir William Wilde.

The scandal transfixed Dublin society. The young woman in ques-tion was a patient of Sir William's by the name of Mary Travers. According to her version of events, she had been coming to Sir William for treatment for about four years when, in October 1862, at the age of twenty-two, she was rendered unconscious by him with the aid of a handkerchief soaked in chloroform; when she came to, she realised she had been violated. Miss Travers kept this alleged occurrence secret for a couple of years and even continued going to Sir William's consulting-rooms as a patient. But then she started a campaign of denigration against him, through letters to the news-paper and privately published pamphlets. Provocatively, she hired newspaper-boys to hawk this scurrilous material outside meetings or social gatherings at which Sir William or his wife and young sons were present. Having at first ignored these taunts, Lady Wilde finally wrote to Miss Travers's father to complain, using such strong terms that she found herself being sued for libel.

Mary Travers's evidence did not stand up to cross-examination. She contradicted herself and never satisfactorily explained why she had waited so long to take action against Sir William. He, for his part, did not take to the witness stand, which led many observers to assume that there had been at least some element of impropriety in the affair – perhaps a short-lived sexual relationship, with Mary Travers's consent, which he had then terminated, inciting in her all the bitter resentment and wish for vengeance felt by a woman scorned.

Mary Travers won little admiration or sympathy with her performance in court. But Lady Wilde also gave a bad impression. When asked why she had at first taken no notice of Miss Travers's allegations against her husband, Speranza replied haughtily that she 'really took no interest in the matter. I looked upon the whole thing as a fabrication.' That answer went down extremely badly with the jury, who would have expected any respectable lady to have been mortified by a young woman's accusations of sexual and professional misconduct by her husband. They were shocked by Lady Wilde's apparent indifference; but then Francesca Wilde was no ordinary lady. As she liked to say, 'respectable' was not a word she tolerated in her household.

The jury found Lady Wilde guilty of libel, but showed its contempt of Miss Travers by awarding her a mere farthing in damages. Nonetheless, for the Wildes the consequences were more serious than that. Sir William had to find £2000 to cover his wife's costs and the couple's social standing took a severe knock. It was galling to have Dublin street-boys singing coarse limericks about Sir William's amorous exploits, and one or two of the more strait-laced Dublin families decided that this time the Wildes had put themselves beyond the pale. But others continued to frequent the parties which Lady Wilde gave in their spacious house in Merrion Square. And Speranza remained defiant.

Oscar, just ten at the time, could not avoid being teased over the matter by other boys, but Lady White taught both Oscar and his elder brother Willie that there was nothing to be ashamed of about appearing in court where right was on one's side. She felt exactly the same way about people being sent to prison – a view that was widely shared by Irish nationalists, several of whom ended up behind bars because of their espousal of the cause of home rule. Indeed, going to prison could be a form of glorious martyrdom in Ireland; it was a disastrous concept to have been implanted in the young Oscar's mind.

Speranza's nationalistic writings were not her only literary endeavours. She was an extremely accomplished linguist, not only in French and Italian but also in such languages as Swedish; several of her translations appeared in newspapers and books. When Sir William Wilde died in 1876 (while Oscar was still at Oxford), leaving unfinished a book he had been writing on the Franco-Dutch watercolourist Gabriel Beranger, Lady Wilde completed the text; the Wildes' Dublin home contained several examples of Beranger's work.

Sir William's will left his family in a far less comfortable financial position than they had been expecting. The big house in Merrion Square and several other properties that Sir William had owned turned out to be heavily mortgaged. Even after the required period of mourning for her husband, Speranza could not have afforded to have entertained in the way that she had in the past, offering hospitality to the cream of Irish literary and academic society. In 1879 she decided to follow Oscar and his brother Willie to England, apparently subduing for good her anti-English sentiments in the process.

Lady Wilde subsequently occupied a series of houses and apartments in Mayfair and Chelsea, often sharing with Willie, who had abandoned an unpromising career in law in order to become a journalist. She proudly watched Oscar's rise to literary and social eminence. When she first arrived in London, Oscar was known as Lady Wilde's son; within a decade, she was known as Oscar Wilde's mother. He became the star attraction of the salons she organised on Saturday afternoons – far less grand than those over which she had presided in Dublin, but nonetheless attracting an eclectic mix of local and foreign visitors.

Newcomers at these salons were often taken aback by the fact that the curtains of the reception rooms were always drawn; the occasions took place in subdued candlelight. This was said to be so that people would not notice that Lady Wilde had lost her former statuesque beauty. That did not mean that she was no longer striking. On the contrary, being six feet tall and possessing unusually large hands, she was both impressive and disconcerting. Some people commented cruelly that she looked liked Oscar in drag; the jibe was all the crueller because it was true. Her clothes were similarly the subject of frequent unflattering descriptions, being both voluminous and hopelessly out of date. Considering Oscar's own profound interest in the way women dressed (for a while he virtually dictated what his wife Constance wore), it might seem surprising that he was unable to prevent his mother from becoming something of a laughing-stock because of her appearance. But he was far too much of a loving son to criticise her.

As Oscar became more famous and more deeply immersed in his demanding personal life, he was a much less frequent visitor to Lady Wilde's home, even though from 1888 she lived in Oakley Street, Chelsea, but a short walk from Oscar's and Constance's 'house beautiful' in Tite Street. Willie's frequent presence acted as something of a disincentive. During Oscar's early days in London, Willie had been of certain use; as a critic and gossip columnist, he was able to give his younger brother more publicity than objectively he deserved. But as Oscar's celebrity grew, an element of sibling rivalry crept in: Oscar began to suspect, not always incorrectly, that Willie was either the source or at least a purveyor of unhelpful news and views about him; an unfavourable unsigned review of *Lady Windermere's Fan* in the *Daily Telegraph* had the stylistic stamp of Willie's work. Moreover, whatever admiration Oscar may have had for Willie in their boyhood days evaporated as Willie lurched from one personal disaster to another. As the elder son, he had inherited the Merrion Square house, but he was unable to keep it up, so sold it. By August 1888 his

Oscar 1891: conquering London and Paris

André 1891: first steps on to the literary scene

The formidable Speranza, Lady Wilde

Lady Wilde caricatured by Harry Furniss
in *Punch*

André and his domineering mother,
Juliette Gide

Constance Wilde, before the marriage
to Oscar turned sour

André's cousin, honorary sister, later wife,
Madeleine Rondeaux

The 'divine' Sarah Bernhardt, Oscar's
first choice for Salome

Robbie Ross: Oscar's seducer and devoted friend

Oscar and Bosie at the height of
the infatuation

André kitted out for
travel

André's devoted Algerian servant,
Athman

Pierre Louÿs: erotic writer, erratic friend

(*Left*) Caricature in *Punch* of Oscar as a French conscript when he threatened to become a French citizen. (*Right*) Alfred Bryan caricature of Oscar as a doughty lady

Bosie in Cairo, 1897

The 'mad, bad' Marquess of Queensberry

Constance and the favoured son, Cyril

Oscar just before his downfall, 1895

André in less serious mood, by Henri Bataille

Oscar released, cutting an imposing figure in Naples, 1897

personal finances were so bad that he was declared bankrupt, finding sanctuary and maintenance with his mother, who was herself having to come to terms with straitened circumstances.

Willie was, like Oscar and their father, a splendid talker, much appreciated by men and old ladies. But he was often gauche when flirting with women. So Lady Wilde was pleasurably surprised when he landed a wealthy American widow, Mrs Frank Leslie, who was sixteen years his senior but an undeniable catch. He wooed her and pursued her to New York, marrying her there in October 1891. It was all too good to last. Mrs Leslie – a forceful woman who doubtless hoped to be rejuvenated by this new alliance – was horrified to discover that Willie was the nineteenth-century equivalent of a couch potato. He reasoned that as his wife had been left a sizeable legacy by her first husband, there was no reason for him to exert himself. He spent most of his time in New York in gentlemen's clubs; not one to be taken for a ride, the new Mrs Wilde manoeuvred him back to London in 1892 and set about getting a divorce, tartly informing friends that Willie had been no use to her either by day or by night. Deprived of funds, Willie started singing for his supper (or at least drinks at the bar) by performing a mocking parody of his brother's works. Oscar got to hear of it and decided to break off all contact with Willie, despite Lady Wilde's earnest entreaties. Their common devotion to her was the only thing that remained between the two brothers.

Oscar therefore could not turn to Willie for support, much less understanding, when he returned to London from Algiers at the beginning of February 1895, worried about the possible pending disaster. Nor could he speak openly to his mother who, for all her love and goodwill, would have been unlikely to have sympathised with the situation into which he had got himself, mainly because of the potential impact on Constance and the children. Robbie Ross was a devoted and intimate friend, but he was too young and too much in awe of Oscar to give the equivalent of family counsel.

Wise counsel was exactly what Oscar needed. The Marquess of Queensberry was closing in on him, like a lion that had sniffed its prey. Yet Queensberry was a predator demented and unpopular enough for him to have been chased away if he had been handled properly. George Alexander at St James's Theatre heard that the Marquess was planning to demonstrate displeasure and insult the playwright at the opening night of *The Importance of Being Earnest* in a way he had done once before: to present a bouquet of vegetables.

Oscar's play opened on St Valentine's Day; the weather was bitterly cold, snow was falling and the capacity audience hurried into the theatre from their carriages. Alexander had sensibly arranged for policemen to be stationed around all the theatre doors to ensure that Queensberry would not get in. After waiting outside for a while, the powerless Marquess left his bunch of carrots and turnips (described by Robert Sherard as a 'phallic bouquet') at the stage door and left muttering, to plan his next move.

Dressed in a smart coat with black velvet collar and sporting a green carnation, Oscar was a little nervous about his play's reception; when he had watched one of the last rehearsals, he had informed George Alexander archly: 'Yes, it is quite a good play. I remember I wrote one very like it myself, but it was even more brilliant than this.' The first-night audience did not share the author's reservations. The applause was thunderous and, with the notable exception of George Bernard Shaw, the critics were enthusiastic. Lady Wilde had not been present; bizarrely she had seen none of her son's plays, preferring not to stir from home. But she wrote to Oscar:

> You have had a splendid success and I am so glad. Someone said you were now the foremost man of the day and I am very proud of you. If you can send me the typewritten copy I would be glad to read the play with all its brilliant dialogue . . . I have seen many of the reviews for the new play. All good. You are indeed the success of the day and no-one gets such long notices.

Another absentee from the première was Lord Alfred Douglas, who was still in Biskra with André Gide and the little *caouadji* with whom Bosie had absconded from Blidah, Ali. Ali had turned out to be a very beautiful, fair-skinned boy with a smooth brow, a small mouth and (according to Gide's memoirs) the eyes of a *houri*.[1] André was not attracted to the lad himself; he considered him too effeminate and too aware of his own physical charms. But André was fascinated by Bosie's evident felicity in being with Ali, despite the fact that they could not communicate verbally, as Ali spoke nothing but Arabic. Gide's memoirs make no reference to the hardly incidental detail, which André injudiciously communicated to his mother at the time, that Ali was at most twelve or thirteen years old. This admission prompted an agitated letter from Mme Gide by return of post, asking why André felt it necessary to spend so much time in Bosie's company, when surely the young English Lord was more than capable of looking after himself.

Rather like a lepidopterist who had acquired an obsession with a particularly exotic sub-species of butterfly, André had in fact decided to observe Lord Alfred at very close quarters, becoming an accomplice to the young aristocrat's debauchery. On arrival at Biskra, André had discovered that the cardinal's room he had inhabited at the Hôtel de l'Oasis the year before had been occupied by someone else. So instead he took a suite of three rooms at the newly built Hôtel Royal (about which Playfair's travel guide raved). The apartment was on the ground floor, with its own independent entrance, though André often preferred to go in and out by the window, partly to avoid some of the crowd of boys who hung around outside the street door.

André, Bosie and Ali each had his own room, though Bosie and Ali were functioning as a couple. As Lord Alfred was getting frustrated at not being able to talk to his boy-lover, André asked Athman – the servant he and Paul Laurens had employed the year before – to

1. A voluptuous nymph in the Islamic paradise.

act as an interpreter. André reckoned that Athman, being an Arab, would be neither surprised nor shocked by the nature of the relationship. Athman accepted this responsibility with alacrity, largely because it gave him the opportunity of seeing André. But in the daytime, André was happy for Bosie, Ali and Athman to go off for carriage-drives around the Biskra oasis, while he stayed in his room and wrote. André noted, not without pleasure, that Ali was making Bosie suffer, just as Bosie had made Oscar squirm. Ali became involved with a local shepherd-boy, which Bosie just about tolerated, despite flushes of jealousy. But when Ali went to bed with the very same Mériem whom André, Paul Laurens and Pierre Louÿs had all enjoyed, Bosie was distinctly piqued. 'Boys, yes boys, as much as he likes,' Bosie told André. 'But I will not stand for his going with women!'

The curious little Hôtel Royal *ménage* – of which Mme Gide so strongly disapproved – could have continued longer than it did, had not Bosie heard from his elder brother Percy of his father's attempt to ruin the première of *The Importance of Being Earnest*. Instantly enraged, Lord Alfred unceremoniously dumped his Arab catamite, and headed for London, cabling Oscar that he was on his way. Unable to resist the temptation of seeing his treacherous paramour again, Oscar wrote back, c/o Thomas Cook's:

[? 17 February 1895]

Dearest Boy, Yes: the Scarlet Marquess made a plot to address the audience on the first night of my play! . . .

He left a grotesque bouquet of vegetables for me! This of course makes his conduct idiotic, robs it of dignity.

He arrived with a prize-fighter! I had all Scotland Yard – twenty police – to guard the theatre. He prowled about for three hours, then left chattering like a monstrous ape. Percy is on our side . . .

I had not wished you to know. Percy wired without telling me. I am greatly touched by your rushing over Europe. For my own part I had determined that you should know nothing.

The following day, unbeknownst to Oscar, the Marquess set the time-bomb which would explode in the playwright's face: a visiting card, on which Queensberry had scribbled half illegibly the words 'To Oscar Wilde posing somdomite [*sic*]', depositing it with the porter at Oscar's club, the Albemarle. The club porter, not quite understanding the message, but realising it was meant to offend, placed the card in an envelope to await Oscar's next visit, which did not occur for another ten days. In the interim, Oscar was staying at the Avondale Hotel in Piccadilly with Bosie, until one of their inevitable rows occurred, this time over Bosie's desire to invite another young man to join him at the hotel, at Oscar's expense. This disagreement led to Bosie's moving out in a huff. Richard Ellmann, in his biography of Wilde, considered – on the basis of evidence that Queensberry later gave in court – that what the Marquess hoped to gain by leaving his offensive card for Oscar was an interview, to give him an ultimatum to separate from Bosie; in the event, Queensberry got much more. As the distressed Oscar wrote to Robbie Ross:

> [28 February 1895]
> Since I saw you something has happened. Bosie's father has left a card at my club with hideous words on it. I don't see anything now but a criminal prosecution. My whole life seems ruined by this man. The tower of ivory is assailed by the foul thing. On the sand is my life spilt. I don't know what to do.

Flight to Paris was one option Oscar considered, but the manager of the Avondale Hotel would not allow him to take his baggage away until he had settled the colossal bill that he and Bosie had run up, which he was unable to do. Robbie Ross called round to see him late that evening and advised him not to respond to Queensberry's provocation. By then, Oscar was adamant. He intended to see the solicitor Charles Humphreys the next day, to ask if there were grounds for libel. Bosie accompanied him to the solicitor's office, goading him on; Bosie was exhilarated by the prospect of seeing his father humiliated in court.

Any wise lawyer conversant with the full facts of the affair would have advised Oscar to swallow his pride and drop the whole matter. But Humphreys was not made aware of the truth. Oscar and Bosie lied about the nature of their relationship and withheld vital information about their lifestyles. Robbie urged them to take both Humphreys and Bosie's brother Percy into their confidence, but they refused. Assured by his client of the validity of his case, Humphreys advised that a prosecution for libel was likely to succeed. Oscar was worried that he did not have the money to finance such a prosecution, but Bosie overruled that objection by insisting that his brother Percy and his mother Lady Queensberry would be happy to pay the costs.

Accordingly, on 1 March, the Marquess was arrested and charged with publishing a libel against Oscar. At the committal proceedings, he justified leaving the offensive card by saying that he had intended to save his son from Oscar's corrupting influence, and that he stood by what he had written, claiming the message read that Oscar was 'posing as a sodomite'. Queensberry hired private detectives to find evidence of Oscar's homosexual activities, so that he could confidently enter a plea of justification when the case came to trial. One of those detectives encountered a cooperative female prostitute, who complained that Oscar and his friends had been bad for business because of the way they had made sex with boys fashionable. She pointed the detective in the direction of Alfred Taylor's rooms in Little College Street, Westminster, where he managed to get hold of the names and addresses of Alfred Wood, Alfonso Conway and other boys with whom Oscar had consorted.

Unaware of the evidence that was being accumulated by Queensberry's team, Bosie persuaded Oscar to take him to Monte Carlo for a week. It was foolish to go at such a sensitive time, and even more foolish to come back. In Monte Carlo, Bosie indulged his taste for gambling, as usual at Oscar's expense, while Oscar fretted. They then suffered the humiliation of being asked to leave their hotel by the manager, following complaints from other British guests.

Back in London, Oscar enlisted the help of Frank Harris, who agreed to testify as an expert witness that Wilde's writings, such as *The Picture of Dorian Gray*, were not immoral. But when Harris heard that Queensberry's lawyers were likely to produce details of Oscar's intimate correspondence with Bosie, as well as the fact that Oscar had been successfully blackmailed over these letters, he warned Oscar that he was bound to lose his case. He urged him to follow the example of other prominent homosexual men faced with likely ruin and to flee to France, ideally taking Constance with him. George Bernard Shaw sat in on a discussion that Oscar had with Harris at the Café Royal, and for a while Oscar seemed swayed by Harris's arguments. But then Bosie arrived, was apprised of the gist of the conversation and angrily denounced Harris as being no friend of Wilde's. Bosie then stormed out, followed by Oscar, muttering 'It's not friendly of you Frank, it's really not friendly.'

On 30 March, Queensberry's lawyers entered their plea of justification for the alleged libel; it contained no fewer than fifteen counts, only two of which were linked to the supposed immorality of Wilde's literary work. The others specified twelve different youths whom Oscar was accused of soliciting for sex. Like a character in a story by the Charles Dickens whom Oscar so despised, he found himself confronted by the ghosts of his past. Yet even then, Oscar did not withdraw. The French artist Henri de Toulouse-Lautrec, who was visiting London at the time, found him to be outwardly confident and vociferous in his contempt for British morals and attitudes.

When the libel trial opened, on 5 April, Oscar performed with bravura, often provoking the public gallery into laughter with his wit and repartee. Following in the footsteps of his mother, he was using the court to score points against the British establishment and English narrow-mindedness. But unlike her, he was condemning himself in the process. When Oscar was championing the artistic merit of his work, he easily bested the defence counsel. Buoyed by the reaction he was getting from the gallery, he made Queensberry's lawyers seem like philistines. He even indulged in self-mockery and self-caricature, partly out of show, but perhaps also to try to trivialise some of the defence's arguments in favour of their plea of justification. When asked whether he had ever adored a young man, for example, he replied to guffaws from the public that he had never adored anybody except himself.

Oscar maintained his composure as he was questioned about the valets, grooms and other low-class boys he had fêted in London and Paris. However, it was a different matter when the defence counsel asked whether he had ever kissed a boy called Walter Grainger, a servant in the house in Oxford where Bosie had had rooms when he was an undergraduate. Caught off-guard, Oscar replied flippantly: 'Oh dear no. He was a peculiarly plain boy. He was, unfortunately, extremely ugly. I pitied him for it.' In those few words, Oscar effectively exposed himself as a homosexual; like a terrier, the defense counsel started to harry him relentlessly. Moreover, the counsel indicated that he would call as witnesses for Queensberry some of the boys that had been referred to by name.

It had now become obvious to lawyers on both sides in the case that not only was Oscar going to lose his libel action, but also that he would be open to prosecution himself because of the sexual activities that had come to light. Oscar's legal team offered to keep the trial going, by allowing the defence to call its witnesses, so Oscar would have time to get away to France. But Oscar insisted on staying. He was advised therefore that the only sensible course of action was to concede defeat in the case, which in the event meant accepting Lord Queensberry's plea of justification, in other words admitting that the Marquess had been justified in the public interest of accusing Oscar of posing as a sodomite.

As soon as Queensberry was acquitted, the machinery was put

into place to prosecute Oscar, though it was allowed to operate slowly enough to give him several hours to pack a few things and leave the country. Instead, he prevaricated. He installed himself in the Cadogan Hotel, where Bosie had taken a room, and fended off the urgings of Robbie Ross, Reggie Turner and other friends that he should catch the boat-train for France. At 5 p.m. a newspaper reporter arrived and informed Oscar that a warrant had been issued for his arrest. There was still just time to flee. But Oscar settled back in his chair and declared: 'I shall stay and do my sentence, whatever it is.'

It would be an exaggeration to say that Oscar was embracing his martyrdom, like St Sebastian tied to a tree and shot with arrows (though later he sometimes saw himself in that role). A half-packed suitcase by his side was evidence that he had at least considered the possibility of flight. Yet as he had told André Gide in Algiers, Oscar felt that he needed things to be brought to a head. His passion for Bosie and the feasting with panthers could not continue in the same way; some tragic catharsis was required. But there was another important element to Oscar's refusal to save himself: the noble tradition and the honour that were embodied in his mother, Lady Wilde. The reported details of her younger son's waywardness came as a great shock to her. But she wanted him to hold his head up high. If he fled, he would be no son of hers.

At 6.10 there was a knock on the bedroom door at the Cadogan Hotel. A waiter came in, followed by two detectives. 'We have a warrant here, Mr Wilde,' one said, 'for your arrest on a charge of committing indecent acts.'

CHAPTER NINE

Madame Gide

On 19 February 1895, the day after Lord Alfred Douglas left Biskra to join Oscar in London, André wrote to his mother to let her in on a scheme that had been hatching in his mind for some time: to take Athman back with him to France. There, André argued, Athman could assist Mme Juliette Gide's devoted maid Marie in running the household at the Château de La Roque. André had not just raised the matter with Athman, who was overjoyed; he had even got permission from Athman's mother, whom Mme Gide had met when she had been in Biskra herself. André also apprised Madeleine of the plan, seemingly oblivious to the fact that neither she nor Mme Gide would receive the news gladly.

Deprived of his employment as companion and interpreter to Bosie and the little *caouadji* Ali (who had been whipped and sent home in disgrace by Bosie, for paying too much attention to girls), Athman had found a lucrative alternative source of sustenance by becoming a pimp for European tourists anxious to sample the delights of the street of the Oulad Nail. As Athman boasted to André, he often got paid thrice over, receiving a commission from the Oulad Nail, a tip from the client, and a ten-franc supplement on the girl's fee, which he incorrectly translated to the gullible tourists. André was displeased, not so much that Athman had become a procurer, but rather because of the little dishonesties involved. As André explained to Athman, the boy must remain worthy enough to be introduced to his friends in Paris. André justified to himself his decision to take Athman to France on the grounds that he would be rescuing Athman from a life of sin; for Mme Gide, however, the whole scheme was further evidence that André was slipping into a life of sin himself.

In Gide's writings, Mme Gide often comes over as a domineering puritan, obsessed with moral and financial correctness, and constantly interfering in her son's existence. To a degree, that picture is true, as her letters bear testimony. They are full of niggling advice and detailed financial accounts, often offered with a touch of reproach. Yet there is no doubt that she dearly loved André; after her husband's death, André was the centre of her life. She did whatever she could to encourage and ease his writing and his intellectual pursuits. She managed his finances rather expertly, by giving him a monthly allowance, topped up from time to time with extra amounts.

Gide later criticised his mother for keeping too tight a hand on the purse-strings and for denying him the right to exercise direct control over monies that were rightly his once he had achieved the age of twenty-one. She was worried, not without justification, that he could all too easily become a spendthrift. In 1895, by his own calculation, André was using up two-thirds of his monthly allowance just on buying books and music. Moreover, when he received a modest legacy from his grandmother, he immediately blew half of it by buying a plot of land in Biskra, arguing that this was a good investment for the future, given the way the oasis was becoming such a popular winter resort. In reality, the aim of that purchase was to put down deeper roots in North Africa, which was hardly likely to please Mme Gide, who already regretted how much time André was spending away from home.

In April 1895 Mme Gide turned sixty; she was far from strong, and worrying about André's physical and moral well-being added to her burdens. The almost uninterrupted flow of letters that passed between mother and son while he was in Algeria was both a comfort and a cause of distress for Juliette Gide. When André was ill or spiritually low, she suffered with him; but when his mood improved with a rapidity and unpredictability verging on manic depression, she was often equally alarmed. Her hints that it would be best for everyone if André returned home became all the more insistent as André's spirits rose with the advent of the North African spring.

In fact, since Lord Alfred Douglas had left Biskra, André had been living through a period of lyrical exaltation, getting up early in the morning and setting off into the desert, notebooks and pencils in hand. Sometimes he would follow dried-up riverbeds; on other occasions he would clamber up great sand dunes, sitting at their crest until nightfall, his heart as light as a feather. He would laugh as he remembered how Bosie used to stare into the *caouadji* Ali's face and demand yet again that Athman inform the boy that his eyes were like those of a gazelle. Or he would scribble rapidly in his notebook, transforming the real-life Oscar Wilde into the character of Ménalque, the half-sinister mentor figure of *Les Nourritures terrestres* (a title of which, incidentally, Mme Gide heartily disapproved, perhaps suspecting some of the truly earthly concerns the book would contain).

As George Painter pointed out in his study of André Gide, *Les Nourritures terrestres* is a hymn to the joy of life, 'or rather, to the life in which everything is joy; to the pleasures of the senses – or rather, to the state of being in which everything gives pleasure to the senses'. In a letter to his friend Christian Beck, written in 1907, twenty years after his book's first publication, Gide himself called *Les Nourritures terrestres* 'the harvest of my tuberculosis: it was the epoch of my greatest fervours.'

As in so many of Gide's books, the first-person narrator of *Les Nourritures terrestres* travels on a journey of self-discovery, visiting many of the places that had made such an impact on André himself. In Florence the narrator comes across a colossal villa, jutting out from the hillside, like the prow of a mighty ship. This is home to Ménalque, who is based not only on Oscar Wilde but on des Esseintes, the hero of Joris-Karl Huysmans' novel *A rebours*, which had had such a powerful influence on Wilde himself. There is also an element of André in Ménalque: a newly liberated and cynical, adventurous and worldly-wise André, impatient with some aspects of his earlier self. The composite André-Oscar-Ménalque figure is able to utter at the end of *Les nourritures terrestres* a statement that has become one of the most famous and unsettling of all Gide's pronouncements: 'I hated the family, the home and all places where men think they can find rest . . . Each new thing must find us always and utterly detached . . . Families, I hate you.'

That was a revolutionary stance to take in *fin-de-siècle*, bourgeois France; in relation to Mme Gide, it was nothing short of treachery, though fortunately for everybody concerned, she did not live to see it in print. André's resentment against his own small family, as opposed to families in general, was growing while he was in Algeria because he felt Mme Gide was unfairly enlisting the help of Madeleine and her sisters and his male cousin Albert Démarest to persuade him to return home.

André had started fantasising of a future life divided between France and Algeria, with extensive travels elsewhere. The winters would be spent in Biskra and on his plot of land he would build a house, of which the ground floor would be arranged as a Moorish café. Athman would be appointed its manager. André spared his mother that last detail, which was probably as well; as it was, she was beginning to wonder whether the desert sun was turning his mind. She even asked him whether he was not suffering from fever.

Mme Gide viewed with concern André's declaration that his youth was now over. Many parents find it difficult to come to terms with the developing maturity of their offspring, but in this particular case

Juliette Gide feared that André's independence from her protective control could lead him to follow the dangerous path of Oscar Wilde and Alfred Douglas. In keeping with the times, she did not articulate precisely her fear that André might be being corrupted (as she would see it) into becoming gay, but her letters leave one in little doubt that that is what was at the back of her mind. She greeted with relief the news that Bosie had left Biskra, but warned André obliquely that as London and Paris were so near, he should not fall into the temptation of seeing Lord Alfred when he returned to Europe, thereby compromising his own position.

Mme Gide's fears on this account grew after Paul Valéry called to see her in Paris at the end of February, and acquainted her with the gossip that was now rife about Oscar Wilde because of his relationship with Bosie (this was the week before Lord Queensberry left his insulting visiting card for Oscar, triggering off the libel case). According to Valéry, Oscar Wilde had become – as Mme Gide duly reported to her son – a 'Roman emperor of extreme decadence', and he was bringing the utmost reprobation of British society down upon himself. In response, André begged his mother to keep him posted with what developed next. This request reflected much more than curiosity at the fate of a friend who was bringing doom upon himself; as André and his mother were both well aware, the evolving Wilde affair was a warning to André about the potential nature of his own risks.

The most immediate danger, in Mme Gide's eyes, was posed by André's determination to bring Athman to Paris, where they would inevitably become the object of intense scrutiny and probable ridicule, not to mention malicious speculation. Rather than say so outright, Mme Gide began a campaign, through her letters, to try to persuade André that taking Athman out of the environment in which he had been raised was nothing short of cruelty. How would Athman cope with the cold weather and pale light of France, she asked? Or the 130 stairs that led up to the servants' quarters in the sixth floor of their Paris residence, where male and female servants lived together in such close proximity? Furthermore, among many of the expenses that André would incur by bringing Athman to Paris, the boy would have to give up the Arab dress he was used to and be provided with European clothes. Even then, she reasoned, he would be treated like a plaything by many people, including André's friends, and he would be the butt of cruel jokes at the hands of others. And how on earth would he manage during Ramadan?

Madeleine – probably at Mme Gide's instigation – joined the fray, softening the blow to André by saying how much his project to bring Athman to France had made her laugh, but then adding more seriously that she was totally opposed to the idea, because there was a ninety per cent chance that it would be a disaster for the boy. With percipience she suggested that André wanted to go through with the scheme for his own sake, not for Athman's. Then she warned that Athman would be destroyed if he were taken out of his usual context: '[10 March 1895] those people have their own place; and only in his own place is Athman a happy and attractive child.'

André was deeply irritated by many of his mother's and Madeleine's urgings. He was determined not to let this damage his relationship with either of them, but he countered their arguments with accusations that they did not understand the situation. In his view the fifteen-year-old Athman had enough experience and was now ripe to become the most perfect valet one could possibly have – someone who would be devoted and almost like a friend. Far from impinging on the domestic work of Marie and other staff in Paris and at La Roque, as Mme Gide said she feared, Athman could help out by doing some of the more menial and masculine tasks like cleaning shoes, carrying water up to people's rooms and bringing dishes from the kitchens to the dining-room.

André became so exasperated by his mother's continued opposition (and her criticism of his plans for the land he had bought at Biskra) that on 12 March he wrote to her in an uncharacteristically peremptory tone:

I find your advice unbearable, in that it seems not so much to be trying to provide light for the path ahead but rather to modify my behaviour, and that sometimes makes me think that you understand LIFE in a way that is so different from mine that it is almost useless for me to listen to your advice, other than out of deference, so long as I know that you won't, before formulating it, have taken into account the most important thing: the reasons and the passions which make us act as we do . . . If I set about living the life you advise, it would be a constant lie vis-à-vis my thoughts . . . Resign yourself to not being able to suppress from my existence all those oddities which might sprout there like grass (I call them 'oddities' to please you, because for me they don't seem like that, but rather something that is really natural).

He threatened that if his mother did not welcome him together with Athman at the Gides' Paris home, or failed to persuade Marie to treat the boy properly, then he would go and stay with Athman somewhere else. If this threat was designed to invoke contrition in his mother, it failed. She was adamant in her refusal that Athman sleep in the Paris apartment. And what would people think, she asked André, when they heard that an only son had abandoned his widowed mother, in order to go and live with an Arab boy, a 'half-savage', whose very cleanliness she was now questioning? What would Madeleine, whom he still aspired to marry, make of it all?

Both sides continued to pile on the emotional blackmail until the matter was resolved, in Mme Gide's favour, by her maid Marie, who wrote to André to say that the day he brought his 'little negro' into the Gides' home, she would leave. Knowing how helpless Mme Gide would be without the woman who had looked after for so many years, André capitulated. He telegraphed Mme Gide to say that when he arrived home in May, Athman would not be with him.

André had not the heart to break the news to Athman immediately, but the boy quickly sensed that something was wrong. He watched André as he brooded and frowned in silence. When André plucked up the courage to tell him that they would not be going to France together after all, he tried to soften the blow by taking Athman on holiday as far as El Kantara for a few days. The apricot trees were in bloom at El Kantara; the air was full of the humming of bees. Crops were beginning to send up tender green shoots in the irrigated fields, while above the settlement the tall palm trees swayed. For two days, André and Athman savoured this paradise, basking in the pleasure of each other's company. Gide never let on whether they had become lovers, but certainly, he was in love.

On the third morning, when it was time for André to go, he could not find Athman anywhere. He had to leave without saying goodbye. But as the train pulled out of the station, he caught sight of Athman in his white burnous sitting on the banks of the dried-out riverbed, his head in his hands. The boy did not look up as the train passed. As Gide recalled in his memoirs: 'for a long time, as the train was carrying me away, I watched his little motionless grief-stricken figure, lost in the desert, an image of my own despair.'

Mme Gide was gratified that, as she saw things, when it came down to a choice between herself and Athman, André had chosen her, even though that meant frustrating his own will. However, it is doubtful that things were quite as simple as that. Having only weeks before existed in a state of euphoria, André now found himself once more in turmoil, even tending to violence. When he got to Algiers, he was joined by Pierre Louÿs, who had spent most of the winter convalescing from illness in Spain; Pierre now discovered how much his friend had changed. They had hardly been a quarter of an hour together before they were quarrelling openly, not just about what to do and where to go, but also over Oscar Wilde and his relationship with Bosie.

Algiers was redolent of the memory of the nocturnal adventures André and Oscar had enjoyed together in the city only two months earlier, but the newspapers quickly brought André down to earth: he read about the opening of the Queensberry libel trial in London on 3 April; two days later it had collapsed and it was Oscar who was now cast in the role of guilty party. On 5 April Queensberry was acquitted; that evening, as we have seen, Wilde was arrested at the Cadogan Hotel. The following day Oscar appeared at Bow Street Police Court and was charged with offences under Section Eleven of the Criminal Law Amendment Act of 1885. Bail was refused and he was taken to Holloway Jail (not then a prison only for women) to await trial at the Old Bailey.

For the first few days in prison Oscar kept up his spirits by thinking of Bosie, or so he told his good friend Ada Leverson ('The Sphinx') and her husband Ernest:

[9 April 1895]
I write to you from prison, where your kind words have reached me and given me comfort, though they made me cry, in my loneliness. Not that I am really alone. A slim thing, gold-haired like an angel, stands always at my side. His presence overshadows me. He moves in the gloom like a white flower.
With what a crash this fell!

Wilde's name was removed from the boards outside the theatres where his two plays *An Ideal Husband* and *The Importance of Being Earnest* were playing; shortly, under public pressure, the plays themselves were taken off. The full vindictiveness of British middle-class self-righteousness began to be felt. With notable exceptions such as the Leversons, friends who had earlier been proud to count Oscar among their intimates now abandoned him; acquaintances who had fought to get him to attend their parties at the height of his success now denied even knowing him. Moreover, as Oscar's friend Henry Harland waspishly noted, hundreds of homosexual and bisexual English gentlemen took the precaution of fleeing the country for the Continent, lest their sins catch up with them too.

Among the departures was Robbie Ross. Newspapers had reported that he was with Oscar when the police came for him at the Cadogan Hotel. Robbie had had to resign immediately from the Savile Club, and he knew that he would now be shunned by 'good' society; but at first he wanted to stay behind, to be of whatever assistance he could to Oscar. His mother was more realistic. She pointed out that he could not help what was clearly a lost cause and that he might unwittingly bring about his own downfall in the process. She clinched her argument by offering to contribute £500 to Oscar's defence costs if Robbie left at once. Duly persuaded, Robbie went to France, as did Reggie Turner, Maurice Schwabe and several other members of Oscar's gay coterie. Bosie stayed, determined, if he could, to visit Oscar every day in prison.

Even in France, where many people considered homosexuality more a cause for humour than censure, some of Oscar's erstwhile friends dropped away. The newspaper *Le Figaro*, commenting on Wilde's predicament, mentioned that three well-known French writers, Catulle Mendès, Marcel Schwob and Jean Lorrain, were intimates of his. Schwob reacted to this revelation by challenging the author of the article to a duel. Lorrain, who had dedicated a short story to Wilde only four years previously, flatly denied that he knew the scandalous playwright at all well. Others did behave more nobly. In Holloway Oscar heard from Robert Sherard – who stood loyally by him, despite his complete lack of understanding of or sympathy for homosexuality – that Pierre Louÿs, Stuart Merrill and the poet Jean Moréas had all expressed sympathy. (So too had Sarah Bernhardt, though she demurred when Sherard suggested that she manifest that sympathy in more concrete terms than words by buying the rights to *Salomé*.)

Missing from the list of French sympathisers cited by Sherard is the name of André Gide. This might seem odd, given that he had sprung to Wilde's defence in the face of Pierre Louÿs' criticism during their encounter in Algiers, the very time of the Wilde débâcle.

Perhaps André wished to save his mother embarrassment by having his name publicly linked to Oscar's, notwithstanding the anguish he had otherwise been giving her by his recent letters. Despite the renunciation of Athman, André was still causing alarm – so much so that Mme Gide implored him to tone down his language and purify his thoughts before he got home. As she complained in desperation in a letter dated 8 April:

> My dear child, I have received your long letter. I am incapable of replying to it, but I have the strong feeling that there are many sophisms in what you are saying. Life! Knowing life . . . It seems to me that P[ierre] Louÿs and Oscar Wilde would speak like that. Can you promise me that you are not going to trumpet your experiences, that you'll keep them to yourself? Let's agree that you are going through them as if through fire; would that be the same for those who might be tempted by your example to try those same experiences? I so much want you to promise me that you won't pass on your experiences . . .

Mme Gide seems to have been unaware that Pierre Louÿs was actually in Algiers with André at the time, at least for a few days. Furthermore, presumably not having been told of André's recent experiences with boys, Pierre insisted on taking him to a brothel there. André was not keen on the idea, but allowed himself to be dragged along; the establishment, exotically called the Andalucian Sisters, had nothing Arab or even Spanish about it. The place struck André as plain sordid; Pierre declared that that was exactly why it appealed to him so much. Half-heartedly, André decided that now he was there, he had better try to go through with things; he was also curious to see if he would be able to perform more effectively this time than he had with the young Oulad Nail whore En Barka in Biskra one year previously.

André chose the prettiest girl in the place and found that he could function normally as a man after all, even if he did not derive much pleasure from it. Hardly had he finished, though, than he started to worry (unnecessarily, as it turned out) that he might have caught syphilis from her. Far from reassuring him, Pierre opined that that was highly likely; as she was so much prettier than any of the other girls there, she would undoubtedly have been chosen for sex by many more customers. However, André should not worry, Pierre continued, because many great French literary men owed three-quarters of their genius to having got the pox. André was unable to enter into the spirit of this jibe; he felt a hatred of Louÿs welling up inside him, and was only too pleased when soon after this escapade, Pierre decided to carry on with his travels alone.

André lingered in Algiers, pondering his future, not least in the sexual domain. He now knew for sure that he liked boys, but Oscar's tribulations were terrible warning signals about the potential dangers that might lie ahead. Brothel-crawling and passionate heterosexual affairs, à la Louÿs, were clearly not a viable or desirable alternative; neither could he see himself fitting into the role of conventional husband and father. That left either celibacy or Madeleine, or, more appealingly, celibacy *and* Madeleine. Sex had nothing to do with the love he felt for her and his continuing determination to marry her.

Partly because Madeleine's help had been elicited in getting André not to bring Athman to Paris, he was now hearing from her far more regularly than he had for a year or more. Her letters helped nurture the pure sentiments he felt for her. As André wrote to his mother at this time, he saw in Madeleine 'a radiance of celestial and infinite wisdom'. Having for so long dissuaded André from pursuing the idea of marriage to his cousin, Mme Gide was now coming round to the idea that it might actually be rather a good thing. Perhaps Madeleine could put André back on the straight and narrow. It was nonetheless worrying for Mme Gide that André seemed so reluctant to leave Algiers. She wondered if he had dropped Athman only to become embroiled in some other, equally unsuitable liaison, perhaps with another local girl like the Mériem she had seen heading for his room in Biskra.

According to *Si le grain ne meurt*, André had in fact regained a sense of exaltation with Pierre Louÿs' departure. Every day he awoke at dawn in a state of fervour, joy and frenzy; every moment seemed like an hour, every sensation became ethereal. Far from relinquishing his experiences of the preceding months, as his mother wished, André was assimilating them. He had not just become emancipated; for all of Wilde's current difficulties, André had begun internally to absorb the influence of Oscar to justify his own follies, and to base on reason what he had seen previously as his madness.

Fortified by his new self-confidence, André returned to France in mid-April, stopping first at his uncle Charles Gide's home at Montpellier. Juliette Gide had made her brother-in-law a party to some of her fears about her son; he also knew of André's earlier ménage at Biskra with Mériem and Paul Laurens. Charles Gide lamented the fact that André had no true profession or job to keep his mind more healthily occupied. Perhaps marriage to Madeleine might help to calm him. There could be no guarantee, however, that either or both of them would be truly happy if they wed.

By the time André arrived in Paris on 19 April, Mme Gide had come to the conclusion that if Madeleine herself now viewed André's suit more favourably, then she should withdraw all her former objections. If André married his cousin, he would not be alone after his mother's death. Accordingly, it was arranged that Madeleine would come to Paris for a few days in May, so the two cousins could see if they wanted to enter into an engagement.

On André's part, an added incentive to take this plunge was given by the distressing news from London. Constance Wilde had left town, taking the little boys Cyril and Vyvyan with her so that they might escape some of the publicity and hostility. On 24 April, despite valiant efforts by some of Oscar's closest friends to avert his bank-ruptcy, the contents of the Wildes' house in Tite Street (except for some books and manuscripts that Robbie Ross had managed to retrieve) were sold at knockdown prices amidst disgraceful scenes of ribaldry, in order to meet some of the claims by creditors. The following day, at the urging of Oscar Wilde's lawyers, Lord Alfred Douglas left for France, heading first for Calais, where he joined Robbie Ross and Reggie Turner, then moving on to Rouen and Paris. He had indeed visited Oscar daily in Holloway Prison, but now that the trial was imminent, it was better that he was out of the way. At their last meeting, Oscar kissed the end of Bosie's finger through an iron grating.

The trial opened on 26 April, with Oscar defended by Sir Edward Clarke, who had offered to represent him without a fee. Oscar's case was tied in with another against Alfred Taylor, because Taylor had procured youths to commit acts of indecency with Wilde. Nobly, Taylor had refused to save his own skin by giving evidence himself against Oscar, but otherwise the linking of the two men – including charges of conspiracy – was hardly beneficial to Oscar's cause. Much of the evidence produced was familiar to those who had followed the Queensberry libel case closely, but this time it was all set out in much more graphic detail, a surprising amount of which was reported in the more sensational press.

A reporter from the *New York Times* noted that Oscar looked careworn and anxious as the procession of boys came forth to give their evidence against him. He admitted knowing them, but denied in the face of their testimony (some of it admittedly inconsistent and tainted) that he had had indecent relations with them. It was not a convincing performance and he showed none of the wit that he had displayed at the outset of the Queensberry libel case. Only once did Oscar rise to the occasion in this trial, when the prosecution brought up literary matters, such as his floridly romantic letters to Bosie and the homosexual material that had appeared in the magazine *The Chameleon*, including Bosie's two poems. When Oscar was asked what was the 'Love that dare not speak its name', he replied:

The 'Love that dare not speak its name' in this century is such a great affection of an elder for a younger man as there was between David and Jonathan, such as Plato made the very basis of his philosophy, and such as you find in the sonnets of Michelangelo and Shakespeare. It is that deep, spiritual affection that is as pure as it is perfect. It dictates and pervades great works of art like those of Shakespeare and Michelangelo, and those two letters of mine, such as they are. It is in this century misunderstood, so much misunderstood that it may be described as the 'Love that dare not speak its name', and on account of it I am placed where I am now. It is beautiful, it is fine, it is the noblest form of affection. There is nothing unnatural about it. It is intellectual, and it repeatedly exists between an elder and a younger man, when the elder man has intellect, and the younger man has all the joy, hope and glamour of life before him. That it should be so the world does not understand. The world mocks at it and sometimes puts one in the pillory for it.

This speech provoked a spontaneous burst of applause from the public gallery; it was a fine moment in otherwise gruesome and sordid proceedings. As the prosecutor pointed out, its lofty sentiments hardly applied to the motley collection of rent-boys, pimps and blackmailers who had earlier appeared in the witness stand. It was a tremendous statement of defiance, that has rightly entered the annals of homosexual emancipation. But in terms of saving Oscar from the fate that awaited him, it was whistling in the wind.

On 29 April, the eve of the end of the trial, Oscar wrote from jail to Bosie, in France:

My dearest boy, This is meant to assure you of my immortal, my eternal love for you. Tomorrow all will be over. If prison and dishonour be my destiny, think that my love for you and this idea, this still more divine belief, that you love me in return will sustain me in my unhappiness and will make be capable, I hope, of bearing my grief more patiently. Since the hope, nay rather the certainty, of meeting you in some world is the goal and the encouragement of my present life, ah! I must continue to live in this world because of that.

In his summing up, the judge directed the jury to acquit Wilde and Taylor on various charges which he considered tenuous or unproved. But he put four questions to them relating to charges that they might feel substantiated. These included accusations of indecent acts with Edward Shelley, the publishers' boy; with Alfred Wood, the boy Oscar had shared with Bosie (though Lord Alfred's name was kept out of the proceedings); with Frederick Atkins, whom Oscar had met through Maurice Schwabe; and with Charles Parker, who had caused a stir with some of the gentlemen in the court at the Old Bailey by turning up in army uniform.

The jury was out for nearly four hours. They had reached agreement on only one charge, concerning the alleged indecent acts with Frederick Atkins, and found Oscar not guilty. Confronted with the jury's inability to reach a verdict on the other instances, the proceedings were brought to an end and a new trial was ordered. The ordeal was not yet over.

CHAPTER TEN

The Sphinx

NEARLY FOUR WEEKS were to elapse before Oscar faced his retrial. The first few days were an agony of uncertainty, as initially it was unclear whether he would be granted bail, though there was no obvious legal reason why he should not be. Then it was a matter of raising the necessary money. On 4 May bail was set at the punitively high level of £5000, half of which was allowed to be posted by Oscar on his own behalf. Raising the rest was problematic. Bosie, Robbie and Reggie Turner were all in France; many other erstwhile friends had fallen away. Ada Leverson and her businessman husband Ernest remained true friends, but Ernest was prevented by the terms of his business partnership from offering surety. Frank Harris – who again visited Oscar in Holloway Jail – was debarred because he was not a householder. However, Bosie's brother Percy stepped into the breach, raising half of the outstanding amount. The rest came from someone who was only a slight acquaintance of Oscar's, but whose socialist Christian principles were affronted by the way Oscar was being treated: an Anglican minister by the name of Stewart Headlam. That act of charity lost Headlam a lot of friends, both within and beyond ecclesiastical circles, as well as causing his maid to hand in her notice.

Even if the Leversons were unable to intervene financially, they did much to boost Oscar's morale in those difficult days spent in prison awaiting bail. They both sent books and a little flurry of letters and telegrams passed between Oscar's cell and the Leversons' home in Courtfield Gardens, South Kensington. Oscar could talk openly with Ada, his 'Sphinx', about his love for Bosie, his 'Prince Fleur-de-Lys':

[6 May 1895]
My dear Sphinx, I have not had a line today from Fleur-de-Lys. I suppose he is at Rouen. I am so wretched when I don't hear from him, and today I am bored, and sick to death of imprisonment . . .

Your kindness and Ernest's make things better for me. I go on trespassing on it more and more. Oh! I hope all will come well, and that I can go back to Art and Life. Here I sicken in inanition.

The following day the bail hearing at Bow Street police station went in Oscar's favour. He was released and checked into the Midland Hotel at St Pancras, where he hoped he was unknown. But the vindictive Marquess of Queensberry had sent some of his thugs to shadow Oscar and to hound him from wherever he came to rest. When these louts arrived, the manager of the Midland Hotel told Oscar he had to leave. Other hotels similarly turned him away. As Ada Leverson commented in her annotated volume of correspondence with Oscar, *Letters to the Sphinx*: 'He was like a hunted stag, with no place to find refuge.' Oscar was therefore forced to swallow his pride and head for Oakley Street, to beg shelter from Lady Wilde and his brother Willie. Willie – unconsciously echoing the Sphinx, as well as mixing his metaphors – recorded later that Oscar 'came tapping with his beak against the window-pane, and fell down on my threshold like a wounded stag.'

Oscar was spiritually crushed by the realisation that he had become a pariah. Within a matter of days, during which he slept on a camp-bed in the corner of a room Willie had given him, he became physically ill as well. Robert Sherard came over from Paris to see how he was bearing up. Oscar's plaintive cry: 'Oh, why have you brought me no poison from Paris?' hardly reassured him. Sherard tried to persuade Oscar to get away from London, preferably away from England altogether, but Oscar would not budge, despite the palpable tension with Willie. Oscar knew that Willie had sold some of his letters to Oscar's lawyer, as a means of raising some ready cash. Moreover, when Oscar heard that Willie had been supposedly defending his reputation around town – on one occasion declaring with absurd irrelevance that one could safely leave any girl alone with Oscar – the playwright moaned that his brother 'would compromise a steam-engine'. Oscar bore this hateful situation partly because he thought he had nowhere else to go, but also out of loyalty to his mother, who was pleased to have both of her sons under her roof once again, even in these terrible circumstances.

Fatally for Oscar, both Lady Wilde and Willie firmly believed that Oscar should stand and face the music at his second trial, no matter what the outcome; only that would be proper conduct for an Irish gentleman. By contrast, almost all Oscar's remaining friends wanted him to jump bail and escape to France. Even Percy Douglas, who could ill afford the prospect of losing his surety, was of the opinion that Oscar should slip away, if there was the slightest chance of his being convicted.

Frank Harris decided to bring things to a head. He managed to persuade Oscar to go out to lunch, in a private room at a restaurant in Great Portland Street. There Harris revealed that he had arranged with a sympathetic Jewish businessman to have a yacht put at Oscar's disposal. According to Harris's account, the yacht was ready and waiting to sail at Erith in Kent; Oscar could leave immediately. But Oscar refused. His mother had said she would denounce him if he avoided the trial. More significantly, as he had indicated to André Gide in Algiers, something inside himself was driving him to bring matters to a head.

The Leversons also coaxed Oscar out of the unhealthy environ-ment at Oakley Street by having him over to dinner. His misery was so evident that Ada decided bravely, with her husband's support, to invite him to come to stay with them. They were aware that in doing so they would risk opprobrium. They even summoned their servants together, to warn them who was coming and to offer them the opportunity of leaving their service if they preferred. Unlike the Revd Headlam's maid, the Leversons' domestics stayed.

On the appointed day Ada went to fetch Oscar in a little pill-box brougham. The Leversons' young son was away in the country at the time, so they had been able to have the servants prepare the nursery floor for Oscar's occupation: three rooms and a bathroom, making it almost like a self-contained flat. At Oscar's request, the toys scat-tered about were left, as they reminded him of the many joyful hours he had spent with his own two little boys (whom he would never see again). So when Oscar's solicitor called for a consultation about the impending trial, he found Oscar surrounded by dolls' houses, a rocking-horse, golliwogs and a blue-and-white nursery dado with fluffy rabbits and other toy animals lined up on it.

Oscar had his breakfast, lunch and tea up in his rooms, as well as receiving his visitors there. These included his faithful barber, who came daily to shave him and wave his hair. But each evening at 6 o'clock, Oscar would go downstairs, properly dressed for dinner, a fresh flower in his buttonhole. Often, when he was alone with the Sphinx, he paced the room, a cigarette in his hand. He improvised prose poems as he stalked, on one occasion suddenly stopping and asking Ada for writing materials so that he could note one down. She was unable to find any, prompting the affectionate reproof: 'You have all the equipment of a writer, my dear Sphinx, except pens, ink and paper.'

The easy intimacy between Oscar and Ada had developed quite rapidly over the previous three years. Ada was an admirer of Oscar's wit and writings, but she also parodied them in a number of places, notably in *Punch*. Unlike many of that magazine's satirical assaults on Wilde, however, Mrs Leverson's were never meant unkindly. Oscar was quite flattering about even some of her more feeble parodies; one, based on his long poem *The Sphinx*, Ada entitled *The Minx*. Having decided Ada herself was not a minx, Oscar dubbed her the Sphinx instead. They shared an extravagant sense of humour, as well as a taste for paradox and puns. But Ada's greatest asset, as far as Oscar was concerned, was that she was a confidante to whom he could say absolutely anything. She could sympathise where others would only have condemned. At the same time, Ada, who was trapped in a marriage to a husband whom she found increasingly uncongenial, asked nothing from Oscar except his friendship and amusement in return.

One day Constance came to the Leversons' house to see Oscar, to beg him to leave the country. When she left two hours later, in tears, Ada knew that the mission had been in vain. Hoping that Oscar might heed her advice even if he ignored his wife's, Ada sent a note up to him, urging him to save himself while he could. He returned the note when he came down that evening for dinner, commenting briefly: 'That is not like you, Sphinx.' The subject was closed.

The long days of confinement in the Leversons' nursery seem to have turned Oscar's mind to religion. In his letters to Bosie an element of Christian martyrdom began to appear and his effusions of love became less neo-classically romantic as they took on a character that was more sacred than profane:

[? May 1895]

As for you, you have given me the beauty of life in the past, and in the future if there is any future. That is why I shall be eternally grateful to you for having always inspired me with adoration and love. Those days of pleasure were our dawn. Now, in anguish and pain, in grief and humiliation, I feel that my love for you, your love for me, are the two signs of my life, the divine sentiments which make all bitterness bearable. Never has anyone in my life been dearer than you, never has any love been greater, more sacred, more beautiful . . .

Dear boy, among pleasures or in prison, you and the thought of you were everything to me. Oh! keep me always in your heart; you are never absent from mine. I think of you much more than of myself, and if, sometimes, the thought of horrible and infamous suffering comes to torture me, the simplest thought of you is enough to strengthen me and heal my wounds . . . Let destiny, Nemesis, or the unjust Gods alone receive the blame for everything that has happened.

Every great love has its tragedy, and now ours has too, but to have known and loved you with such profound devotion, to have had you for a part of my life, the only part I now consider beautiful, is enough for me. My passion is at a loss for words, but you can understand me, you alone. Our souls were made for one another, and by knowing yours through love, mine has transcended many evils, understood perfection, and entered into the divine essence of things.

. . . Now I think of you as a golden-haired boy with Christ's own heart in you. I know how much greater love is than everything else. You have taught me the divine secret of the world.

Bosie wrote from France imploring Oscar to join him. But as Oscar told the poet W.B. Yeats – who called to present various letters of sympathy and encouragement from a number of prominent Irish writers – he had to stay. On the eve of the opening of the retrial, Oscar asked Ada Leverson to leave a sleeping draught on the mantelpiece for him, saying that he had no intention of taking it, but that its presence would have a magical effect. The following morning, Oscar sought assurances from the Sphinx that she would write to him if the worst came to pass.

This time the proceedings at the Old Bailey took six days. Oscar's defence counsel successfully argued that his client should be tried separately from Alfred Taylor. But the advantage of that manoeuvre was largely lost when the Taylor case was taken first and the defendant was speedily found guilty. The Marquess of Queensberry, who was present, sent a gloating telegram to his daughter-in-law (Percy's wife), remarking that it was Wilde's turn next. When Percy ran into his father in the street by chance later that week, the two men came to blows and were bound over to keep the peace. The French press, which was following the whole Wilde affair with passionate interest, confused Percy with Bosie, reporting that it was Lord Alfred who had struck his father. Characteristically Bosie sent off a telegram from Rouen to *Le Figaro* demanding an apology, while wishing that he himself had been involved in the incident.

The same tawdry collection of witnesses was produced as at the previous trial, but for all their blatant individual untrustworthiness, their cumulative effect was damning. Oscar's counsel, Sir Edward Clarke, appealed to the jury not to allow the unpleasantness of the accusations and what he called the 'torrent of prejudice' that had recently been sweeping through the British press to cloud their judgement of the evidence. If they felt the charges against Wilde had not been proved, Sir Edward continued, they would be able by their verdict to save him from absolute ruin and could leave him, 'a distinguished man of letters and a brilliant Irishman, to live among us a life of honour and repute, and to give in the maturity of his genius gifts to our literature, of which he has given only the promise of his early youth.'

This plea found no response in the judge who, in his summing-up, declared that this was the worst case he had ever tried. The jury withdrew with the judge's condemnation of the heinous nature of Oscar Wilde's supposed crimes ringing in their ears. After a little more than a couple of hours of deliberation, they returned with a verdict of guilty on all counts, except the charge relating to Oscar's alleged relations with Edward Shelley.

Sentence was passed immediately. Puffed up with righteous indignation, the judge informed Oscar and Alfred Taylor:

> It is no use for me to address you. People who can do these things must be dead to all sense of shame, and one cannot hope to produce any effect upon them . . .
>
> I shall, under the circumstances, be expected to pass the severest sentence that the law allows. In my judgement it is totally inadequate for such a case as this. The sentence of the Court is that each of you be imprisoned and kept at hard labour for two years.

Oscar blanched and swayed. A lone voice in the public gallery cried out 'Shame!' Oscar was heard to mutter 'My God, My God'; the judge gestured to the warders and the prisoner was led away. That evening the Marquess of Queensberry hosted a celebration dinner, laughing in his triumph.

Almost uniquely among the British press, *Reynolds's News* protested at Queensberry's presence at the trial and made the point that Oscar had hardly been guilty of corrupting the young male prostitutes who had comprised most of the witnesses. While such newspapers as the *Daily Telegraph* were pandering to the prevailing mood of philistine self-congratulation ('Open the windows! Let in the fresh air!' it trumpeted), *Reynolds's News* concentrated on the enormity of the punishment. In the second week of June Oscar was transferred to Pentonville Jail, where he had to sleep on a plain plank bed raised just a few inches off the ground. At first he had no mattress and little other bedding. Insomnia was inevitable. The food was of such poor quality that diarrhoea was for many prisoners an almost permanent condition. The stench in the cells was often overpowering. The 'labour' imposed under Oscar's sentence initially consisted of six hours a day on a treadmill, twenty minutes on and five minutes off. Later he would graduate to only slightly less numbing activities such as oakum-picking. Normal exercise consisted of one hour a day, walking in the open air in single file with the other prisoners, among whom all communication was forbidden.

The French press explained to its readers what 'hard labour' meant, prompting an outraged letter from Madeleine Rondeaux to her cousin André Gide:

> [30 May 1895]
>
> Have you seen the sentence passed on [Oscar Wilde and Alfred Taylor]? I'm enclosing a newspaper cutting about it. If the details are correct, the punishment of *hard labour* is worthy of being added, in a supplementary chapter, to those in the sinister *House of Death* – or otherwise has been forgotten by Dante. It's awful, isn't it?

However, André was temporarily numbed to the enormity of what was happening to his friend on the other side of the Channel by the death of his mother on 31 May. André had been summoned to La Roque three days previously, to find his mother apparently unconscious of the people around her. Her look was vague and it seemed to André that her body no longer belonged to her. When her heart stopped beating, André found himself overwhelmed by conflicting feelings of distress and freedom. This was typical of the ambivalence that had governed their relationship. It was not just the woman who had brought him into the world who had now died before his eyes, but a symbolic figure of Christian faith and moral purity who had expired, provoking sentiments of both exhilaration and fear.

While Oscar was struggling to adapt to the brutality of his sentence at Pentonville, André was griefstricken over his mother's death. He began distributing her jewels and other possessions, not only to close relatives but also to people who had hardly known her. It was as if he were atoning for Mme Gide's six decades of penny-pinching, as well as celebrating his sudden wealth.

Barely a fortnight after Mme Gide's death, André and Madeleine became engaged, deeply shocking the sensibilities of many of their relations. The uncles' and aunts' disquiet would have been all the greater had they been a party to some of the correspondence now passing between the two cousins. In one letter towards the end of June, Madeleine referred to herself as André's 'friend, sister and fiancée', acknowledging that 'sister' might strike people as strange, but avowing that was what she felt herself most strongly to be. A few days later she commented ominously: 'I don't fear death, but I do fear marriage.'

André spent July at La Roque, most of the time alone with his mother's maid Marie, who had been as shocked as anybody by the unseemly haste of the engagement, for which Marie blamed André. On 28 July she confided in a letter to Madeleine that André had often been the subject of her prayers. She went on: 'even his writings made me sigh to heaven, because I could not understand his point of view and must have heard from someone that what he was writing was not good. I really suffered over this.'

Madeleine herself confessed to her fiancé that some passages in *Le Voyage d'Urien*, for example, had made her close the book. How, she asked him, could he have written such things, when his own life had been 'so intact, so pure'? The question pricked André's conscience, as he recalled many of the incidents that had taken place during his North African travels. Probingly, Madeleine asked why he feared telling her his inner thoughts, as they were such close friends. But André could not bring himself to confide in her. He was frightened that she would break off the engagement if she knew his secrets; that would be intolerable, as she was now his only anchor in a world in which he was essentially alone. Moreover, in contrast to the freedom from moral constraints he had enjoyed in Biskra, he now felt guilt.

Not for the first time, the developments in Oscar Wilde's life were serving as a disturbing warning for André, who was not allowed to ignore what was happening to his friend. The author Maurice Quillot wrote to inform him that he was dedicating his new book *Madame Aesthète* to 'the Martyr Oscar Wilde', while in the French press a series of articles started to appear, defending the Irishman's reputation and damning the savagery of British justice. In a long article in the *Mercure de France*, Hugues Rebell commented indignantly:

> One asks oneself what crime Oscar Wilde could have committed in order to be treated this way, whether he had betrayed England, tried to assassinate the Queen or to blow up Parliament. One is astonished to learn that Oscar Wilde has committed no crime, that he probably did not even commit the unnatural act of which he stands accused – at least, his guilt has as yet not been proved. It was merely necessary, in order for him to be condemned, that there came along to insult him a man whose sad conduct is known by all London, a kind of furious madman whose brutalities caused his wife and sons to leave him. Lord Queensberry, jealous at seeing his son prefer the society of a poet to that of his gross and cruel father, did not shy, in order to satisfy his hatred, from making suspect a liaison which Wilde's talent and spirit were sufficient to explain.

Other writers, including Stuart Merrill, Henri de Régnier and Octave Mirbeau joined the fray in Oscar's defence. Merrill attempted to rally enough support to present a petition for clemency to Queen Victoria, but too few people of sufficient standing were prepared to put their own reputations on the line. Some, to Merrill's disgust, even made light of the affair. The novelist Jules Renard noted caustically in his posthumously published journal that he would be ready to sign a petition in favour of Oscar Wilde, providing Wilde made the solemn undertaking never to write again.

Once again, André's name was conspicuously absent from those who spoke up on Oscar's behalf. Perhaps internally he could justify that failure by pleading the pressure of coping with his mother's loss and shouldering the new responsibilities that had come his way. Of all those responsibilities, none was greater than his now firm commitment to take Madeleine as his wife. As Gide later recalled in his memoirs, at the time he sincerely believed that he would be able to give himself completely to her. If that was to be the case, his homosexuality would have to be suppressed.

CHAPTER ELEVEN

Madeleine

MADELEINE RONDEAUX was a complex creature. She herself recognised that she had two distinct personalities. One she christened 'Marie': wise, serious and reasonable, aware of her responsibilities and always mindful of the moral basis of her existence – the Christian Gospels. The other personality, 'Marthe', was altogether more frivolous: cheerful, enthusiastic and emotional – a lover of poetry and romanticism. Much of Madeleine's prime was affected by the creative tension between 'Marie' and Marthe', though 'Marie' nearly always vanquished in the end. 'Marthe' was flattered and excited by proposals from at least three young men: André and two local suitors in Normandy. 'Marie' turned them all down. André was meant to abandon his attempt after the first rebuff, as the two other young men duly did; then, after a seemly period of chagrin, he should have tried successfully somewhere else. But André refused to play by the rules. He kept on proposing. 'Marie' similarly kept turning him down, until eventually she was won over and agreed with 'Marthe' that they did want to marry André, for he appealed to both of them in a way no-one else could.

André and 'Marie' could pray together, united in a Protestant fervour all the more ardent for being a minority persuasion in Catholic France. André and 'Marthe' could read aloud to each other from eighteenth- and nineteenth-century French and German literature, many volumes of which were locked away in glass-fronted cabinets in the Gide household, at least while André's mother was alive and kept custody of the key. 'Marie' sang hymns in church; 'Marthe' reclined on the sofa, listening to André playing pieces by Chopin – of whom Mme Gide strongly disapproved as someone likely to induce impure thoughts in young minds. Or else 'Marthe' sat on the window-seat of one of the front rooms at the Château de Cuverville, contemplating the huge cedar tree that dominated the entrance to the property, and in which she had climbed as a girl.

André complicated matters by inventing other personalities for Madeleine, notably the 'Emmanuèle' who figures in several of his works, beginning with the *Notebooks of André Walter*. Madeleine was displeased with this portrayal of herself, not so much because it distorted her into an almost two-dimensional figure of virginal purity, delicate health and offended sensibility, but because 'Emmanuelle' clearly echoed aspects of the 'Marie' side to her nature. To make matters worse, André used some of their correspondence as the raw material for several passages in his books, which Madeleine felt abused the intimacy of their relationship. She frankly disliked the *André Walter* poems. Yet throughout the years they were together, first as loving cousins and then as man and wife, she nurtured André's vocation as a writer.

Their common passion for literature was an immensely strong bond. Cut off from intellectual society, Madeleine had no-one else to talk to in depth about the books or the poems and articles that impressed her. None of her four younger siblings at the chateau – Jeanne, Valentine, Edouard and Georges – cared deeply enough about books to be a satisfying interlocutor. André, in that sense, was perfect; an ideal 'third brother', with whom she could enjoy animated conversations, or merely sit in the comfort of supportive silence as each pursued his or her reading or thoughts. André had several male friends, notably Paul Valéry, with whom he could savour that kind of intellectual rapport. But Madeleine was the only female equivalent.

The mutual support André and Madeleine gave each other was emotional as well as intellectual. Madeleine had been made prematurely worldy-wise and disillusioned with humanity by her mother's behaviour. Mme Mathilde Rondeaux lived largely for pleasure and must have felt stifled by the aura of moral rectitude, hard work and parsimony that her husband Emile caused to be permeated throughout the household. The family lived according to the norms of the late nineteenth-century Protestant upper middle class, carefully maintaining its place in Normandy society and playing a role in public life. Cuverville offered limited scope for Mathilde Rondeaux's amusement, so she made the most of the weeks spent at the family residence in Rouen. The gossip of her mother's flirting with army officers and other attentive men reached Madeleine's ears in the painful years of her own early adolescence. Then in 1881, when Madeleine was thirteen and André not yet twelve, Mathilde eloped with one of her admirers, taking her sixth child, a baby girl called Lucienne, with her, never to return.

André's father, Paul Gide, had died the year before, so the two cousins were thrown together in their sense of loss. Moreover, there was an ineffable sadness about Madeleine's demeanour after her mother's disappearance that appealed strongly to André's romantic disposition. Whether consciously or not, André made it his mission to save Madeleine from a cruel world, to protect her and make her happy.

Emile Rondeaux's death in 1890 made Madeleine the head of the household at Cuverville; she had already been in charge of much of the domestic administration since her mother's departure. The responsibilities gave her a maturity beyond her years, which made her all the more attractive to André, who had no patience with girlish silliness or helplessness. Madeleine's and André's relatives often cited her duty towards the household and looking after her younger siblings as a major reason why Madeleine should not contemplate marriage, not even to André. Remaining a spinster seemed to be what fate had allotted her. Her duty was to accept that graciously.

Soon after Juliette Gide's death in 1895, when André and Madeleine announced their determination to press ahead with the marriage, it was not only the apparent abnegation of those responsibilities, and the indelicate haste of the engagement, that disturbed the remaining older generation of Rondeaux and Gide relatives. Several of them were worried about both the propriety and the genetic advisability of first cousins marrying. André was summoned to see Aunt Claire – who lived in the grandest of all the Rondeaux family's magnificent properties – to discuss that indelicate matter. Fortunately, André's cousin Albert, who had thoughtfully done some research into the subject, was present at this frosty interview and was able to cite legal and scientific evidence to neutralise the objections raised. Madeleine fared less well when she too made the required family visits to the Gide relatives. At Montpellier, at the home of M. and Mme Charles Gide, she parried the latter's concern about the medical desirability of the union by saying this would not matter if it was to be an unconsummated *mariage blanc*. André's aunt was deeply shocked. But a *mariage blanc* was what he and Madeleine envisaged from the start; true to their intentions, they did indeed never make love.

The few people who had read *Les Cahiers d'André Walter* might have realised that this would be the case, because in that book the narrator André tells Emmanuèle: 'I don't desire you. Your body makes me uneasy, and carnal possessions appal me.' As Madeleine's love for André was sisterly, rather than that usually existing between two people on the verge of marriage, she may have found this disturbing statement paradoxically reassuring. But she was far less happy with something André had said to her in 1893: that part of his literary and personal vocation was to be an 'object of scandal'. At the time she had asked him why, fearing there was more to this declaration than the usual writer's craving for fame. Now, two years later, on the eve of the wedding, with the Oscar Wilde scandal still ringing in her ears, she might usefully have asked André a supplementary question about his desire to be an object of scandal: 'How?'

The marriage celebrations, at the beginning of October, were small and intimate, partly in deference to André's mother's relatively recent death, but mainly because the couple wanted things that way. There was a civil ceremony at the Château de Cuverville – with few people except close members of the family present – followed by the necessary paperwork at the local town hall. Lastly, there was a church service at the nearby village of Etretat. Madeleine's mother, Mathilde Talabart, was not present; the breach with her five elder children had never been healed. Also absent, more surprisingly, was André's uncle Charles, who had often assumed the role of André's benign family mentor since Paul Gide's death. However, Charles Gide and his wife did invite the newly-weds to begin their honeymoon at their house outside Montpellier, where André had spent such pleasant days before his first trip to North Africa two years earlier.

Indeed, the whole honeymoon, which lasted eight months (a protracted time, even by late nineteenth-century upper-middle-class standards), was a pilgrimage to places where André had known earlier happiness or excitement. The honourable pretext was that he wished to introduce his new wife to individuals and settings that had been significant in his recent past, some of which he had already told her about; the hidden agenda was to test her resilience to those people and places that would remain significant for him, despite his changed status. Marrying Madeleine was the fulfilment of one of André's most persistent dreams, but that did not mean that he felt any obligation to abandon his other fantasies.

Switzerland was the first major stop on the itinerary; inauspiciously, Madeleine almost immediately fell ill, at Neuchâtel, where André had wanted to show her the tranquil charms of the lake. For a few days he tolerated her weakness with loving forbearance, sitting at her bedside for hours. But when she started to recover, he hurried her on too quickly to St Moritz, to experience the glories of the Swiss Alps under snow and ice. The petite Madeleine was no natural mountaineer and the exertion of sleigh-rides and Alpine trekking was too much for her; she was soon laid up again, in the restorative luxury of the Hotel Kuhn. The manager there was taken aback that the honeymooners requested separate bedrooms. Bored with ministering to his sick spouse, and irritated by the realisation that travelling with her would be much more limiting than his expeditions with Paul Laurens, André sat in his room, resenting the hotel's comfort almost as much as he resented Madeleine's frailty. Asceticism had firmly established itself as an important element in his well-being.

The rage that grew inside him during those long, dark weeks in St Moritz in November and early December was further fuelled by the Swiss. The more Madeleine eulogised their honesty and correctness and reliability, the more André found them unbearably stultifying. As one can gather from relevant passages in Gide's largely autobiographical novel of 1902, *L'Immoraliste (The Immoralist)*, it was at this time that André suddenly realised that having only recently been liberated from his mother's moral strictures by her death, he had voluntarily hitched himself to someone equally virtuous, and, at times, reproving. He had only himself to blame for this, though it was Madeleine (like her fictional counterpart Marceline in *L'Immoraliste*) who would have to suffer many of the consequences. One side of André's character still admired and cherished virtue, but the other – moreover the one that was once more on the ascendant – wanted to pursue the path of moral deconstruction and amorality opened up by Oscar Wilde in Paris four years earlier.

Unable to see Oscar, or even to enter into correspondence with him, given the restrictions of his imprisonment, André invented and polished dialogue with him in the artistically transformed figure of Ménalque in the pages of *Les Nourritures terrestres*. André had taken up again the manuscript he had started in North Africa in 1893, determined not to leave St Moritz until he had finalised the section on Ménalque – a clarion call to voluptuousness so at odds with the situation in which André now found himself that Madeleine was not surprisingly shocked and hurt when he read the finished pages aloud to her. Familiar with the details of Wilde's disgrace, and sensitive to the thinly veiled pederastic references in the piece, Madeleine could not fail to be concerned. As the narrator of *Les Nourritures terrestres* tells his confidant Nathaniel near the beginning of the book:

> Ménalque is dangerous; fear him; he is reproved by wise men, yet children are not afraid of him. He teaches them to love more than just their families – and, slowly, to leave them. He makes their hearts sick with the desire for bitter wild fruits and troubled by a strange love. Ah! Ménalque, I would have liked to have followed you yet more along other routes. But you hated weakness and aspired to teach me to leave you.

Although only part of a work in progress, the main 'Ménalque' chapter was published in the magazine *L'Ermitage* the following month, January 1896, prompting an enthusiastic response from André's friend Paul Valéry.

By then, André and Madeleine had left Switzerland for the warmer and more agreeable climate of Italy. They hired a carriage to travel through the Apennine villages, where little boys ran alongside them laughing and begging. André was flushed with pleasure at the sight of the scruffy lads, but Madeleine felt excluded from his joy. It was if he became another person when there were beautiful children around; furthermore, this other André was a person of whom the 'Marie' side of Madeleine could only disapprove, and by whom the more joyful 'Marthe' side of her personality felt rebuffed. For the moment, however, Madeleine bit her tongue.

André had written almost nothing in his diary during 1895, apart from a few pious exhortations such as 'Suppress the idea of merit in oneself'. But when he and Madeleine arrived in Florence in mid-December, he started to compose extensive travel notes. The couple went to view the churches and art galleries he had largely neglected on his previous stay in the city. He found himself so fired by some of the paintings and sculptures of youths that he would sometimes return alone, standing for hours in front of Donatello's marvellous David, for example, savouring the softness of the boy's cheeks, his small delicate body and oriental grace. Meetings with his real-life young writer friend Roberto Gatteschi and a new acquaintance, Gabriele d'Annunzio (then working on a series of novels with Nietzschean heroes), could not drive from André's mind the thoughts evoked by the statue, the painful nostalgia for the 'oriental grace' of North Africa. His obsessive longing for the ardour and emptiness of the desert, the special shade of palmeries and the Arabs' long and voluminous white robes – and what lay underneath – so troubled his senses that he found himself unable to sleep. He wandered the streets at night, often following people he thought looked particularly interesting, so he could observe them more closely. Plagued by migraines and weariness, Madeleine stayed in her hotel room for hours on end. The guilt André sometimes felt at leaving her rarely drove him back to keep her company.

In Florence, André resisted the temptation to go beyond mere observation of local youths. But if Gide's memoirs are to be believed, in Rome, where he and Madeleine next progressed, a demon seemed to take hold of him. Recklessly, on the pretext of needing models for the photography that had become one of his hobbies, he invited boys he had picked up on the Spanish Steps to pose for him at the small apartment he and Madeleine rented in the Piazza Barberini. For small sums of money, many of the boys were willing to do more than just pose. André showed Madeleine some of his rather unsuccessful early academic photographic portraits of his favourite model, Luigi, and other boys whom he got to ape classical postures, as if to prove to her that his pastime was innocent. In one of Gide's later autobiographical works, *Et nunc manet in te . . .*, he accused his younger self not only of blindness to the risks involved and to Madeleine's sensitivity, but also of dismissing the importance of these Roman sexual encounters because, he claimed, neither his heart nor his spirit was involved. Those were reserved for Madeleine – or so André deluded himself.

The couple continued their journey south, reaching Naples by the end of January. Both of them were keen to go by boat through the grottoes of Capri, which had already acquired the status of a romantic touristic site, despite the rapaciousness of the boatmen. But for André there was another, more dangerous attraction on that island: Lord Alfred Douglas, who had taken a year's lease on a small villa in the Strada Pastano. André had bombarded Bosie with letters during the previous year, avid for any news of Oscar, though it was not until September, when Douglas had arrived in Capri, that he bothered to reply, urging André to pay him a visit. They probably saw each other in Naples, rather than in Capri, as Bosie had recently become disenchanted with the island, which was being swept by rainstorms. With typical extravagance, he moved out of the villa he had rented on Capri to take up residence at Parker's Hotel Tramontano in Naples, before settling into another villa, at Posilipso, on the outskirts of the city.

Far from being chastened by Oscar's downfall, Bosie was as intemperate as ever. His mother, Lady Queensberry, had asked a Roman Catholic priest, Father Sebastien Bowden, to give him spiritual advice through the post, in the hope of calming him down. But as the priest wrote resignedly to Bosie's and Oscar's friend More Adey, 'my fears are that AD is at present so self-willed and blinded as to be humanly speaking beyond Redemption.'

Bosie attributed much of his present instability to the fact that he was tortured by the separation from Oscar; he was quite convinced that he was suffering just as much as Oscar was in prison. As Bosie had written to André, he was miserable because he was sure the British prison system was going to kill Oscar. Oscar had responded badly to the regime at Wandsworth Prison, even though in several ways it was less rigorous than that at Pentonville, from which he had been moved in July. At Wandsworth, Oscar was obliged to spend some time in the prison hospital because of dysentery and malnutrition. The sickness was a blessing in disguise, as it gave Oscar relief from the greatest physical hardships of his incarceration.

As Bosie informed André, he had written to Queen Victoria pleading for mercy for Oscar, claiming that Oscar was the innocent victim of the Marquess of Queensberry's hatred. The plea was to no avail. While she did not credit the existence of lesbianism (which was why lesbianism had not been outlawed in Britain, along with male homosexuality), she did acknowledge homosexuality between men, and was not amused. The British public and press were in no mood for leniency in Oscar's case either. Moreover, well-substantiated rumours suggested that the authorities in England were making an example of Oscar by keeping his punishment harsh, so as to deflect criticism over the careful omission from his trial proceedings of the names of several high-ranking personalities, including Lord Rosebery (who had nonetheless had to resign as Prime Minister largely as a result of the Wilde scandal).

Meanwhile, Oscar had begun to feel very resentful that Bosie was enjoying himself in southern Italy while he was languishing in jail. As had so often been demonstrated in the past, when the two of them were together, Lord Alfred exerted a fatal yet irresistible magnetism over Oscar. But in prison, Oscar was out of range. There was not even direct contact between them by letter. The one message from Bosie that did reach Oscar was verbal, when he was being escorted from prison to attend bankruptcy proceedings against him. An attendant whispered to him that 'Prince Fleur-de-Lys' sent his greetings. Before his imprisonment, Oscar would have been charmed to hear this; at that moment, the message only compounded his feeling of being the casualty of Bosie's detestation of his father, and provoked a bitter laugh.

One of the worst humiliations to which Oscar was ever subjected took place when he was transferred yet again, in November 1895, this time to Reading Gaol. He and his guards were obliged to change trains at Clapham Junction, where he was kept standing in his hideous prison uniform, handcuffed, for about half an hour in the early afternoon, providing a butt for the sarcastic comments of passengers on trains passing through that busy interchange. When someone recognised the prisoner, the comments became all the more ribald. One man walked up to him and spat in his face. The incident marked Oscar for the rest of his life, causing him to weep at the memory.

The cruel treatment of the fallen Oscar Wilde revolted many people in France, where it was censoriously reported. The number of articles appearing in French newspapers attacking the barbarity of the British increased (doubtless fuelled by the continuing rivalry and mistrust that existed between these two imperial powers). Several British newspapers responded to these attacks by criticising the French for the way that the Jewish French army officer Alfred Dreyfus had been court-martialled, formally humiliated and sent off to Devil's Island penal colony for life, despite – as several British observers correctly surmised – having been framed. Blind to their own prejudices, the British and the French contentedly condemned each other's. The anti-gayness of the British and the widespread anti-Semitism of the French provided considerable opportunity for mutual recriminations as the Wilde and Dreyfus affairs developed simultaneously.

Oscar was touched by the continuing efforts of several friends on both sides of the Channel to draw attention to the injustice of the severity of his treatment. But he became increasingly angry with Alfred Douglas's attempts to assist that campaign, alarming news of which reached him through the occasional permitted visits and letters from friends. *En route* from Rouen to Italy, in the summer of 1895, Bosie had stopped in Paris where the prestigious literary review *Mercure de France* had commissioned him to write his version of the Oscar Wilde affair. Bosie leapt at the chance. This was his golden opportunity to get even with his father, or so he thought. He wrote the article, in English, in Italy, quoting in it three of the intimate letters that Oscar had written to him while on remand in Holloway Prison, as evidence of the 'purity' of their relationship. The completed article was duly sent off to the *Mercure de France*, for translation and anticipated publication. The translator informed Robert Sherard of its contents and Sherard was able to contact Oscar to see if he approved before the article was set in type. Oscar was extremely annoyed and urged Sherard to prevent its publication unless the letters were omitted. Without informing Bosie, Sherard told the editor of Wilde's objections. The magazine was still prepared to print the article without the letters, but Bosie – livid that Sherard had, as he saw it, gone behind his back – withdrew it, on the grounds that without the letters it was meaningless. Partly because of this incident, Bosie complained to André that Oscar's friends had influenced his lover against him. Yet it seems mainly to have been through months of agonising reflection that Oscar's love for Bosie turned to hate.

It is significant that André made no mention in his travel notes of meeting Bosie at this time, possibly because he used to read these aloud to Madeleine when he considered them sufficiently polished. He was doubtless anxious not to be asked too many probing questions about his conversations with Bosie (whose pain over the separation from Oscar had not curbed his appetite for local boys). Presumably André told Madeleine he was meeting Bosie, however. And she would have been aware of the renewed friendship between her husband and Lord Alfred through the letters that Bosie wrote to André as he and Madeleine continued their travels through Sicily to Tunis. Bosie felt that in André he had found someone who offered him not only sympathy but no sense of rivalry – an ease that he did not feel with Robbie Ross, who had been staying with Bosie until André arrived.

On St Valentine's Day, 1896, Bosie was able to write ecstatically to André that he had read in the newspapers that Oscar's play *Salomé* had at last been successfully staged, at the Théâtre de l'Oeuvre in Paris, thanks to the actor-manager Aurélian-François Lugné-Poë, who himself took the role of Herod. Salome was played not by Sarah Bernhardt, as Oscar had always hoped, but by Lina Munte. News of the production of course filtered back to Oscar in Reading Gaol. In his eyes, this was yet more evidence of France's superiority over perfidious Albion. When he was allowed to write to Robbie Ross, Oscar instructed him:

> [10 March 1896]
> Please write to Stuart Merrill in Paris, or Robert Sherard, to say how gratified I was at the performance of my play: and have my thanks conveyed to Lugné-Poë; it is something that at a time of disgrace and shame I should be still regarded as an artist. I wish I could feel more pleasure: but I seem dead to all emotions except those of anguish and despair. However, please let Lugné-Poë know that I am sensible to the honour he has done me.

It was not just in his travel notes that André made no allusion to Douglas or Wilde at this time. More strikingly (as had happened when he had encountered Oscar and Bosie in Florence two years earlier), André omitted to tell his regular correspondent Paul Valéry, even though the two friends were discussing Gide's 'Ménalque' in their letters. It was not just a matter of avoiding drawing attention to his friendship with the scandalous pair. He also seems to have wanted to keep different parts of his life separate from each other: his friends, his lovers, his wife. Madeleine would have been startled to learn that she was not mentioned either in the letters André wrote to Valéry from Italy.

Indeed, André often gave the impression to others that he was travelling on his own, as at times he probably wished he was. Yet he was still anxious to get Madeleine's approval of the places he loved. Unfortunately, the arrival in Tunis was disappointing for someone who was hoping to show it off. In just three years, the city had changed considerably. Trees were being planted along wide Frenchified avenues and in squares; zinc was replacing clay for roofs. Street lights were removing much of the mystery of formerly dark corners and entrances. Only in the souks was the atmosphere still captivating, though André searched in vain for the café where the Sudanese ex-slaves used to gather. As a substitute, he quickly became an *aficionado* of the popular street theatres in the Arab quarters, where hordes of children gathered to watch mimes and shows. Each morning he filled his pocket with salted, dried melon-seeds, later distributing them among eager little hands.

But it was Algeria – and not least Biskra – by which André really wanted Madeleine to be enchanted. Above all, Biskra meant Athman. Too impatient to wait until the couple arrived at Biskra, Athman went to the station at El Kantara to meet them. Now seventeen years old, and resplendently dressed in white and blue silk, with a blue jacket and an enormous brown turban – an outfit that had exhausted all his money – Athman was an impressive sight. André barely recognised him. However, the youth's dogged devotion had not changed. At El Kantara and at Biskra, he accompanied André and Madeleine on carriage-drives, or waited patiently with the horses while the two of them went off for walks among the palm trees. Soon their party grew. There were other Arab boys who tagged along. Then one of André's friends, the writer Francis Jammes, arrived from France. In such an environment, in which Madeleine, as well as the men, talked for hours about books, Athman's own pretensions to literary greatness were inflated. He spent hours copying passages from books that had been recommended or else he experimented writing verse. Sometimes the boy's lyricism took more original forms. One evening, accompanying André and Jammes into the desert to savour the odour and aura of the silent night, he suddenly threw off his burnous, secured his flapping underclothes and turned cartwheels in the sand.

For André (and Jammes), Athman was a non-ending source of amusement, which was half of his attraction. The seriousness with which he took himself only made him more of a clown. Determined to function as much as possible on equal terms with his French companions, he devoured a volume on the lives of great men – and then proceeded to season his conversation with historical allusions. He took to writing to contemporary artistic figures in France, sternly informing the artist Degas, for example, that he would be happy if Degas disliked Jews and agreed with him that Poussin was a great painter. For a while, carried away by his reading of *The Thousand and One Nights*, in particular the story of *Aladdin*, he signed all his letters 'Athman, or the wonderful lamp'.

Madeleine could not help but be charmed by her surroundings. She liked Athman and she was genuinely delighted by the exoticism of the place. When she and André made an expedition to Touggourt, they went by camel. The beasts' swaying motion sent her into fits of giggles. The clarity of the light and the warmth of the spring air relaxed her and made her happy, just as they did André. She overcame her Norman inhibitions about any lack of cleanliness, or about eating with one's hands out of a common dish. 'Marthe' was in the ascendant over 'Marie'; she was letting her spirit of adventure develop.

And yet there were moments when Madeleine was brought up sharp, and her joy at the spontaneity and colour of the Arab life going on around her was submerged by sadness and disquiet. André was usually the cause. One image of him troubled her for years to come. They had been travelling by train and as it pulled into a station, begging children ran alongside, echoing the experience they had had driving with the horse-and-carriage through the Apennines the previous autumn. Expectant little faces looked up at their carriage windows; skinny brown arms were held out. As if oblivious to Madeleine's presence, André leant out and took hold of the arms of the running children, and ran his fingers up and down their soft skin. Then suddenly he withdrew as if stung by guilt; he blushed scarlet, sat back in his seat and mopped his brow. Madeleine looked at him anxiously, without saying a word. But later she wrote to him: 'You looked like a madman, or a criminal . . .'

CHAPTER TWELVE

Constance

AMONG the many disturbing images that went through Madeleine Gide's mind, there was that of Constance Wilde. If Oscar was a warning to André of the dangers of trying to flout convention, Constance's experiences were equally a salutary lesson in how one could be dragged down by one's husband's indiscretions. Constance's tragedy was in many ways as great as Oscar's and perhaps even more cruel. For she was truly innocent, caught up in a drama not of her own making.

Because of Oscar's dominating personality and brilliant literary output, whose reputation now stands as high as ever, Constance has remained eclipsed. But she was a much more remarkable woman than posterity generally acknowledges. Had she not been, Oscar would never have married her. To an extent, when he did so, he was acquiring a lovely new possession, which he could show off for other people's admiration. As a young woman, she was very beautiful: slim, fair-skinned, with thick brown hair and violet eyes. For Oscar, there may also have been an element of finding a replacement for his lost sister, Isola – a near contemporary of Constance's – whom he had loved dearly but who died while still a child. That does not mean that

Oscar was looking for a sister-wife, like André's Madeleine. There was a considerably more 'normal' attachment between the Wildes when they were first married. The problem, as already noted, was that during Constance's second pregnancy, she physically revolted Oscar, and his carnal desire for her was never rekindled. Besides, boys had intervened.

Oscar subsequently so marginalised his wife that she appeared to be of little importance, either for him or for anybody. That impression was reinforced by several of Oscar's gay coterie (though not Robbie Ross, to his credit). They laughed at Constance behind her back, seeing her as the fooled spouse who, for a while at least, provided Oscar with a smokescreen behind which he could carry out his homosexual liaisons. For some of the misogynists among that circle, Oscar's often unwitting punishment of his wife for being a woman was a source of pleasure and mirth.

Yet Constance was no fool. Unlike her elder brother Otho, Constance had been denied a formal education, but she made up for that by reading widely and listening to the many intelligent men – and sometimes women – who frequented the rather grand households of her paternal grandfather Horatio Lloyd in London and her mother's family in Dublin. Born in London, she had a foothold in both cities; she could thus relate both to Oscar's origins and to his first adopted home. Moreover, she was no strait-laced puritan. Her father Horace came from a family of principled Liberal stock. She adored him, despite his regular disappearances and his sometimes bohemian ways and all the gossip of his alleged marital infidelities.

Constance was much less close to her mother, Adele, who did not really seem comfortable in the maternal role. Hence Constance's relief when she found a substitute mother in Lady (Georgina) Mount-Temple – a relation by marriage – with whom Constance was often parked as a young girl, at Babbacombe Cliff in Devon. The house, now a hotel (as indeed is Grandfather Lloyd's substantial dwelling in Lancaster Gate in London), was a masterpiece of pre-Raphaelite art and crafts. It was designed by John Ruskin and decorated by William Morris and Edward Burne-Jones; like her father, Constance greatly admired it, returning there frequently after her marriage, as did Oscar. The house undoubtedly sharpened her interest in interior design. Though Oscar often liked to pose as his wife's educator in such matters, she in fact knew almost as much as he did on the subject.

She was moreover politically far more mature than her husband, whose romantic socialist leanings could easily be swept aside, either by the need to turn a memorable epigram, or not to offend some distinguished personage – often a socially well-connected female – whom he wished to flatter or entertain. Constance, in contrast, was a staunch Liberal, like her forebears. She was active in the Chelsea branch of the Women's Liberal Federation after her marriage and campaigned for women's suffrage. Intellectually, she could not compete with Oscar who, after all, had brilliant academic credentials. But she was an attentive listener, able and willing to chide her husband when he was talking tosh.

When Oscar turned his back on Constance, literally and metaphorically, she began to devote herself almost wholly to the future well-being of their two sons, Cyril and Vyvyan. All of her behaviour in the last decade of her life has to be viewed with that in mind. She never stopped loving Oscar, even after his disgrace. But her protective love for her children sometimes had to take precedence. Many people assumed that after Oscar's fateful trials, Constance would divorce her husband; certainly, several of her relatives and friends urged her to do so. At times she too thought that might be for the best, for the children's sake. But her love stopped her making the decisive break.

Cyril, then about to celebrate his tenth birthday, was at boarding school in Dublin when the trials took place. Constance had been trying to keep their father's predicament secret from both boys, but Cyril saw news of the affair posted on billboards. By looking up various words in the dictionary, he discovered the gist of the charges and was greatly upset. His mother knew he would be ragged unmercifully as the trials came to their inevitable climax, so decided to send both boys to safety and, she hoped, obscurity in Switzerland, where her brother Otho was living. Unwilling to abandon Oscar immediately herself, Constance hastily hired a very religious and reportedly reliable French governess to accompany the boys. Vyvyan, aged only eight, was kept in the dark about the reason for the sudden departure and did not learn of the nature of his father's offences until he was in his teens. Sadly, the governess turned out to be totally irresponsible, leaving the boys locked in a hotel room in Paris without toys or adequate food while she went off to church or to see friends. When they reached Switzerland, and checked into a hotel in Glion, she failed so badly to keep the boys under control that the management complained.

Constance joined the boys and the governess at Glion at the end of May 1895. Arriving in the late evening after a long journey through France, in pain from a back injury sustained when she had fallen downstairs a few months previously, she was horrified to find the boys playing outside the hotel, unsupervised; the governess was up in her room, calmly reading. After an angry altercation, she was dismissed. This left Constance alone to field Vyvyan's awkward questions. She fibbed that Oscar was detained on business in London and would join them when he could. As for the toy fort and soldiers her sons asked after, she had not the heart to tell them they had been boxed up to be sold with the rest of the contents of the House Beautiful in Tite Street in the demeaning auction organised in response to clamouring creditors.

For several summer weeks, there was the opportunity for quiet repose. But then the hotel manager started to receive complaints from other guests that the wife and children of the immoral Oscar Wilde were lowering the tone of the place by being residents there. Accordingly, he asked them to leave. Constance was still using her real married name, but at the suggestion of her brother Otho, she now agreed to have it changed to one of his names, Holland – again, largely for the sake of the boys. Otho also invited the homeless trio to come to stay with him and his wife at Bevaix, on Lake Neuchâtel.

In the middle of September, Constance set off for London, to visit Oscar in Wandsworth Prison. She was nervous about the encounter. Robert Sherard, who had already been to the jail, warned her about Oscar's poor physical and mental condition, as well as describing the horrors of the prison itself. But the reality was still a frightful shock. There was a jostling crowd of prisoners' relatives and friends, who rushed forward into the visiting hall at the sound of a bell. A grill and a gap of about a metre separated the prisoners and their visitors; they had to shout to each other to be heard. Oscar looked shambling and pathetic in his ill-fitting prison garb. He was ashen-faced and clearly unwell. As Constance wrote to Robert Sherard the following day:

> [22 September 1895]
> It was indeed awful, more so than I had any conception it could be. I could not see him and I could not touch him, and I scarcely spoke . . . He has been mad the last three years, and he says that if he saw Lord A. he would kill him. So he had better keep away, and be satisfied with having marred a fine life. Few people can boast of so much.

Oscar extracted a promise from her that he could join her and their sons on his release. Separation from the boys was especially painful for him. Subsequently, Constance confirmed to her lawyers that she did not wish to proceed with a divorce.

Given Constance's own uncertain health and the strain that she was going through, it seemed unwise to subject herself to the rigours of a Swiss winter. So she and her sons and her brother and his wife moved into an apartment in the little village of Seri near Genoa. The house had been found for her by her friend Margaret Brooke, Ranee of Sarawak, who was married to Sir Charles Brooke, the second

White Rajah of that part of northern Borneo; the Ranee spent much of her time in Italy. However unpleasant many British people might be to the Hollands – as they were now called – Constance did benefit from the solicitude of several devoted and kind friends, like the Ranee, as well as from Otho's loyalty. Mercifully, Oscar's bankruptcy did not leave her destitute as she had a modest income through a legacy from her grandfather Horatio Lloyd. She made the new home as comfortable as possible. But she was suffering increasingly from pains in her back and in her fingers and she was having trouble with her digestion. She put the latter down to the local food, though other causes might well have been her worry over Oscar's condition, and the bitter knowledge that Lord Alfred Douglas was living scot-free and unrepentant further down the Italian coast.

In February 1896, just days after Bosie had bid farewell to André Gide in Naples, Constance received a letter from her sister-in-law, Lily Wilde, informing her of Lady Wilde's death following a bad bout of bronchitis. Oscar had not yet been told, and despite her own poor health, Constance felt she must make the journey back to England to tell him personally. Finding it unthinkable that she should have to break the news by shouting it across a crowded visitors' room of the kind she had experienced at Wandsworth, she took the precaution of writing to R.B. Haldane, a sympathetic member of the Home Office committee that investigated prison conditions, asking that her visit to Oscar at Reading Gaol should take place in a private room. The request was granted.

Reading Gaol looked forbidding from the outside, but Constance was greeted civilly by the officers on duty. She was shown into a room usually used by solicitors when they were being briefed by their inmate clients. Oscar was brought to her there, looking thinner and more haggard than he had been four months before. His nails were broken and his hands scarred and dirty from picking oakum, one of the mindless tasks imposed on prisoners of his category. She embraced him and held him tightly, fighting back her tears. She could not condone or even comprehend the sexual need that had driven her husband to take stable-boys and other lower-class youths and male prostitutes into his bed. But she still had a powerful desire to touch him.

Oscar knew the object of Constance's mission even before she told him. The previous day, while Oscar's cell was being swept out, a spider suddenly ran across the floor and a warder stamped on it. Transfixed by this careless act of tempting fate, the superstitious Oscar hallucinated that he heard the scream of a banshee. Then a vision of Speranza, Lady Wilde, appeared. She was dressed in a hat and overcoat, which Oscar invited her to take off. But she shook her head sadly and vanished, which Oscar interpreted as an intimation of her death. During her last days, the real-life Lady Wilde had asked if Oscar could be brought to see her before she died, but that was something prison regulations did not allow. Once she realised that she would never see him again, she declared in resignation: 'May the prison help him!', and turned in her bed to face the wall.

In the solicitors' room at Reading Gaol, Oscar's and Constance's conversation moved on to more pleasant matters, such as the health of the children and plans for their education. Oscar urged her to appoint a guardian for them in his absence, preferably a family friend who had a legal background. Constance then agreed that Oscar should have an income from her of £150 a year after his release, and a one-third interest in her marriage settlement should she predecease him. They both knew that any moneys that might come his way from future editions of his books or productions of his plays – assuming such things could happen in his lifetime – would be swallowed up by creditors. Constance acknowledged that whatever her husband may have done, their marriage was still valid enough for her to be obliged to support him, albeit modestly. Those arrangements made, Oscar then spotted the warder beckoning with his finger; like a dog, Oscar meekly obeyed and left the room, without looking back.

Having returned to Italy briefly, Constance then moved on to

Germany, where a family friend, Carlos Blacker, helped to find suitable schools for Cyril and Vyvyan; both Blacker and the Ranee of Sarawak thought a German education would benefit the boys. Moreover, if their true identity was discovered (something that Cyril was determined to try to prevent), it would not matter too much. Oscar's work was still highly regarded in Germany, despite the scandal; indeed, Germany would be in the vanguard of his rehabilitation as a literary figure of stature.

Unfortunately, the first two schools turned out badly; the boys, notably Cyril, got involved in fights, not for being Wildes, but for being British, resulting in their expulsion. Eventually Cyril settled down more happily at a sporty, English-style college called Neuenheim, while Vyvyan was despatched to the gentle and religious surroundings of the Jesuit Collegio della Visitazione in Monaco, thanks to the intervention of another of Constance's high-placed friends, Princess Alice of Monaco. Constance herself went back to Italy again, moving into a villa just outside Genoa, found for her by the Ranee of Sarawak. The villa was considerably more comfortable than the Seri apartment; this was not so much a luxury as a necessity, as her physical condition was continuing to deteriorate. She consulted a specialist, who diagnosed a form of spinal paralysis, the only available treatment for which was rather risky – and not necessarily successful – surgery.

Oscar's own health was a matter for growing concern. His work duties now included tending the garden at Reading Gaol, which ought to have been beneficial; certainly, in the summer months, it brought more colour to his face. But as Robbie Ross discovered on one of his visits to Oscar, the playwright had become almost emaciated. His hair had greyed and thinned; there was a distinct bald patch at the back of his head. He complained of anaemia and gout; in cold weather, one of his ears bled and gave him great pain. It had been injured in a fall in the chapel at Wandsworth and the resultant abscess had never been properly treated. At Reading, the doctor was unsympathetic, sometimes accusing Oscar of malingering. Oscar found it hard to bear his physical illness, but worst of all, as he told Robbie, he feared madness.

Oscar's mental agitation was evident in an anguished plea he started writing shortly after passing the halfway mark in his prison term, in June 1896. In that he came close to repudiating the views he had held about homosexual love, as expressed in his extempore defence at the Old Bailey of the tastes he had claimed were shared by Plato, Michelangelo and Shakespeare. In his petition from Reading Gaol, he declared in contrast that he had been suffering from sexual madness, pleading that this was a disease which needed curing, not a crime that merited punishment. He wrote that he did not attempt 'to palliate in any way the terrible offences of which he was rightly found guilty'. But he begged that the authorities would take note of the danger of his impending insanity, growing deafness from the abscess in his ear, and the possibility of blindness from being obliged to read by insufficient gaslight. The then Governor of Reading Gaol – a martinet by the name of Colonel J. Isaacson, who believed in reforming characters by chastising inmates for the slightest deviance from rules or any evidence of slipshod comportment – duly passed Oscar's petition for clemency on to the Home Office. But the Colonel completely undermined its effect by appending a note from the prison doctor attesting that in his view there was nothing seriously wrong with the prisoner at all.

A few days after Oscar's petition was submitted, he watched a hangman cross the prison yard, carrying gardener's gloves and a little bag. A scaffold was tested and on the morning of 7 July, a murderer by the name of Charles Wooldridge – who had killed his wife in what the French would have considered a *crime passionnel*, born of jealousy – was duly hung. The condemned man went to his death without flinching. The image loitered in Oscar's mind, worrying him throughout the summer, evoking a phrase that kept recurring in his thoughts: 'each man kills the thing he loves'. As he brooded, he became convinced that that was exactly what Alfred Douglas had done to him. Oscar had no wish to see Bosie dead, but he was distressed that his lover looked as if he would escape any punishment for completely ruining someone else's life.

In retaliation, Oscar could only wound Bosie by making him aware of the extent to which his feelings about him had changed. He refused to allow Douglas to dedicate a book of poems to him, which almost, but not quite, dissuaded Bosie from publishing the book at all. Oscar also pressed – unsuccessfully – for the return of the many letters and presents that he had given the young lord during the heyday of their association. As the months passed and Oscar got no response to his petition to the Home Secretary, his bitterness against Bosie grew like a poisonous weed. As he wrote to Robbie Ross, succumbing to Bosie had been the great mistake of his life:

> [November 1896]
> I admit I lost my head. I let him do what he wanted. I was bewildered, incapable of judgement. I made the one fatal step. And now . . . I sit here on a bench in a prison cell. In all tragedies there is a grotesque element. He is the grotesque element in mine. Do not think I do not blame myself. I curse myself night and day for my folly in allowing him to dominate my life. If there was an echo in these walls it would cry 'Fool' forever.

The one great alleviating factor in the nightmare of Oscar's second year behind bars was Colonel Isaacson's transfer away from Reading during the summer of 1896 and his replacement by a far more humane Governor, Major J.O. Nelson, who treated his most famous charge with both courtesy and respect, which reduced Oscar to tears of gratitude. Major Nelson saw to it that Oscar had access to far more reading material than had previously been the case. The prison library was not richly endowed in worthwhile literature, but Oscar was able to submit lists of books he would like to read, many of which were approved by the authorities, and subsequently provided by Oscar's friend More Adey. They included works by Froissart, Huysmans and Goncourt, as well as a French Bible, plus German and Italian grammatical works. In those moments when Oscar was not convinced he was going to die in jail, he clearly had his mind focussed on Continental horizons: France, Italy, Germany and Switzerland, in that order.

Unlike André Gide, who had become addicted to the exoticism of North Africa as a conduit to personal liberation, Oscar in his prison day-dreaming sought the reassurance of a world he knew and which knew him, but which would not spit on him, as did England. Little brown Arab boys were all very well, but Oscar could never have tolerated the self-imposed exile from European civilisation that André savoured in large doses, both in the Maghrib and, later, in sub-Saharan Africa. Oscar favoured the European Continent because it could provide both youthful companionship and the sort of intellectual and social environments he had so appreciated in London. Why settle for the second best of an 'either-or' situation?

Moreover, on the Continent, so Oscar believed, he could reconstruct his life with Constance and the boys, without ruling out agreeable marginal distractions. Constance had settled for the time being in Italy, but she could presumably be equally at home in France. Dear friends like Robbie Ross and More Adey already spent a significant amount of their time in those two countries, which would mean that on his release, Oscar would not necessarily be cut off from his friends at all. However, what Constance realised (and Oscar seems to have pushed from his mind) was that Alfred Douglas also had chosen France and Italy as his bases. Knowing her husband's defencelessness when he was in Bosie's vicinity, she wondered whether either country would be large enough to keep the two men apart.

The important thing, Oscar and Constance were agreed, was to get Bosie out of his system. The method Oscar proposed was unusual, but singularly appropriate. Prison regulations allowed him to write a set number of letters, so he would write one to Bosie; not just an ordinary letter, but an immense epistle that would review critically their past five years, together and apart. Thus *De Profundis* was conceived. Major Nelson was apprised of the plan, and decided to cooperate by gently bending prison rules (something that would have been unimaginable with his predecessor). The 'letter' could be of indeterminate length, and although Oscar would not be able to keep the entire manuscript with him, he would be given the opportunity of rereading and revising the text as he went along. It was a massive undertaking: a therapeutic exercise, an essential element in a programme for Oscar's survival and rehabilitation, as well as a unique contribution to English literature. As the project developed, it became clear that it was neither objective nor forgiving. Therein lies its passion.

Composed between January and March 1897, *De Profundis* begins with a chide to Bosie for not writing to Oscar all the time he was in prison, and warns him that there will be much in the extended letter that will wound him to the quick. 'If it prove so,' Oscar writes, 'read the letter over and over again till it kills your vanity.' He points out that far from being a youthful innocent when the two friends first met, Bosie was already in the gutter, consorting with rent-boys. Almost as severe a fault was the way in which Bosie virtually stopped Oscar writing; he prevented that peace and solitude so necessary to the writer's Art by constantly bothering Oscar and demanding to be entertained. A typical day in London in the autumn of 1893, for example, when Oscar ought to have been working, involved Bosie turning up at midday for drinks, then lunch at the Café Royal or elsewhere, which usually lasted until 3.30 p.m. At tea-time, Bosie appeared again and stayed until it was time to change for dinner, at the Savoy or at Tite Street. Supper at Willis's would round off the day.

'When I compare my friendship with you to my friendship with such still younger men as John Gray and Pierre Louÿs,' Oscar continues, 'I feel ashamed. My real life, my higher life was with them and such as they.' Bosie had not only monopolised Oscar's time at the expense of his Art, he had also brought about his financial ruin, goading the older man on in extravagance. Between the autumn of 1892 and Oscar's imprisonment in May 1895, Oscar spent more than £5000 with or on Bosie – more than many workmen would earn in a lifetime. Worse still was the ethical degradation Bosie brought about in Oscar, by making the playwright's will-power subject to his own. 'Your meanest motive, your lowest appetite, your most common passion, became to you laws by which the lives of others were to be guided always, and to which, if necessary, they were to be without scruple sacrificed.'

Having given in to Bosie on small things, Oscar found himself incapable of exerting his own will-power when issues of greater moment arose, notably as a result of Bosie's feud with his father. Instead of taking wise counsel in London when the crisis with Queensberry developed, Bosie had dragged Oscar off to Monte Carlo, leaving him outside the casino while he gambled, at Oscar's expense. Back in London, Bosie had forced him to ignore the urging of his friends to go abroad to avoid disaster.

Every three months or so, during the course of their relationship, Oscar had tried to break away from Bosie's spell, on one occasion fleeing London for Paris at barely a moment's notice, having invented some absurd pretext to explain his sudden departure to Constance. Later, when Bosie was in Greece (as recalled in *De Profundis*), Oscar had tried to sever their link, but Bosie sent a telegram to Constance, begging her to use her influence to make him renew contact. 'Our friendship had always been a source of distress to her, not merely because she had never liked you personally, but because she saw how your continual companionship altered me, and not for the better.'

Constance had compassion; the relationship between the two men resumed. And when Bosie's eldest brother Francis Drumlanrig died in the supposed shooting accident, Oscar himself was moved to strengthen it further. 'The gods are strange. It is not of our vices only they make instruments to scourge us,' the letter continues, drawing on *King Lear*. 'They bring us to ruin through what in us is good, gentle, humane, loving. But for my pity and affection for you and yours, I would not now be weeping in this terrible place.'

Oscar could and would have saved himself by leaving for the sanctuary of Paris at the end of April 1895, instead of bringing the libel action against Queensberry, had not the Avondale Hotel impounded his luggage for the non-payment of the bill (run up with Lord Alfred's assistance). There were also the assurances from Bosie that his family would finance the legal action which Oscar could not afford on his own. Bosie's motive was to try to get the Marquess of Queensberry sent to prison, supposedly as retribution for the wrongs the Marquess had inflicted on Bosie's mother. But if Bosie really wanted to know how a wife would react to her husband's being in jail, Oscar argued, he should write to Constance and ask her.

It was not Queensberry who turned the tables by putting Oscar in prison but Bosie, as Bosie's hatred for his father determined events. Bosie's hatred, vanity and greed had ruined Oscar's life, but at first Oscar could only respond with love. 'I knew, if I allowed myself to hate you, that in the dry desert of existence over which I had to travel, and am travelling still, every rock would lose its shadow, every palm tree be withered, every well of water prove poisoned at its source.' But Love ceded way to Hate, as Oscar heard not a word directly from Bosie (not even when Lady Wilde died), while learning from others of the things Bosie was doing, such as living at ease in Naples and trying to get unhelpful articles published in the French press.

Yet *De Profundis* emphasises Oscar's need to forgive Bosie for his own sake; by writing the letter he was not trying to plant bitterness in Bosie's heart but rather to pluck it out of his own. Besides, Oscar recognised that some of the blame for his ruin lay within himself. The 'pitiless indictment' against Bosie is mirrored by an unwritten indictment without pity against himself. 'Terrible as what you did to me was, what I did to myself was far more terrible still.' Only humility can redeem. As Gide was to point out in his memoirs of Wilde, so Oscar himself acknowledged that the gods had given him almost everything: 'genius, a distinguished name, high social position, brilliancy, intellectual daring'. But he had spoilt himself by surrounding himself with smaller natures and meaner minds.

In his despair in prison, neither Religion nor Reason could help him. And yet the figure of Jesus Christ was of comforting relevance. 'I remember saying once to André Gide, as we sat together in some Paris café, that while Metaphysics had but little real interest for me, and Morality absolutely none, there was nothing that either Plato or Christ had said that could not be transferred immediately into the sphere of Art, and there find its complete fulfilment.' Bosie's fault, when he was at his worst, was to be remote from the 'secret' of Jesus and simultaneously from the true temper of the artist. The latter part of *De Profundis* expounds on the relationship between Christ and Art, philosophising about Christianity and the Bible, ancient Greece and contemporary French literature; Verlaine's poems, Baudelaire's *Fleurs du mal* and Hugo's *Les Misérables* are all owed to Christ.

Major Nelson, the kindly Governor of Reading Gaol, must have been gratified by these musings, as well as by Oscar's revelation that he was studying the Gospels, in Greek, every night after he had cleaned his cell and polished his eating-tins. As Richard Ellmann pointed out, in his magisterial biography of Wilde, Major Nelson was hoping that *De Profundis* would be a kind of late nineteenth-century *Pilgrim's Progress*. One can view it like that; the Christian themes concentrated in the latter part of the text inevitably give the impression that Oscar was working with that aim in mind. But in fact that is not what *De Profundis* is essentially about, as even a religiously disposed reader such as André Gide would discern. Rather, it is an exercise in coming to terms with something terrible in one's past: the how and why of what happened, so that the writer can then move on to start life afresh. The new beginning would be physically marked by Oscar's release from prison, but the psychological and intellectual restart was at least as important.

De Profundis – of seminal importance to an understanding of Oscar's life and relationships – is also a hymn to friendship. In counterpoint to the destructive force of the passion between Oscar and Bosie, there is the recognition of the positive force of true friendship and intellectual companionship, as provided by such people as Pierre Louÿs (who had tried in vain to make Oscar realise that he should opt for friendships such as his, rather than the relationship with Bosie) or André Gide. Those friendships were mainly, but not exclusively, with men; there are glancing references to loyal women friends such as Ada Leverson and Adela Schuster, an immensely supportive (and affluent) Wilde devotee in Wimbledon. There are even intimations of Constance's high value as a friend, as well as a wife. But interestingly, the one person who emerges from *De Profundis* as the friend *par excellence* – overshadowing Constance and everyone else – is Robbie Ross, the boy who had first seduced Oscar into the homosexual way of life, and who was now himself a figure of some importance in the arts world. As a measure of Oscar's trust in Robbie, he designated him his literary executor. Robbie would be waiting on the other side of the prison gate when Oscar was released, so he declared in *De Profundis*.

Oscar was scheduled to be let back out into the world on 19 May 1897, from Pentonville Prison, following the tradition that prisoners were discharged from the place they had first been incarcerated. The previous day, the transfer from Reading was accomplished. Oscar was allowed to wear normal clothes, and was not handcuffed, so he would be spared the sort of humiliations he had experienced on previous occasions. According to a contemporary article in the *New York Times*, when Oscar arrived at Twyford railway station and beheld a spring bush in full bud, he undermined the prison authorities' well-intentioned efforts to have him pass unrecognised by throwing up his arms and exclaiming: 'Oh beautiful world! Oh beautiful world!' One of the warders with him shushed him beseechingly: 'Now, Mr Wilde, you mustn't give yourself away like that. You're the only man in England who would talk like that in a railway station!'

CHAPTER THIRTEEN

Berneval 1897

THERE WAS considerable discussion among Oscar's friends as to who would be outside Reading Gaol to collect him. In the event, the two people who were given the responsibility were Stewart Headlam – the clergyman who had stood bail for him at his trials – and More Adey. Despite what he had written to Bosie in *De Profundis*, Oscar himself decided it was better that Robbie Ross join him on the Continent, rather than in England, so as to protect Robbie's reputation and the Ross family's feelings. Before the trials More Adey had not been a particularly close friend of Oscar's, though he was part of the smart London gay set that included Lord Alfred Douglas and Robbie, as well as being an intimate of Max Beerbohm's. At times Bosie had asked More to intercede on his behalf with Oscar. During Oscar's imprisonment More took on a greater significance in his life, because he acted in a voluntary capacity to try to defend Oscar's personal interests, while Robbie concentrated on the literary side. More's tasks included dealing with Oscar's solicitors, of whom Humphreys was a source of increasing irritation to his client.

The most important of the personal interests More had to deal with was the delicate matter of Oscar's relationship with Constance.

More acted as one of the conduits for news and information between husband and wife, as well as trying to maximise the financial benefits Oscar would receive from his wife's marriage settlement. This involved a great deal of work and some tricky decisions, some of which unfortunately provoked hurt feelings all round. In particular, Constance's advisers were anxious that she be able to buy Wilde's half-share in their marriage settlement from the Official Receiver (who had taken charge of it at the time of Oscar's bankruptcy). Oscar was at first willing for that to happen, but More, Robbie and other friends thought he would be better off if they purchased it for him. Oscar agreed that they were right, but Constance was very bitter about the change of heart. This so soured relations between the Wildes that in December 1896 Oscar wrote to More that Constance was inflicting mental and physical suffering on him by fighting her corner, ranking her alongside the Marquess of Queensberry for causing him anguish. All thoughts of rejoining her on his release were cast aside. There was once more talk of divorce.

The most painful thing of all for Oscar was that Constance chose as guardian for their two boys a member of her own family, a cousin called Adrian Hope. In many ways, Hope was a good choice for the boys, but he had the major disadvantage of believing that it was in Cyril's and Vyvyan's interest that Oscar should be kept well away from them. Oscar begged More to put pressure on the courts to give him some right of access at least to Cyril, who was always his favourite, but it was to no avail. Similarly, More was asked to try to ensure that the boys were not turned against their father, but there was little he could do about that.

During the last fortnight of Oscar's incarceration, he wrote several very long letters to More Adey, setting out in detail his financial anxieties for the future. More and Robbie had told him he would receive enough money (on top of the planned allowance from Constance) to be able to live comfortably, if modestly, in France or Italy for eighteen months or more, by which time it was hoped that he would have found the possibility to earn money again by his pen. Then it transpired that the lump sum would be far less than had been expected, which was the cause of great arguments. In fact, Oscar became almost paranoid about money; he felt everyone was trying to stop him getting his due. He was quite convinced that Ernest Leverson, who had been administering some funds on his behalf, could not be trusted. And he had almost given up hope that the Douglases – not least Bosie, of course – would ever contribute significantly to his upkeep, despite the family's bringing about Oscar's ruin and the reckless generosity he had displayed towards Lord Alfred.

However, on the day of Oscar's release, such material worries and personal recriminations were temporarily forgotten. Stewart Headlam and More Adey took Oscar in a cab to Headlam's house, where he was able to change his clothes and adopt the pose with which he was going to face the world. Ada Leverson came round to see him and was amazed to find him looking well and debonair, 'like a king returning from exile'. His conversation was sparkling and his wit was light; he even joked about his time at Reading. But later it became clear that this was all a brave façade. The religious turn of mind which permeated the second half of *De Profundis* had apparently not yet abandoned him. He declared that he wanted to go into a Catholic retreat for six months and sent off a note to the community in Farm Street, Mayfair, asking them to accept him. When a reply was sent back, turning him down, he burst into tears.

With hindsight, one could surmise that the wish to enter a place of contemplative seclusion immediately after emerging from a term of enforced solitude and hardship must have been a whim or maybe a panic attack at having to face the future. Oscar knew that Robbie was waiting for him in Dieppe. Yet through his prevarication, he missed the ferry that would take him into exile, just as two years before he had deliberately not seized the opportunity to catch the boat that would have saved him his prison ordeal.

Accompanied by More Adey, Oscar now was obliged to catch the overnight ferry from Newhaven, which chugged into Dieppe at 4.00 a.m. on 20 May. Robbie and Reggie Turner were on the quayside to greet him. Oscar was carrying a large envelope, containing the manuscript of *De Profundis*; the instructions he gave Robbie were that once it had been copied, he should keep the original and send a copy off to Lord Alfred. In principle, there was no intention that the letter should be published, at least for the foreseeable future.

Robbie had booked a room for Oscar at the Hotel Sandwich in Dieppe, in the name of Sebastian Melmoth, the pseudonym Oscar had decided to adopt until his real one became more widely acceptable again. 'Sebastian' he had chosen for its suggestion of martyrdom, while Melmoth was drawn from the title of a book by his great-uncle, the Revd Charles Maturin, *Melmoth the Wanderer*.

Robbie and Reggie (who, Oscar impishly pretended, had exchanged their two names in order to disguise themselves) had filled his hotel room with welcoming flowers and books. Robbie was also able to pass on the encouraging news that he had after all been able to raise about £800 from well-wishers to help Oscar survive. Like a child let loose in a sweetshop, Oscar almost immediately started spending money on luxuries such as perfumes; this prompted swift reproach from Robbie, who was put in the invidious position of having to try to stop his friend frittering away resources which would not easily be replenished.

As before his downfall, Oscar loved to entertain. A number of French artists and poets made the journey to Dieppe specially to see him, which on at least one occasion prompted a dinner in a restaurant that became so animated that Oscar later received a formal letter from the municipality warning him that any misconduct could lead to his being expelled from France.

As it was, Oscar had to suffer a number of insults and rebuffs, sometimes from local tradespeople and restaurateurs, who were frightened his presence would shock other customers. Usually, however, the slights he received came from British visitors to the town. From strangers that was unpleasant, but something that could be shrugged off; from former friends from London or Paris it was intolerable. Aubrey Beardsley (who blamed the Wilde scandal for destroying the *Yellow Book* to which he had contributed) scuttled down an alleyway to avoid meeting him. The portrait painter Jacques-Emile Blanche cut him dead in the street.

Occasionally there was the compensation of the kindness of strangers who came to his defence when he had been slighted. The Norwegian landscape painter Fritz von Thaulow loudly asked Oscar to do him the honour of dining with him and his wife, after some English prigs had insulted him in public. Even with the compensation of such gallantry, it was not a situation Oscar wished to prolong, particularly after first Reggie and then Robbie left to return to England. Accordingly, Oscar moved out of Dieppe to the small nearby community of Berneval-sur-Mer, where he could enjoy true anonymity. He rented two rooms in the Hôtel de la Plage there and set about getting to know the locality. The stony beach was backed by cliffs reminiscent of Dover; the few visitors were almost invariably French and not at all fashionable. There he felt he could be safe. Within days of his arrival, he felt so settled that the hotel proprietor, who was also an estate agent, suggested he find a chalet for Oscar to live in. Nonetheless, shadows from the past fell even on Berneval.

On his arrival in Dieppe, Oscar had written contritely to Constance, asking her to consider a meeting, as well as allowing him to see the children. She replied promptly but evasively; her health was getting steadily worse and Italy was so far from northern France. She did not rule out the possibility of a family reunion, but she did not encourage it either. From then on, consciously or unconsciously, the couple played cat-and-mouse games with each other, forever denying each other the prize they held in their hands: the two boys, in Constance's case; the restoration of a visible marital relationship in Oscar's.

Far less welcome – or so Oscar made out to Robbie – was the sudden reappearance, at least on paper, of Lord Alfred Douglas. Bosie managed to get a first letter delivered to Oscar in Dieppe; it was the first of many. In it Bosie berated Oscar for not loving him any more, while he himself had remained emotionally (though certainly not physically) faithful. For a while Oscar rejected Bosie's requests for a meeting, which, he believed, could only be fatal, as well as putting his allowance from Constance at risk. She had no intention of subsidising the reprise of a partnership that had destroyed her home.

Yet less than a week after Robbie Ross had left Berneval for England, leaving Oscar to his own devices, Oscar was responding amicably to Bosie's barrage of letters. Bosie had sent him some books to read, including André Gide's recently published *Les Nourritures terrestres*. It is unknown whether Oscar recognised himself in the character of Ménalque. What is certain is that he did not think much of the work as a whole, as he informed Bosie:

> [? 2 June 1897]
> André Gide's book fails to fascinate me. The egoistic note is, of course, and always has been to me, the primal and ultimate note of modern art, but *to be an Egoist one must have an Ego*. It is not everyone who says 'I, I' who can enter into the Kingdom of Art. But I love André personally very deeply, and often thought of him in prison.

Oscar had equally been in André's thoughts, both during his travels in North Africa and back at home in Normandy and Paris; he divided his time in France between the two. Once André learnt that Oscar was installed at Berneval, guilt over past neglect – tinged with curiosity – drove him to make an unannounced visit there to see his old friend. He arrived on 20 June. The weather was terrible, making Berneval look unattractive and singularly uninteresting; with a typical disregard for chronological accuracy, in his account of the visit, contained in his essay *In Memoriam* incorporated into his book *Oscar Wilde*, Gide said it took place when winter was hardly over.

He turned up at the Hôtel de la Plage at lunch-time, only to discover that Oscar had gone off to Dieppe to see the von Thaulows, who had consolidated their first impetuous dinner invitation into a supportive friendship. M. Melmoth would return only that evening, André was told. So he spent hours walking on the desolate beach, wondering what had made Oscar choose such an apparently Godforsaken place.

Oscar did not get back until 11 o'clock that night, by which time André had checked himself into the Hôtel de la Plage. He was so unimpressed with his fellow guests that he had dined alone, immersed in a book. A carriage drew up and Oscar entered, flustered and loud. Somewhere during the day he had been separated from his overcoat. Barely registering any emotion at André's unexpected presence, he declared that the previous day the hotel servant had brought him a peacock feather as a present, which he knew presaged some misfortune. The hotel proprietor now fussed around, getting some hot grog to restore Oscar's spirits. By the time the two friends were settled down to talk in Oscar's sitting-room, André's sense of nervous anticipation had been completely deflated.

He noted with surprise that the Oscar before him was not the same figure he had last seen in Algiers: the frenzied man of letters heading full tilt for the disaster he felt obliged to confront. Instead, the Oscar of Berneval was almost the Oscar of Paris 1891: the same voice, the same laugh of amusement, the slightly weary look. Physically, he had deteriorated. His skin was ruddy, like a workman's; his hands were rough, though incongruously his thick, coarse fingers still wore the aesthete's rings that André recognised, notably an Egyptian scarab. His teeth were in a terrible state.

Oscar told André that prison had completely changed him, as he had hoped it would. Bosie could not be made to understand that;

Lord Alfred expected Oscar to want to pick things up exactly where they had left off. But Oscar's life was a work of art, and an artist should never do the same thing twice.

He defended his decision to settle in Berneval rather than move to Paris, as André would have expected. The public remembers only what one has most recently done, Oscar argued; if he went to Paris now, he would be viewed everywhere as the convict. He needed to produce a new work before he ventured out into French literary society once more. Besides, he was enjoying playing the role of the eccentric English gentleman who had landed in the community of Berneval like some great exotic bird. He had become friendly with the priest at the local church, which gloried in the name of Our Jubilant Lady. Together they would chat for hours. The local customs officers had also become friendly with Oscar. Worried that they would become extremely bored through having so little to do – or so Oscar informed André – he kept them supplied with novels by Alexandre Dumas *père*.

Slightly irritated by this idle prattle, André, in true French intellectual's style, tried to steer the conversation in a more serious direction, asking Oscar if he had read Dostoyevsky. This sparked off one of Oscar's fine discursive monologues on what for him was the essential element that made Russian literature truly great: pity. In prison, pity had given Oscar the will to live.

For the first six months or so, he had found his own situation so awful that he had contemplated suicide. But then he had seen how much worse things were for some of his fellow inmates. There was the young man who was mentally deranged and who kept breaking prison rules, which led to his being regularly beaten. Oscar still shuddered at the memory of his screams. Then there were the small children who had been thrown into jail for stealing a rabbit or some other minor offence. They lay down whimpering in their cells, frightened and hungry. One of the first things Oscar had done on his release was to write to the Home Office and to several newspapers attacking the barbaric practice of imprisoning children. Oscar thanked God for making pity change his life. He had gone into prison with a heart of stone, he claimed; he had lived only for his own pleasure. God had shown him how pity transformed the world. Now his model was St Francis of Assisi. André promised to send him the best biography of that saint that he could find.

André was fascinated to see that far from wanting to put prison behind him, Oscar still had several of his criminal companions in mind. In particular there was the young man at Reading who had defied the rule against talking during the exercise hour, when the prisoners shuffled round the yard, one behind the other. The young man told Oscar how much he pitied him, because he was suffering more from his sentence than ordinary mortals would. Much moved by this compassion, Oscar thanked him, but unfortunately he had not yet learnt how to speak without moving his lips. The two of them were summoned, separately, to see the Governor, at that time still Colonel Isaacson, and were asked who had spoken first, as he should receive the heavier punishment. Both took the blame. Once out of prison, Oscar wrote to the young man and sent him money. In several instances, he intervened on other prisoners' behalf.

André and Oscar did not get to their respective beds until the early hours of the morning. Yet Oscar did not seem particularly tired the following day. He was keen to show André a house he was going to rent, the Chalet Bourgeat. There he planned to write two new plays with biblical themes: *Pharaoh* and *Ahab and Jezebel*.

When the carriage came to take André away, Oscar climbed in to accompany him part of the way to the station. He raised the matter of *Les Nourritures terrestres*, praising it politely. André could tell that was not truly how Oscar felt about it. However, it was only when the carriage stopped to drop Oscar off that the Irishman said suddenly: 'Listen, dear, now you've got to promise me something: *Les Nourritures terrestres* is good, very good. But, dear, promise me, from now on, never write "I" again. In art, you see, there is no *first* person.'

This was not advice that André heeded. Had he done so, several of his best books would never have seen the light of day.

Back in Paris, André went to see Bosie – who had left Naples in order to get within striking distance of his former lover – to report on how the visit had gone. Bosie scoffed at the idea that Oscar could be happy holed up alone in such a tedious place as Berneval. He needed company just as much as he needed peace to write; once he had completed the planned *Pharaoh* play, he would summon Bosie to join him – or so Bosie believed.

For a while, the gentle charm of Berneval continued to hold Oscar there. The day after André left was Queen Victoria's Diamond Jubilee. Far from bearing a grudge against the Empress who had turned a deaf ear towards his plea for clemency, Oscar determined to celebrate the event in style. He had the main function room at the Hôtel de la Plage decked out in Union Jacks and coloured lights and held a party for his new friends: the priest, the customs officers, the postman and the schoolmaster and fifteen little boys from the village. The celebrations put him in enormous good humour, as was evident in the account he sent Lord Alfred the following day:

[23 June 1897]

My darling Boy, . . . My *fête* was a huge success: fifteen *gamins* were entertained on strawberries and cream, apricots, chocolates, cakes and *sirop de grenadine*. I had a huge cake with *Jubilé de la Reine Victoria* in pink sugar just rosetted with green, and a great wreath of red roses round it all. Every child was asked beforehand to choose his present: they all chose instruments of music!!!

6 accordions

5 trompettes

4 clairons[1]

---

1. bugles.

They sang the Marseillaise and other songs, and danced a *ronde*, and also played 'God save the Queen': they said it was 'God save the Queen', and I did not like to differ from them. They also all had flags which I gave them. They were most gay and sweet. I gave them the health of *La Reine d'Angleterre*, and they cried 'Vive la Reine d'Angleterre!!!!' Then I gave 'La France, mère de tous les artistes',[2] and finally I gave Le President de la République: I thought I had better do so. They cried out with one accord 'Vivent le Président de la République et Monsieur Melmoth!!!'[3]

Two things are striking about this letter. First, the infectious enthusiasm of a father compensating for the separation from his own sons by entertaining fifteen young boys; second, the warmth of the tone to Bosie. Over the previous weeks, Oscar's correspondence with Lord Alfred had started to resume some of its earlier intimacy; even at a distance, Oscar was once more beginning to fall under his spell, so much so that he even issued an invitation to Bosie to come and visit him, preferably under a pseudonym. Oscar seems to have been careless of the consequences that the news of any reconciliation would have when it got back to Constance, as it inevitably would. Somehow, one of Oscar's solicitors got wind of the proposed visit and resigned in disgust. With the Marquess of Queensberry threatening to come to France and shoot Oscar should he and his son ever get together again, Oscar suddenly got cold feet and called the visit off.

This was just as well, as Oscar had work to do. Keeping Bosie at bay meant that he was able, within a period of about two weeks beginning 8 July, to compose *The Ballad of Reading Gaol* (inspired by the hanging of Charles Wooldridge), which is both his finest poem and a magnificent polemic. The Chalet Bourgeat, into which he had

2. 'France, mother of all artists'.
3. 'Long Live the President of the Republic and Monsieur Melmoth!'

moved, was conducive to work. It had a garden and two large bal-
conies, where Oscar spent much of his days and several balmy nights,
drinking in the healthy sea air. His writing was unperturbed even by
the stream of sometimes tortuous letters he was receiving from
Bosie and the feedback he was getting from Bosie's intemperate correspondence with Robbie Ross.

There was more than an element of truth in Bosie's belief that
Robbie was trying to keep Oscar away from him. Robbie knew that
it could be possible for Oscar to see either Constance or Bosie again,
but not both. There was considerable procrastination all round. But
by the end of August Oscar had made his choice: he would meet
Bosie in Rouen.

Bosie told André Gide that Oscar wrote to him every day in the
run-up to that encounter, though only a few of the letters survive.
Oscar and Bosie fell into each other's arms at Rouen station and
spent the night together at a hotel in the city. When Oscar returned
to Berneval, he received a loving telegram from Lord Alfred, which
prompted a note in reply that left no doubt that the infatuation had
been rekindled:

> [? 31 August 1897]
> My own Darling Boy, I got your telegram half an hour ago, and
> just send you a line to say that I feel that my only hope of again
> doing beautiful work in art is being with you. It was not so in the
> old days, but now it is different, and you can really recreate in me
> that energy and sense of joyous power on which art depends.
> Everyone is furious with me for going back to you, but they don't
> understand us.

Everyone was indeed furious. Constance was not just angry but
humiliated. By now a very sick woman, her one hope of happiness
in which to end her days was shattered. Robbie Ross also felt let
down. He had been working hard to try to provide for Oscar condi-

tions that would give him a certain security and calm in which to work. Linking up with Bosie again was the surest way of undermining that security and destroying calm. The turmoil was immediate. Less than a week after leaving Bosie in Rouen, Oscar was writing to Robbie that he simply could not stand Berneval any more. 'I nearly committed suicide there last Thursday – I was so bored.'

Another supposed reason for his disenchantment with Berneval was that the weather had turned grey and English. So he decided he was going back to Rouen (where in fact the weather was worse), theoretically to work on an old project of his, a play called *A Florentine Tragedy*. Robbie would not have been fooled by this explanation. It was obvious that the attraction of Rouen lay in its having been where Oscar had refound the terrible, burning passion that was and remained the most exciting thing in his life. 'Of course I love him as I always did, with a sense of tragedy and ruin,' Oscar confessed to Robbie. Even though Bosie was no longer in Rouen, perhaps his aura would still be there. Then, when the necessary practical arrangements had been made, Oscar would follow in Bosie's footsteps, first to Paris and then to Naples, where they could live together. Oscar always did have a penchant for fairy stories in which there was a handsome prince and people lived happily ever after.

In his letters to other friends, Oscar spoke of the need to go to southern Italy to find the sun. But it was Bosie who was his sun; to repeat a hackneyed but totally appropriate image, Bosie was the flame to which the moth Oscar was inevitably drawn. As one of the best-informed spectators of this new act of the tragedy, André Gide could only shake his head and count his blessings that his passions were physical not emotional – or so he continued to convince himself.

CHAPTER FOURTEEN

Paris 1897–1900

HIS MIND made up, Oscar packed his bags at Berneval, extricated himself from his financial obligations regarding the chalet there and set off for Paris on 15 September 1897. There were many people in Paris he wanted to avoid, assuming, probably correctly, that they would make obvious their displeasure at being reminded of his existence. But he needed to find some friend who could help him out of his most pressing current difficulty: raising the £10 fare to Naples, where Bosie (who had gone off for a holiday at Aix-les-Bains with his mother, Lady Queensberry) would join him. Pride probably prevented Oscar's turning to André Gide at this stage; as he had played the role of André's mentor, it would be a little awkward suddenly to turn mendicant. Besides, it was often difficult to track André down. Instead, Oscar chose the Irish-American poet and novelist Vincent O'Sullivan, who lived in Paris and had visited Oscar in Berneval about six weeks previously. O'Sullivan responded to a summons to call on Oscar at his hotel. They then went out to lunch at a discreet little restaurant where Oscar executed a neat manoeuvre that was to become his Paris speciality.

First he entertained O'Sullivan with amusing stories. One was about an English newspaper correspondent friend of his in Paris called Rowland Strong. The previous year, when Strong had heard that Verlaine was dying – so Oscar recounted – Strong could not face the squalor in which he knew the celebrated poet was eking out his existence, so sent his manservant instead to see how he was. The manservant returned, as ever imperturbable. 'Well?' asked Strong. 'I saw the gentleman, sir,' the valet replied, 'and he died immediately.'

Thus O'Sullivan was in a mellow mood when, towards the end of the meal, Oscar suddenly revealed that he was passing through a crisis. Prison had left him troubled and all that some of his friends could think of was for him to bury himself in some obscure mountain village to write, whereas what he really needed to restore his spirits and fuel his inspiration was a spell in the sun of southern Italy. 'I shall go to Italy tonight,' Oscar declared, according to O'Sullivan's book of reminiscences *Aspects of Wilde*. 'Or rather, I would go, but I am in an absurd position. I have no money.'

O'Sullivan was a push-over. At his insistence, they took a cab straight from the restaurant to the Banque de Paris, where he withdrew the sum Oscar said he needed. Far from feeling put upon, O'Sullivan looked back on his act of generosity with satisfaction. 'It is not every day that one has the chance of relieving the anxiety of a genius and a hero,' he wrote. Few of those who were stung by Oscar for money over the next couple of years were so gracious.

Oscar and Bosie met as planned in Aix-les-Bains and travelled together to Naples, where they checked into the Hotel Royal des Etrangers. They had insufficient funds on them to cover the excessive bill they started runing up, but Lord Alfred's title was worth a respectable amount of credit. Meanwhile, Oscar dreamt up a ruse for raising cash: getting a commission of £100 from Dalhousie Young (an Englishman who had written a brave essay in defence of Oscar Wilde at the time of his imprisonment) to write the libretto for an opera based on the story of Daphnis and Chloe. Oscar must have

known that he would never see the project through, though he and
Bosie did jointly produce some rather feeble texts. Discouraged,
Dalhousie Young abandoned the project, which is probably what the
two collaborators had always intended.

By the end of September, the couple were installed in a villa at
Posilipso. Being in Italy, Oscar had intimated to Carlos Blacker that
he would like to visit Constance, but as soon as she knew that he was
living with Bosie, she said that was out of the question. She was so
hurt that her anger boiled over in an uncharacteristically strident
letter to her husband:

> [29 September 1897]
> I *forbid* you to see Lord Alfred Douglas. I forbid you to return to
> your filthy, insane life. I forbid you to live at Naples. I will not allow
> you to come to Genoa.

Neither side could make the other budge. Accordingly, in
November, Oscar's allowance from Constance was stopped, on the
grounds that he had broken the terms of the associated agreement.
To make matters worse, Lady Queensberry also decided to flex her
financial muscles by threatening to cut off Bosie's very generous (yet
somehow inadequate) allowance of £1000 a year unless he and
Oscar separated. To add force to her argument, she offered to send
£200 to Oscar if he broke with her son. The lovers discussed the
obvious attractions of this offer, eventually deciding that they out-
weighed the disadvantage of not being able to live together. Bosie
moved out and went to Rome, with an alacrity that made Oscar
suspect that all the younger man's protestations of love were as
empty as his promises of material support. There had been some
serious rows before Bosie had left, giving Oscar the impression that
Lord Alfred no longer found him truly interesting or admirable;
objectively, Wilde was now a has-been rather than a star. The more
he thought about this, the more bitter Oscar became. The pendu-

lum of his affections swung violently away from Bosie, as it had in the past. Yet again he decided that it would be better if they did not see each other.

At least Oscar had the imminent publication of *The Ballad of Reading Gaol* to distract himself from emotional and family problems. From Naples he conducted a lengthy correspondence with the publisher, Leonard Smithers, commenting on every aspect of the long poem's production. It was to be published semi-anonymously under his Reading cell-number designation, 'C.3.3.'.

By accident or design, Oscar timed his return to Paris to coincide with the publication of the *Ballad*, in February 1898. He took a room in the modest Hôtel de Nice in the rue des Beaux-Arts on the Left Bank. It was well below his usual standards, but this was what he would have to get used to. Fortunately, his morale was boosted by the speedy arrival of excellent British press notices for the *Ballad*. Smithers had cautiously printed only 400 copies as a first run, but advance orders before publication date made him realise his mistake. Other printings and editions followed briskly. One, in March, was a *de luxe* edition of ninety-nine copies, signed by Oscar, which he despatched to friends and professional colleagues. It was a way of saying 'thank you' to people such as Robbie Ross and More Adey and the von Thaulows in Dieppe, as well as showing others that prison had not killed his output. With some friends, such as Frank Harris and Robert Sherard, Oscar used the book rather like a visiting card, enclosing his new address and a personal note urging them to look him up. The reaction to the poem was almost uniformly positive. Frank Harris, for one, responded by sending a cheque, which was particularly gratifying.

By April several times more copies of Oscar's *Ballad* had been sold than André Gide's *Les Nourritures terrestres*, though the latter had now been out for a year. Yet André, who had been living with Madeleine in Rome for the first few months of the year, saw the *Ballad* as the swan-song of a doomed man destroyed by an obsession. As a counterbalance to *Les Nourritures terrestres* – so André stated to friends such as Paul Valéry – he was now working on a play centred on the biblical character of King Saul. Like Ménalque, Gide's highly fictionalised Saul was a composite figure made up largely of Oscar Wilde and himself. Gide later described the subject of his play as the ruin of the soul and the bankruptcy and annihilation of personality brought about by non-resistance to temptation. In the case of Gide's Saul, the temptations are both aesthetic and sexual. At times, when Saul speaks in the play, it sounds as if it is Oscar Wilde talking: 'The least sound, the faintest perfume takes possession of me: my senses are open to the outside world, and no sweet thing passes unperceived by me.' The sweetest of things so far as Saul is concerned is the young David, for whom Saul feels a suppressed homosexual desire. Saul kills his wife when it looks as though she is about to find out his guilty secret. As the truth dawns on David, he begins to withdraw his affection for the King, who goes mad. Yet David is both attracted as well as repelled by the older man.

André was still working on the play in the late summer or autumn of 1898 when one evening, while walking along a Paris boulevard with a friend, he heard his name called out. He turned to see Oscar hailing him from one of the outdoor tables of a café. André was shocked by the change in Oscar: it was not just that he had become portly and rather seedy-looking, but he no longer had the commanding presence of a recognised personality, albeit a controversial one. In fact, André was quite embarrassed by the encounter. Just two days before Oscar's release from prison, André had been elected Mayor of the small Normandy commune of La Roque, centred on his family chateau. At least for a while, he took his duties as a pillar of the local establishment seriously and he did not want his new façade of respectability and authority undermined. Moreover, so many of his Parisian friends had told him that Oscar Wilde was someone who was no longer 'seen' by the capital's literary society, given his shameless conduct since his release from prison. In Italy, with Bosie, he had enjoyed many of the local working-class youths; in Paris, alone, he was doing the same.

André had no qualms about consorting with the commonest street urchin or shepherd boy when he was in North Africa, where he was unlikely to be seen by any Frenchman who knew him; furthermore, he could argue that the local people were used to that kind of thing. But he was so put out by the possibility of being spotted in Paris with his infamous friend and muse that when Oscar insisted that he and his companion join him for a drink, André deliberately placed himself opposite Oscar, the back of his chair turned to the street, so that he would be less visible to passers-by. Perfectly conscious of what was going on, Oscar winced and asked him to come and sit by his side instead, saying that he felt lonely.

As André scrutinised his host, he noticed that although most of Oscar's clothes were still of good quality, his hat no longer had its previous shine. His collar was dirty and the cuffs of his shirt-sleeves were frayed. Still smarting from André's evident discomfort at being seen with him, according to Gide's memoirs Oscar said reproachfully (and untruthfully): 'In the old days, when I used to see Verlaine, I did not blush from shame. I was rich, merry and crowned with glory, but I felt that being seen with him was an honour, even when he was drunk.'

Then Oscar snapped out of his mood of indignant hurt and began to recount some of his funny stories, before falling back into gloom. As André and his friend selected a reasonably polite moment to get up to leave, Oscar took hold of André's arm and whispered to him: 'I think you ought to know: I've absolutely nothing to live on.'

A few days later, André ran into Oscar again. This time Wilde said how uncomfortable he felt about being unable to get on with any of the literary projects he had started or indeed to start anything new. André reminded him that when they had met at Berneval the previous year, Oscar had said that he would not come to Paris until he had finished his play about Pharaoh. Had he not brought some of his troubles on himself by failing to abide by that intention? Oscar looked at him sadly and murmured: 'One shouldn't be angry with someone who has been *struck*.'

Several other people who had known Oscar at the height of his powers also found him an ineffably pathetic creature during his last two years. But the situation was not that straightforward. Much depended on his state of health and state of mind, and the impression that he, the accomplished actor, wished to give. When he had money, he would rush off to restaurants and cafés with friends and manage to sparkle in conversation, providing he had not drunk too much absinthe, which was starting to have a detrimental effect on his mind. Nor was Oscar as destitute as he made out.

In April Constance had died, without having seen him again. He claimed that, as with the death of his mother, he had a premonition of Constance's demise the day before. He dreamt she came to see him and that he had told her to go away and leave him in peace. In truth, despite several anguished-sounding notes despatched to mutual friends and connections such as Robbie Ross, Carlos Blacker and Constance's brother Otho, Oscar mourned little for his wife. He could not forgive her for having prevented him from seeing his sons. Besides, her death meant that he became the beneficiary of an allowance from her estate of £150 a year, without conditions. It was insufficient to support the sort of lifestyle he led, but it was more than many working men of the time earned.

At least some of Oscar's revenue went on entertaining, and being entertained by, young men. Straitened circumstances did not curb Oscar's appetite for rent-boys, whom he picked up on the boulevards or had passed to him by friends. One favourite was a young soldier called Maurice Gilbert, who looked particularly dashing in his marine infantry uniform; Gilbert was also one of Bosie's lovers, as well as a great favourite of Robbie Ross and Reggie Turner. Oscar became quite besotted with Maurice, who in turn became one of his most loyal and devoted friends. No longer caring what people thought,

Oscar was spotted by at least one scandalised Parisian acquaintance kissing the young infantryman in the street.

Oscar had 'come out' in both actions and words. He had always enjoyed camp badinage with other gay or bisexual friends; now he talked quite openly about homosexual practices with enlightened heterosexuals as well, for example Frank Harris. These conversations were no longer couched in intellectually respectable terms, with allusions to classical homo-erotic love. He now called a spade a spade. Doubtless some of his more outrageous missives were destroyed by their recipients after they had read and been entertained by them. But several letters that have survived speak quite openly of Oscar's various sexual escapades, as well as the intimate lives of those who were close to him. In one letter to Reggie Turner, for example, he reported with relish that Bosie:

> [11 May 1898]
> is devoted to a dreadful little ruffian aged fourteen, whom he loves because at night, in the scanty intervals he can steal from an arduous criminal profession, he sells bunches of violets in front of the Café de la Paix. Also every time he goes home with Bosie he tries to rent him. This, of course, adds to his terrible fascination. We call him the '*Florifer*', a lovely name. He also keeps another boy, aged twelve! whom Bosie wishes to know, but the wise 'Florifer' declines.

Despite all his intentions to the contrary, Oscar had started seeing Bosie again, though the sexual side of their relationship had long since died. Bosie had gone to Oscar to offer his condolences after Constance's death, which Oscar, as ever generous-hearted, decided was a demonstration of genuine love and concern. Bosie settled in Paris for a while, in a flat in the avenue Kléber, where Oscar would visit him. An inveterate gambler, Bosie was losing heavily at the races, which meant that he rarely had any money. When he was flush, he would invite Oscar to expensive restaurants for champagne dinners that cost more than Oscar had at his disposal for a whole week. Money was a constant worry for Oscar, although he had moved out of the Hôtel de Nice into an even cheaper hotel in the same street, the Hôtel d'Alsace, and sometimes survived solely on the breakfast provided there. At the end of every month Robbie sent him his allowance from London; it was usually exhausted after a week. That meant chasing his publisher Smithers for small moneys due, or touching friends for loans. On 10 December 1898, for example, Oscar seized on the arrival of a presentation copy of Gide's essay *Réflexions sur quelques points de littérature et de morale* (*Reflections on Various Literary and Moral Themes*) to write a thank-you letter to his friend which included an outright request for 200 francs. 'You see how the tragedy of my life has become ignoble,' Oscar wrote (in French). 'Suffering is possible, and maybe necessary, but poverty, misery – there's something terrible. It sullies man's soul.'

André responded promptly, sending the requested sum. In his note acknowledging safe receipt of the money, Oscar mentioned that Frank Harris – who was on the verge of selling for a tidy sum the *Saturday Review* that he edited – was going to give him the chance of finding his soul again, as he had offered to send him to the Riviera for the three winter months as his guest. Chided by Harris for producing nothing of literary significance for publication other than an authorised text of *The Importance of Being Earnest*, Oscar had trotted out his feeble old excuse of not being able to create in grey climates. Harris decided to call his bluff by installing him in a hotel at Napoule on the outskirts of Cannes. However, getting Oscar even to leave Paris proved something of a problem. When Harris went to see him in Paris, Oscar kept producing reasons (usually connected with money) for delaying his departure. At least some of the money Harris gave him, supposedly to pay his debts, went to purchase a splendid bicycle for Maurice Gilbert.

When Oscar did eventually get to Napoule – without Harris,

whose business commitments detained him in Monte Carlo – he found literary inspiration as lacking there as it had been in Paris. He toyed with the idea of writing a long piece of verse about the local fisher-boys, who proved to be as amenable as those he had met with Bosie in Naples the previous year. But the project got nowhere. Unable to write, and frustrated at the lack of stimulating conversation with Frank Harris, Oscar was listless and bored – despite the companionship of one particular eighteen-year-old fisher-boy who had taken his fancy. A tearful reunion with Sarah Bernhardt backstage at a theatre in Nice, where she was appearing in *Tosca*, was one of the few memorable occasions in an otherwise tiresome and fruitless three months.

Oscar did however acquire a new, rich young patron in Napoule: an Englishman called Harold Mellor, who lived most of the time in Gland in Switzerland. Oscar was especially taken with Mellor's handsome young Italian servant-cum-boyfriend Eolo, which perhaps helped obscure the fact that Mellor himself was something of a bore, though one who had a morale-boosting admiration for Wilde's work. Mellor invited Oscar to join him at Gland after his time on the Riviera as Frank Harris's guest expired. Not in a position to turn down a free meal-ticket, Oscar headed there at the end of February 1899, making a diversion *en route* to visit Constance's grave at Genoa. As he wrote to Robbie Ross, the grave:

[? 1 March 1899]
is very pretty – a marble cross with dark ivy-leaves inlaid in a good pattern. The cemetery is a garden at the foot of the lovely hills that climb into the mountains that girdle Genoa. It was very tragic seeing her name carved on a tomb – her name, my name not mentioned of course – just 'Constance Mary, daughter of Horace Lloyd, Q.C.' and a verse from *Revelations*. I was deeply affected – with a sense also of the uselessness of all regrets. Nothing could have been otherwise, and Life is a terrible thing.

Oscar's maudlin frame of mind was doubtless partly due to the depressing news that the published version of *The Importance of Being Earnest* was a flop. Hardly any newspapers or magazines reviewed it; Wilde's name was still too tarnished to be given anything but adverse publicity in the British press. Oscar deduced from that that the only way he would ever get any new play of his staged in London – assuming he actually managed to write one – would be if it were presented anonymously.

Meanwhile, Oscar noted wryly, André Gide was churning things out – essays, treatises, short novels and a play – while still achieving only minimal sales. What was the point of writing books, Oscar wondered, if people did not read them? Or of writing plays, if they were not staged? The synopsis of Gide's *Saul*, which Oscar gleefully communicated to Reggie Turner, made Oscar laugh; he would have laughed even louder if he had known that it would take Gide nearly twenty-five years to get it staged.

Like André, Oscar found the Swiss intolerable. He informed More Adey in a letter that they were so ugly that to look at them conveyed melancholy into all his days at Gland. 'At Nice I knew three lads like bronzes,' he continued, seemingly forgetting how tedious he had found the Riviera, 'quite perfect in form. English lads are chryselephantine. Swiss people are carved out of wood with a rough knife, most of them; the others are carved out of turnips.'

While he was staying at Gland, Oscar learnt of the death of his brother Willie. The gulf between them had been so huge for so long that even Oscar could not feign grief. But he did wonder what would happen to the Irish property that Willie had inherited from their father, and which now – as Willie was childless – should pass to him. He assumed, correctly, that unless he managed to keep this windfall secret then creditors would swallow up anything coming his way. The problem was handed over to Robbie Ross who – after years of tireless efforts – would not settle Oscar's outstanding liabilities until well after the playwright's death.

Oscar had not been in Gland long before he realised that his host Harold Mellor was dull, silent, cautious and, worst of all, mean. When Oscar had money, he spent it, mainly on his friends and attractive strangers; Mellor remained rich precisely because he did not. As Oscar complained bitterly to Reggie Turner, revolting Swiss wines were served at meals. Later even those were suppressed in favour of cheaper beer. The only way for Oscar to survive the place was to think of it as a sort of Swiss *pensione*, in which one was never presented with the weekly bill. When he tried to borrow money from his host, he was turned down. By the end of March he could stand it no longer and fled.

He ruled out Paris for the time being, on the grounds of expense. Italy was much cheaper. He informed Leonard Smithers (who was currently preparing *An Ideal Husband* for the press) that he was heading for Genoa. There, as he had discovered on his pilgrimage to Constance's grave, 'I can live for ten francs a day (boy *compris*).' Oscar even wrote ahead to Genoa to book one young seafaring lad, Edoardo – a blond who always dressed in dark blue – so that he would not have to waste time hunting when he got there.

The first postcards Oscar sent to Robbie Ross from Italy were enthusiastic. Villages he visited were picturesque; the locals were friendly. Yet within a month, disillusion had set in. He was bored to a degree that suggested this had become almost a clinical condition. Alarmed by what he took to be Oscar's mental deterioration, Robbie gallantly travelled to Italy, paid his bills and accompanied him back to Paris, where at least he still had some friends with whom he could have stimulating conversations. Bosie, for a while, was in high spirits and was willing to entertain him in restaurants; Bosie's second volume of poems, *The City of the Soul*, was published to acclaim. Perhaps inspired by this example, Oscar himself completed a prose poem called *The Poet*, which a French magazine (today unidentified) agreed to publish with his own name. It was hardly a major comeback, but it was better than nothing.

Increasingly, however, Oscar identified himself with the ghost of Paul Verlaine – a once brilliant literary force who had become a vagabond, a figure of shame. When he drew the parallel in conversations it was hard for his interlocutors not to agree. Oscar's appearance had become less and less attractive, especially after he lost some of his teeth and could not afford a dental plate. The Australian soprano Dame Nellie Melba, who had known Oscar in his heyday, was so shocked by his appearance on meeting him in the street in Paris in the summer of 1899 that when he asked for some assistance, she opened her handbag and gave him all the money she had in it. He had become someone to whom one offered help, not for who he was but for who he had been; he was now an object of pity, a charity case.

The proprietor of the Hôtel d'Alsace, Jean Dupoirier, was so moved by Oscar's state that he advanced Oscar the money to pay off the bill of another hotel where he had been staying since his return to Paris from Rome, and moved him back into the Hôtel d'Alsace, on the implicit understanding that Oscar would pay when he could and enjoy credit when he could not. Frequently during the winter of 1899–1900 he was confined to his bed with a variety of ailments, including what he told friends was food poisoning contracted from infected mussels.

By April 1900 Oscar's morale and finances were so dire that he even accepted an offer of a trip to Italy with Harold Mellor, whose company he knew he could not abide. Typically, Mellor announced before they departed that Oscar would be permitted to incur expenses of £50 and no more. Despite this inauspicious start, the trip proved far more enjoyable than Oscar had dared hope. It was twenty-three years since his last visit to Rome, and the rediscovery of its architecture and art was a revelation; the city also caused Oscar to think more seriously about God than he had done since being an undergraduate at Trinity College, Dublin. Earlier, in the cathedral at Palermo in Sicily, Oscar had told a fifteen-year-old seminarist called

Giuseppe that God often uses poverty as a means of bringing people to Him – a statement Oscar felt was of special relevance to his current self. Oscar being Oscar, however, he added his own special touch to the spiritual enlightenment he was passing on to the young Giuseppe by kissing him passionately behind the high altar daily (or so he boasted to Robbie Ross).

In Rome Oscar was among those blessed by Pope Leo XIII, having acquired by fluke a ticket to the Vatican ceremonies on Easter Day; a complete stranger had walked up to him while he was having tea at the Hôtel de l'Europe and asked him if he would like one. Oscar claimed in a letter to Robbie Ross that the Pope's blessing cured him of lingering problems he was having from the Paris mussel-poisoning, though it is difficult to know how seriously one should take such remarks. Much of Oscar's correspondence with Robbie, even when on religious topics, is full of fantasy and irreverent banter. Some of Oscar's lightness of being in Rome can be put down to the fact that Harold Mellor had thoughtfully left him on his own early on in the visit, returning to Switzerland. Freed from Mellor's presence, Oscar wandered round the city with a handsome but mercenary young local guide, indulging in a new hobby: photography.

This visit to Italy was Oscar's last period of happiness and relative good health. In the second half of May he travelled by way of Naples and Genoa to Chambéry in France, where Harold Mellor picked him up in his motor-car, had him to stay at Gland for ten days and then drove him back to Paris. Oscar had sometimes joked with friends that as part of the punishment for his past crimes, the world would never allow him to see the twentieth century. Yet here he was, tasting the first fruits of the modern age. He was fascinated by what was in those days idealistically termed Progress and spent many happy hours in the summer of 1900 at the great International Exhibition in Paris, sometimes in the company of Maurice Gilbert.

Nonetheless, such pleasurable distractions could not hide the fact that Oscar's health was deteriorating. His skin was covered with scarlet blotches that itched intolerably. What he described as 'mussel-poisoning' some observers put down to more serious complaints, including neurasthenia; some saw signs of tertiary syphilis. He spent longer and longer spells in bed, visited frequently by doctors who disagreed in their diagnoses. What was certain was that the damage to his ear incurred during the fall in Wandsworth Prison was now causing him excruciating pain. He had to have an operation on the ear, which was carried out in his hotel bedroom on 9 October. He found the experience so distressing that he telegraphed Robbie Ross in London, begging him to come to Paris immediately.

When he got to Paris, Robbie found Oscar looking very ill, but garrulous. He entertained Robbie and Reggie Turner and other visitors to his bedside with witticisms about his forthcoming demise, the most oft-quoted of which was his remark to Clare de Pratz that 'my wallpaper and I are fighting a duel to the death. One or the other of us has to go.' Despite telling Robbie that he had nothing left to live for, Oscar hung on to life for most of November. His ear had to be dressed daily and morphine had to be administered to lessen the pain.

On 29 November Robbie realised that the end was near. Recalling that Oscar had said years before that Catholicism was the only religion to die in, Robbie (himself a convert) decided to call in a Roman Catholic priest, to give him a conditional baptism and then to administer the last rites. Oscar was conscious, but unable to speak. At 5.30 a.m. an alarming death rattle began; later that morning, blood and foam started oozing from his mouth. He died shortly before 2 p.m., at which time noxious fluids suddenly burst from all his orifices. The hotel proprietor, M. Dupoirier, helped Robbie and Reggie clear up the mess and to prepare the corpse for viewing. Maurice Gilbert, who was on hand, took a photograph of the body lying in the bed.

André Gide was on yet another of his visits to Biskra when he read in a newspaper the details of Oscar's passing. There was no time to get back to Paris to join the small band of mourners who attended Oscar's burial at the cemetery of Bagneux. Shortly afterwards Gide started to make notes for the first of several essays on Wilde, as the initial step in a process of re-evaluation of the man and of their relationship which would continue intermittently for the next fifty years.

CHAPTER FIFTEEN

André after Oscar

WHILE OSCAR lay dying, André was once more savouring the delights of Algeria, right under Madeleine's nose. Familiarity had not dulled Biskra's oasis seductiveness. Moreover, André by now had another travelling companion with whom to share the fruits of the North African earth: a gay twenty-five-year-old French doctor called Henri-Léon Vengeon, better known under his *nom de plume* Henri Ghéon. The two had met when Ghéon was commissioned to write an article on Gide's *Les Nourritures terrestres*; he went to visit André and they felt a connection almost immediately. There was no sexual liaison between them; they would have found the idea laughable. But Henri Ghéon provided a dual function which was both new and satisfying for André: as a homosexual 'hunting partner' and as a scurrilous confidential correspondent.

Together, late at night in Paris, they prowled the boulevards and the rather *louche* working-class districts, or drank in the cafés round the market area of Les Halles, chatting up barrow-boys, consorting with young drug addicts, befriending waifs and strays. They swapped notes on their conquests and their infatuations, telling each other the boys' names and addresses or regular haunts, as well as their physical attributes and staying-power. Henri also shared André's taste for Arab youths and their exotic home environment; he was captivated by the landscapes and inhabitants of the Maghrib and, like André, in particular fell under Athman's spell. Unlike André, though, Henri was not embarrassed to take Athman back with him to Paris for a visit. The artist Jacques-Emile Blanche painted them at the great international exhibition there. Other Parisian literary acquaintances took up Athman, inflating his vanity further. But he did manage to become what he had set out to be: a lyrical poet and marabout of some repute. He indulged increasingly in hashish, and later he married.

In December 1900, however, Athman was still free to travel with André and Henri down south into some of the wilder parts of Algeria, leaving Madeleine (who did not feel up to the rigours of such a desert safari) behind. André felt that Oscar would have approved. Largely from Oscar, André had learnt to be himself; to give in to his desires, not as an act of submission but as an act of assertiveness; to take possession of Life (of which Oscar sometimes claimed to be King), rather than letting Life and other people rule him. And just as Oscar had often abandoned Constance when he was feasting with his dangerous young panthers in London, so now André abandoned Madeleine to go off with his boon companions to see which little desert fauns he could seduce.

The threesome had said they would be away for a week. During that time Madeleine became quite seriously ill. She counted the hours to her husband's expected return, but he did not reappear. She lay on her bed feeling sick and deserted, until she convinced herself that she would have to provide her own support and pull herself up, not just on this occasion but always. Christmas Eve – the traditional time for the main seasonal festive meal for most Continentals – came and went with no sign of the adventurers. Then, rather sheepishly, having spent twelve days courting boys under the palm trees of El Oued and elsewhere, André, Henri and Athman returned on Christmas Day. As

André wrote to Paul Valéry, with little apparent guilt, his poor wife seemed exhausted from waiting for him.

André did not deliberately torment or humiliate Madeleine any more than Oscar set out to make Constance suffer. To the end of his life André protested that Madeleine was the one person he had really loved, though one has to counterbalance that statement with another admission: that when he looked at his wife, he sometimes thought it was his mother before him. Yet he was aware that his conduct towards Madeleine was a form of cruelty. That comes over clearly in the novel *L'Immoraliste*, however different the two main protagonists in the book may be from André and Madeleine. André spent much of 1901 completing *L'Immoraliste*; when it was published the following year, his friend Paul-Albert Laurens (with whom he had made his first North African foray) summed up the plot with brutal succinctness: 'I am ill; hard luck for me. I get better, hard luck for her!' Gide also revealed in later life that *L'Immoraliste* was intended for a while to be part of a longer work called *La Vie de Ménalque* (*Ménalque's Life*), in which the character largely based on Oscar Wilde was to be the central focus of attention.

Only three hundred copies of *L'Immoraliste* were printed in its first edition. André had accepted the fact that the great French reading public was not interested in his work; at the same time he salvaged his literary respect by declaring that he was writing for future generations, not his own. He did still receive plaudits from some of his literary friends, to whom he carefully sent signed copies. But even some of them were uneasy about the way his work was developing. For example, the conservative Catholic writer Paul Claudel (with whom Gide carried on an important correspondence, which was subsequently published) commented on the appearance of *L'Immoraliste* that now Gide had only one more indiscretion to commit – by which, of course, he meant proclaiming openly the love that dare not speak its name.

Between 1902 and 1907 Gide wrote almost nothing of great substance. He was aware that for much of his thirties, he was, as he put it, between two ages and two morals. As he matured, he followed the path that Wilde had illuminated for him. That meant breaking with some of his past. He disposed of the family property at La Roque and resigned, first as Mayor then as a local councillor for that district. At Cuverville he settled into a room almost as far away from Madeleine's as it was possible to be. Most of the time, however, he was away in Paris or travelling compulsively. He began to build a huge house for himself at Auteuil in the Parisian suburbs: modern, cold and wildly impractical.

In Paris, in 1905, he broke with his much-vaunted principle of keeping love and sex in separate compartments by falling for a tennis-playing teenager whom we know of only as 'M'. At first he willingly shared the boy with Henri Ghéon, until jealousy began to creep in. The affair did not last long; however flattered the youth may have been by the attentions of this rich and peripatetic literary figure in his prime, he was not interested in being a permanent lover. André suffered over that; at the same time, his relationship with Madeleine grew more distant.

The affair with 'M' helped André to understand that there was more to homosexuality than physical lust for boys. As Oscar had done before him, André now read more widely classical Greek and Roman authors to find clearer definitions of and justifications for man-boy love. Reflecting on those authors led André to start constructing a defence of homosexuality (as Claudel had feared might happen) in the form of a dialogue, entitled *Corydon*, the first version of which he published privately for distribution among close friends in 1909. They urged him not to make it more widely known, for the sake of both his reputation and Madeleine's feelings, but over the next fifteen years he continued expanding and revising the text, publishing it openly in 1924.

Concurrently with writing the first version of *Corydon*, André was bringing together in book form his memoirs of Oscar, some of which had already appeared in various magazines over the previous eight years. The book was an act of homage to Wilde, but also to an extent an expiation. As Gide made clear in his preface, in his earliest assessments (contained in the book) he had seriously underestimated Oscar's talents as a writer, while concentrating on the Olympian grandeur of the man. This can partly be explained by the fact that André had not known the great Wildean comedies, except by repute. And he was deceived by Oscar's determination to amuse or shock people into thinking that much of the writing was little more than an entertainment. Oscar himself had compounded André's underestimation of his writing ability by informing him in Algiers that he had put his genius into his life but only his talent into his works.

Much of the fascination of Gide's little book on Wilde lies in the fact that it is all about the man, and not his work, with the single, important exception of *De Profundis*. By pure chance, André had known Oscar at contrasting periods in his career: in the ascendant, at the height of his powers and in the final freefall, in France, Italy and North Africa. André was therefore in a unique position to comment on the playwright's character. But when his *Oscar Wilde* came out, in 1910, it provoked a violent reaction from some of the people who considered themselves to be Wilde experts or close friends and who challenged André's ability to judge.

Robert Sherard, in particular, was incensed. Although, according to some reports, Sherard had finally become aware of the nature of Oscar's physical desires by catching sight through an uncurtained window of Oscar and Robbie Ross making love at Berneval in the summer of 1897, Sherard refused to believe André's accounts of Oscar's behaviour, especially in Algeria. He went so far as to publish a pamphlet entitled *Oscar Wilde Twice Defended against André Gide's Wicked Lies*, which helped guarantee attention for André's book. Robbie Ross then entered the fray, declaring that Gide's portrait of Wilde was the most accurate that then existed. Lord Alfred Douglas, by now well on his way to reinventing the story of his partnership with Wilde in a light that was more flattering to himself and in keeping with his new Roman Catholic persuasion, not surprisingly indignantly disagreed.

The controversy over the accuracy of Gide's recollections continues today, partly because of their internal inconsistencies. At one point, for example, Gide says that his name and Oscar's were next to each other on the hotel board at Blidah in 1895, before he wiped his own name off, intimating the symbolic nature of this coupling. Yet in another place in the book, Gide says his name was at the top of the slate and Oscar's was at the bottom. While this is a minor point, to be sure, one certainly has to treat much of the material with caution: Gide often made mistakes with dates and his use of allegedly quoted speech occasionally sounds more like André himself than Oscar. Nonetheless, Gide's Wilde book is a very significant document concerning their own relationship and the effect that that had on André's development both as a writer and as a person.

The book also coincided with a turning-point in Gide's literary career. Having spent nearly twenty years grappling with Wilde's unsettling teaching, André was now able to produce mature works that radiated his own distinctive personality and style. The appearance of *La Porte étroite* (*Strait is the Gate*) in 1909 provided André with his first commercial success, which took both the author and the publishers by surprise. It was not all plain sailing from then on, however, *Les Caves du Vatican* (*The Vatican Cellars*) was a dismal failure when it first came out in 1914. Such Roman Catholics as Paul Claudel were outraged by the liberties the book took with Church history. Claudel had hoped to encourage André along the road to Rome (like Robbie Ross, Bosie and even, if not entirely convincingly, Oscar); instead, Gide was firmly set on a path that eventually led to all his books being put on the Index of works to be boycotted by good Catholics.

The pressure on Gide to convert to Roman Catholicism was relentless. Several of his French friends had already succumbed, including, disastrously, Henri Ghéon. With all the fervour of the recent convert, in 1916 he wrote earnestly to André, urging him to abandon their previously shared lifestyle of cruising the boulevards and picking up rent-boys and to repent his sins. As luck would have it, Madeleine opened the letter by mistake. Any remaining illusions she had about her husband were completely shattered.

To make things even worse, the following year, André fell heavily in love with Marc Allégret, the sixteen-year-old son of his former moral tutor, the Protestant Pastor Allégret. André's love for the boy was obsessive; he had never known emotional passion quite like it. Unable to stand separation from the lad, he followed Marc to summer camp, and in 1918 took him off to England for three months. Madeleine found out about this from Marc's parents, who had been informed of the nature of their son's relationship with André by some prying supposed well-wisher. Mme Allégret seems to have taken the news in her stride, apparently preferring that Marc indulge in a little adolescent homosexuality, even with a man three times his age, rather than getting involved with a girl. But Madeleine Gide was devastated. She took out the thousands of letters that André had written to her over the years, read them one last time and then ceremonially burnt them in the garden at Cuverville. When André found out, it was as if a knife had been struck into him; the best of himself had been killed, he said.

The relationship between André and Madeleine never recovered, despite their superficial amiability when they were together. They lived increasingly separate lives. She hardly stirred from Cuverville and ceased even to read André's books when they came out. The immolation of the letters was for her a way of marking a watershed in her life. But this did not deter André from pursuing his affair with Marc Allégret. That passion never became as destructive as Oscar Wilde's for Bosie. But André did suffer anguish over the boy, especially when Marc was courted, apparently successfully, by Jean Cocteau.

Cocteau, for all his superficiality, was deeply involved in the world of the performing arts, as well as being a writer. As Marc Allégret gradually realised that his own future lay in the cinema (later becoming a film-maker of considerable renown), Cocteau could give him inspiration and contacts that André did not have. The green demon of jealousy gnawed at André's flesh.

The agony and the ecstasy of André's passion for Marc (which slowly matured into a loving companionship) helped André understand and communicate through his fiction the realities of love's pain, no longer in the idealised romantic form of his earlier works, but rather as an immediate and compelling portrayal of sensations and emotional stratagems with which readers of novels could relate. *La Symphonie pastorale* (*The Pastoral Symphony*), which appeared in 1919, consolidated Gide's reputation not only as a controversial writer but as a considerable novelist. The story concerns a Protestant clergyman who falls in love with a blind girl in his care and is seduced by her, only to have her reject him for his handsome son when she regains her sight. The book helped to enhance Gide's literary status not only in France but in England, where he was elected an overseas member of the Royal Society for Literature, replacing Anatole France on his death in 1924.

Some of the people who were aware of André's sexuality wondered how he was able to write so convincingly about heterosexual passion. Despite his marriage, and his experience with Mériem, the Oulad Nail in Biskra, he had never really loved women in a normal way, unlike the young Oscar Wilde. Yet the situation was not as straightforward as it appeared. For at the very time, in the early 1920s, that André started publishing some of his revelatory memoirs, he was involved with a young woman, Elisabeth van Rysselberghe, the daughter of close bohemian friends of his. André did not just want to have a relationship with Elisabeth, he specifically wanted to produce a child through her – which was exactly what happened: a daughter whom they named Catherine was born in 1923.

The paternity of Catherine van Rysselberghe was kept secret except from André's most intimate friends, largely to try to spare Madeleine's feelings. But Madeleine was no fool. She undoubtedly was aware of André's relationship with Elisabeth, which only added to the weight of the cross she had to bear. Having already burnt André's letters, she did the next best thing to weaken the link between them, by gathering together all the intimate presents that André had given her, including crucifixes and jewellery, then distributing them among relatives and friends.

By the time *Les Faux-Monnayeurs* (*The Counterfeiters*) came out in 1926, André was firmly established as one of the most significant contemporary French writers. That position was further strengthened by his association with what had become a leading forum for intellectual thought, the *Nouvelle Revue française* (*NRF*). Yet André shunned some of the trappings of literary celebrity. He declined an invitation to join the Académie Française, the country's pre-eminent association of writers and intellectuals. In contrast to his earlier days of salon-hopping, he now rarely accepted invitations from socially prominent people who wanted him to grace their parties or dinner-tables. He chose his events and his associations carefully. With the exception of a handful of long-standing close friends, in general (like Wilde) he preferred the company of invigorating young people to that of his peers. Moreover, as a sign of determination to avoid being weighed down with the accumulations of a successful life, he sold his large house in Auteuil, in which he had never properly lived, as well as most of his library, including many books signed for him by friends.

He was also becoming increasingly political, largely as a result of an extended visit in 1926–7 to the Congo, Chad and some neighbouring territories under French colonial control. He travelled in the company of Marc Allégret, who took some remarkable photographs of their progress – duly kitted out in solar topees – through often inhospitable terrain, with a sizeable contingent of porters and servants and a tiny pet potto sloth, Dindiki, in tow. As one might expect, the travel diary Gide produced from this journey dwelt at some length on the nature and antics of the young men in André's temporary employ, but the tone was quite different from that of his writings about North Africa. Now the emphasis was less on the author's susceptibility to the youths' individual charms and more on the injustices and brutality of colonialism, as well as the grotesque distortion of human relations between white and black under such a system. The colonial authorities and several large companies working in the region were appalled by some of André's observations, but undoubtedly the book did help bring about some long overdue reforms. It also brought Gide a new breed of admirer – politicised young people, especially students, who were generally left-leaning in politics.

Not everyone fell under his spell. When André went to Berlin in 1928 and visited Dr Magnus Hirschfeld's famous Institute for Sexual Science – where sexual deviation was treated as a serious subject of research, complete with living human specimens housed on the premises – he was observed most critically by the young Christopher Isherwood, who was then gathering material for his Berlin novels. For Isherwood, Gide, in his characteristic cape and large, artistic hat, was the epitome of everything that was wrong with intellectual 'frogs'. The pose grated on Isherwood's nerves, as he informed his friend Wystan Auden.

Stephen Spender and others were more favourably inclined, as André got swept up into the emotional alliance of European writers and workers who came together to oppose the rise of fascism. Events in Germany and Spain, especially in the early 1930s, tended to polarise to left or right. André found himself hailed as a natural ally of the left; though he never became a Communist, he shared many platforms with Communists and was denounced by the right as a fellow-traveller. Some of his closest new friends were Communists, including Pierre Herbart, with whom Elisabeth van

Rysselberghe set up house. Her mother moved in with André, to help look after him at the sixth-floor apartment he took in the rue Vaneau in Paris, where Marc Allégret often stayed, as well as André and Elisabeth's daughter Catherine.

In 1936 André visited Moscow, where he was fêted and cheered and profiled almost daily in the newspapers. He even gave a funeral oration for the writer Maxim Gorky, who died while he was there. But the more André saw of the Soviet Union, the more he realised how unpleasant much of the reality was behind the comradely façade. Individual freedoms were being sacrificed in the name of the common good. And although the world did not know the extent of Stalin's terror, it was clear that fear, coercion and intolerance were part of the Soviet order. Accordingly, when André returned from the Soviet Union, he sat down to write an exposé of what he had sensed. Many friends implored him not to do it, saying that it would play into the hands of the right, or that it would bring swift retribution from the left. The latter warning certainly proved well founded. Hardly was the book out before Gide was being denounced by Moscow as a typical bourgeois individualist. Leftists in France attacked not just his act of political treason but also his personal life. The book, *Retour de l'URSS (Return from the USSR)*, was a best-seller, bringing him notoriety as well as greater fame.

No-one was quite sure now exactly where André stood politically, least of all himself. When the Second World War broke out and the Germans were advancing on Paris, he was in a quandary about what to do. For a while he was not sure whether to side with the Vichy regime, or to believe in de Gaulle's Free French. As he saw more of Marshal Pétain's government, however, it became inevitable that he would refuse to join the collaborators, though he did intend to keep writing. In celebration of his seventieth birthday, the *NRF* brought out his journal for the past fifty years, minus the pages he had torn out about Oscar Wilde in 1891 and a few other sensitive items. Madeleine could no longer be hurt any more by his revelations; she had died the previous year, a shadow of her former self, almost completely cut off from her husband. André immediately legalised Catherine's status as his daughter.

Unable to stay in Paris, he moved south, first to the unoccupied zone and then on to North Africa, which he had neglected for the past three decades. To the concern of some of his friends – and the local authorities – rather than staying still, he travelled widely, not only in Algeria and Tunisia but also in Morocco and Egypt, moving on to the Middle East at the end of the war.

André returned to peacetime Paris to find himself one of the grand old men of French literature, bombarded with correspondence – to almost all of which he diligently replied – as well as with invitations and offers of honours, many of which he turned down. One he could not resist, however, was an honorary doctorate at Oxford University, which he went to collect in the summer of 1947.

He was looked after at Oxford by Enid Starkie, whose biography of Arthur Rimbaud was published that year. She noted that while most recipients of Oxford honorary degrees look as if they are in pantomime drag when dressed in academic hat and gown, the attire seemed perfectly natural on André Gide, who in his late seventies – almost bald and shorn of the moustache that he had worn as a young man – had the dignified air of an owlish savant.

One of the reasons André had accepted to go to Oxford was because he wanted to make a pilgrimage to Oscar's rooms in Magdalen College. When he was led there, he seemed to go into a trance; mindless of the other people in the sitting-room, he walked slowly round, trailing the fingers of one hand along the wall, as if trying to touch some lingering presence of his former mentor.

Within a matter of weeks Gide was awarded the ultimate accolade, the Nobel Prize for Literature. It was a brave and controversial decision by the Nobel Prize committee, given the Catholic Church's deep hostility to Gide and the still prevalent prejudice against homosexuality in many countries including Britain, where the practice was still illegal (and would remain so for another twenty years). Several commentators at the time made the perceptive remark that the prize had been awarded to Gide partly as an act of atonement to Oscar Wilde for what society had done to him.

Certainly, André Gide's Nobel Prize was an important step in the re-affirmation of the validity and even nobility of homosexual relations, notably as defined in the classical tradition that was so dear to both him and Oscar. The process would continue with the gradual re-evaluation of Oscar Wilde as one of the great figures in English literature and social life, culminating in his inclusion in a window at Westminster Abbey in 1995, on the centenary of his imprisonment for offences that both Church and State had condemned.

André died in 1951 at the age of eighty-two – exactly twice the life-span Oscar had enjoyed. On his death André was at the pinnacle of his literary career, although his output had become slim compared with his earlier almost frenzied activity. The situation could not have been more different from Oscar's passing half a century before, in ignominy and relative squalor. Yet just as their lives had often run in parallel, for all their multifarious differences, so after death the trend continued.

Oscar had been buried modestly at the cemetery at Bagneux; André's body was committed to a grave at the cemetery at Cuverville. But both were later disinterred. Oscar was transferred to a much grander site, at Père Lachaise in Paris, in 1909. His tomb there was graced by a striking sculpture by Jacob Epstein, beside which flowers are still regularly laid. When Robbie Ross died, in 1918, he triumphed over both Bosie and Constance, by having his ashes interred in Oscar's tomb. For his part, out of respect for family feelings and his own earlier love for his wife, André was moved out of his grave and into the vault that housed Madeleine, to lie beside her for eternity.

Both endings would have made Oscar roar with delight.

Bibliography

There is an immense amount of material both by and about André Gide and Oscar Wilde; André was particularly prolific, while Oscar has been a subject of perennial interest. Accordingly, only those works which were of direct use in the preparation of this book are cited in the bibliography below. In Gide's case, the author has worked from the French original; where English translations of books have been published, these have been indicated very briefly in brackets in the bibliography. All translations in the text of *André and Oscar* are the author's own.

A: SELECTED WORKS BY ANDRÉ GIDE

Les Cahiers d'André Walter, Librairie Académique Didier-Perrin, Paris 1891.
Le Traité de Narcisse, Librairie de L'Art Indépendant, Paris 1891.
Le Voyage d'Urien, Librairie de l'Art Indépendant, Paris 1893.
Paludes, Librarie de l'Art Indépendant, Paris 1895. (*Marshlands*, tr. George Painter, 1952.)
Réflexions sur quelques points de littérature et de morale, Mercure de France, Paris 1897.
Les Nourritures terrestres, Mercure de France, Paris 1897. (*Fruits of the Earth*, tr. Dorothy Bussy, 1949.)
L'Immoraliste, Mercure de France, Paris 1902. (*The Immoralist*, tr. Dorothy Bussy, 1930.)

Saul, Mercure de France, Paris 1903.

Amyntas, Mercure de France, Paris 1906.

La Porte étroite, Mercure de France, Paris 1909. (*Strait Is the Gate*, tr. Dorothy Bussy, 1924.)

Oscar Wilde, Mercure de France, Paris 1910. (*Oscar Wilde*, tr. Bernard Frechtman, 1951.)

C.R.D.N. (Corydon), anonymous publisher, 1911. (Corydon, tr. Dorothy Bussy, 1951.)

Les Caves du Vatican, Nouvelle Revue française, Paris 1914. (*The Vatican Swindle*, tr. Dorothy Bussy, 1927.)

La Symphonie pastorale, Nouvelle Revue française, Paris 1919. (Pastoral Symphony, tr. Dorothy Bussy, 1931.)

Si le grain ne meurt, anonymous publisher, Paris 1920. (*If It Die . . .*, tr. Dorothy Bussy, 1950.)

Numquid et tu . . . ?, anonymous publisher, 1922.

Les Faux-Monnayeurs, Nouvelle Revue française, Paris 1926. (*The Coiners*, tr. Dorothy Bussy, 1927.)

Voyage au Congo, Nouvelle Revue française, Paris 1927. (*Travels in the Congo*, tr. Dorothy Bussy, 1930.)

Le Retour du Tchad, Nouvelle Revue francaise, Paris 1928.

Retour de l'U.R.S.S., Gallimard, Paris 1936. (*Back from the USSR*, tr. Dorothy Bussy, 1937.)

Journal 1889–1939, Bibliothèque de la Pléiade, Paris 1939. (Journals of André Gide, tr. Justin O'Brien, 1951.)

Et nunc manet in te . . ., Richard Heyd, Neuchâtel 1947.

Correspondance 1899–1926 (Paul Claudel & André Gide), Gallimard, Paris 1949.

Correspondance 1890–1942 (Paul Valery & André Gide), Gallimard, Paris 1955.

Correspondance avec sa mère 1880–1895, Gallimard Paris 1988.

B: SELECTED WORKS BY OSCAR WILDE

Complete Works of Oscar Wilde, Collins, London 1948.
  notably: *The Picture of Dorian Gray, The Sphinx without a Secret, The Portrait of Mr W.H., Salomé, Lady Windermere's Fan, A Woman of No Importance, An Ideal Husband, The Importance of Being Earnest, The Sphinx, The Ballad of Reading Gaol, De Profundis, The Truth of Masks, The Soul of Man under Socialism, Phrases and Philosophies for the Use of the Young, Letters* (ed. Rupert Hart-Davis), Rupert Hart-Davis, London 1962. *More Letters* (ed. Rupert Hart-Davis), John Murray, London 1985.

C: OTHER BOOKS

AMOR, ANNE CLARK: *Mrs Oscar Wilde*, Sidgwick & Jackson, London 1983.
ANONYMOUS: *Oscar Wilde: Three Times Tried*, Ferrestone, London n.d.
AUSSEIL, SARAH: *Madeleine Gide*, Robert Laffont, Paris 1993.
BARTLETT, NEIL: *Who Was That Man?*, Serpent's Tail, London 1988.
BENTLEY, JOYCE: *The Importance of Being Constance*, Robert Hale, London 1983.
BOISDEFFRE, JEAN DE: *Vie d'André Gide (1)*, Hachette, Paris 1970.
BORLAND, MAUREEN: *Wilde's Devoted Friend, Lennard*, Oxford 1990.
BRASOL, BORIS: Oscar Wilde, Williams & Norgate, London 1938.
BREMONT, ANNA, COMTESSE DE: *Oscar Wilde*, Everett, London 1911.
BROAD, LEWIS: *The Friendships and Follies of Oscar Wilde*, Hutchinson, London 1954.
BYRNE, PATRICK: *The Wildes of Merrion Square*, Staples Press, London n.d.
CROFT-COOKE, RUPERT: *Feasting with Panthers*, W.H. Allen, London 1967.
CROFT-COOKE, RUPERT: *The Unrecorded Life of Oscar Wilde*, W.H. Allen, New York 1972.
DELAY, JEAN: *La Jeunesse d'André Gide (1)*, Gallimard, Paris 1956.
DELAY, JEAN: *La Jeunesse d'André Gide (2)*, Gallimard, Paris 1957.
DESCHODT, ERIC: *Gide*, Perrin, Paris 1991.
DOLLIMORE, JONATHAN: *Sexual Dissidence*, Bloomsbury, London 1991.
DOUGLAS, LORD ALFRED: *The Autobiography of Lord Alfred Douglas*, Martin Secker, London 1929.
DOUGLAS, LORD ALFRED: *Oscar Wilde*, Duckworth, London 1940.
DOUGLAS, LORD ALFRED: *Oscar Wilde and Myself*, John Long, London 1914.
ELLMANN, RICHARD: *Oscar Wilde*, Hamish Hamilton, London 1987.
ELLMANN, RICHARD & EPSEY, JOHN: *Oscar Wilde: Two Approaches*, William Andrews Clark Memorial Library, Los Angeles 1977.
ERVINE, ST JOHN: *Oscar Wilde*, George Allen & Unwin, London 1951.
FIDO, MARTIN: *Oscar Wilde*, Hamlyn, London 1973.
HARRIS, FRANK: *Oscar Wilde*, Constable, London 1938.
HARRIS, GEORGE W.: *The Practical Guide to Algiers*, George Philip, London 1893.
HOLLAND, VYVYAN: *Oscar Wilde*, Thames and Hudson, London 1960.
HOLLAND, VYVYAN: *Son of Oscar Wilde*, Rupert Hart-Davis, London 1954.
HYDE, H. MONTGOMERY: *Lord Alfred Douglas*, Dodd Mead, New York 1985.
HYDE, H. MONTGOMERY: *Oscar Wilde*, Eyre Methuen, London 1976.
HYDE, H. MONTGOMERY: *The Trials of Oscar Wilde*, Dover, New York, 1962.
HYTIER, JEAN: *André Gide*, Edmond Charlot, Algiers n.d.

INGLEBY, LEONARD CRESSWELL: *Oscar Wilde*, T. Werner Laurie, London n.d.

JULLIAN, PHILIPPE: *Oscar Wilde*, Constable, London 1969.

KING, FRANCIS: *Florence: a Literary Companion*, John Murray, London 1991.

KNOX, MELISSA: *Oscar Wilde*, Yale University Press, New Haven 1994.

LANGLADE, JACQUES DE: *La Mésentente cordiale*, Julliard, Paris 1994.

LANGLADE, JACQUES DE: *Oscar Wilde*, Mazarine, Paris, 1987.

LANGLADE, JACQUES DE: *Oscar Wilde*, écrivain français, Stock, Paris 1975.

LEVERSON, ADA: *Letters to the Sphinx*, Duckworth, London 1930.

MELVILLE, JOY: *Mother of Oscar*, John Murray, London 1994.

MERLE, ROBERT: *Oscar Wilde*, Fallois, Paris 1995.

MERLE, ROBERT: *Oscar Wilde, ou la <<destinée>> de l'homosexuel*, Gallimard, Paris 1955.

MIKHAIL, E.H. (ed.): *Oscar Wilde: Interview and Recollections: Vol. 1*, Macmillan, London 1979.

MORLEY, SHERIDAN: *Oscar Wilde*, Holt, Rinehart & Winston, New York 1976.

O'BRIEN, JUSTIN: *Portrait of André Gide*, Secker & Warburg, London 1953.

O'SULLIVAN, VINCENT: *Aspects of Wilde*, Constable, London 1936.

PAINTER, GEORGE: *André Gide*, Arthur Barker, London 1951.

PEARSON, HESKETH: *The Life of Oscar Wilde*, Methuen, London 1946.

PEPPER, CHORAL: *Walks in Oscar Wilde's London*, Peregrine, Salt Lake City 1992.

PIERRE-QUINT, LEON: *André Gide*, Stock, Paris 1932.

PLAYFAIR, SIR R. LAMBERT: *Algeria and Tunis*, John Murray, London 1895.

POLLARD, PATRICK: *André Gide, Homosexual Moralist*, Yale University Press, New Haven 1991.

RANSOME, ARTHUR: *Oscar Wilde*, Martin Secker, London 1912.

REBELL, HUGUES ET AL: *Pour Oscar Wilde*, Elisabeth Brunet, Rouen 1994.

RODITI, EDOUARD: *Oscar Wilde*, New Directions, Norfolk Conn. 1947.

SCHMIDGALL, GARY: *The Stranger Wilde*, Dutton, New York 1994.

SHERARD, ROBERT: *The Life of Oscar Wilde*, T. Werner Laurie, London 1906.

SHERARD, ROBERT: *The Real Oscar Wilde*, David McKay, Philadelphia n.d.

SHERARD, ROBERT: *Oscar Wilde: The Story of an Unhappy Friendship*, T. Werner Laurie, London 1902.

SINFIELD, ALAN: *The Wilde Century*, Cassell, London 1994.

SPEEDIE, JULIE: *Wonderful Sphinx*, Virago, London 1993.

STURGIS, MATTHEW: *Passionate Attitudes*, Macmillan, London 1995.

THIERRY, JEAN-JACQUES: *André Gide*, Hachette, Paris 1986.

TYDEMAN, WILLIAM & PRICE, STEVEN: *Wilde: Salomé*, Cambridge University Press 1996.

VALLET, ODON: *L'Affaire Oscar Wilde*, Albin Michel, Paris 1995.

VARAUT, JEAN-MARC: *Les Procès d'Oscar Wilde*, Perrin, Paris 1995.

VON ECKARDT, WOLF, GILMAN, SANDER & CHAMBERLAIN, J. EDWARD: *Oscar Wilde's London*, Michael O'Mara, London 1988.

WALKER, DAVID: *André Gide*, Macmillan, London 1990.

Index

[Note on abbreviations: AD: Lord Alfred Douglas; AG: Andre Gide; OW: Oscar Wilde; AG's and OW's literary works are indexed under author entries.]

Pierre Louÿs

Gide Fruits of the Earth / Corydon
de Profudis
Hugues Rebell — Great Name!
(Hugues Rebell II — pour moi
n'existe pas?)
Christopher Isherwood